北京的宗教

Religions of Beijing

Religions of Beijing

北京的宗教

Edited by
You Bin and Timothy Knepper

Photography by
Bob Blanchard

Translated by
Phoebe Liang D'Alessandro

主编 游斌 蒂莫西·耐普

摄影 鲍勃·布兰查德

翻译 梁兆枫

BLOOMSBURY ACADEMIC
LONDON · NEW YORK · OXFORD · NEW DELHI · SYDNEY

BLOOMSBURY ACADEMIC
Bloomsbury Publishing Plc
50 Bedford Square, London, WC1B 3DP, UK
1385 Broadway, New York, NY 10018, USA

BLOOMSBURY, BLOOMSBURY ACADEMIC and the Diana logo are trademarks of Bloomsbury Publishing Plc

First published in Great Britain 2020

Copyright © You Bin and Timothy Knepper, 2020

Photography © Bob Blanchard

You Bin and Timothy Knepper have asserted their right under the Copyright, Designs and Patents Act, 1988, to be identified as Author of this work.

Cover design by Tjaša Krivec

Cover image © Frederic J. Brown / Staff / Getty Images

All rights reserved. No part of this publication may be reproduced or transmitted in any form or by any means, electronic or mechanical, including photocopying, recording, or any information storage or retrieval system, without prior permission in writing from the publishers.

Bloomsbury Publishing Plc does not have any control over, or responsibility for, any third-party websites referred to or in this book. All internet addresses given in this book were correct at the time of going to press. The author and publisher regret any inconvenience caused if addresses have changed or sites have ceased to exist, but can accept no responsibility for any such changes.

A catalogue record for this book is available from the British Library.

Library of Congress Control Number: 2020910954

ISBN: PB: 978-1-3501-2710-4
       ePDF: 978-1-3501-2711-1
       eBook: 978-1-3501-2712-8

Typeset by John Fender

To find out more about our authors and books visit www.bloomsbury.com and sign up for our newsletters

Contents

List of Figures vi

Introduction: Religions in Beijing 2
    You Bin
    Timothy Knepper

1. **Baiyunguan Temple**. 8
    By: 陈睿 Chen Rui
    With: Nicole Margheim

2. **Beiding Niangniang Temple** 20
    By: 郑幼敏 Zheng Youmin
    With: Nicole Margheim

3. **Changping Mosque** 32
    By: 马文 Ma Wen
    With: Ireland Larsen

4. **Chongwenmen Church** 46
    By: 陈景枢 Chen Jingshu
    With: Madelyn Bjork

5. **Confucius Temple and Imperial College** 56
    By: 谭泽民 Tan Zemin
    With: Sara Feldman and Rosalind Carey

6. **Dongsi Mosque**. 68
    By: 马斌 Ma Bin
    With: Kameron Tomes

7. **Dongyue Temple** 80
    By: 田丁丁 Tian Dingding
    With: Kelsey Rick

8. **Guangji Temple**. 92
    By: 李瑶 Li Yao
    With: Madelyn Bjork

9. **Haidian Church**. 106
    By: 谷俊锋 王迎梅 Gu Junfeng and Wang Yingmei
    With: Kameron Tomes

10. **Housangyu Church** 116
    By: 张睿 Zhang Rui
    With: Sara Feldman and Kelsey Rick

11. **Huode Zhenjun Temple** 128
    By: 张筱嘉 Zhang Xiaojia
    With: Ireland Larsen and Rosalind Carey

12. **Tanzhe Temple** 140
    By: 于博洋 刘熠然 Yu Boyang and Liu Yiran
    With: Kelsey Rick and Anna Wondrasek

13. **Tianning Temple** 152
    By: 钟秋思 Zhong Qiusi
    With: Sara Feldman

14. **Tongzhou Mosque** 164
    By: 黄婧怡 Huang Jingyi
    With: Kameron Tomes

15. **Xishiku Church**. 176
    By: 丁柏予 Ding Baiyu
    With: Nicole Margheim

16. **Xizhimen Church** 188
    By: 李琳 Li Lin
    With: Ireland Larsen

17. **Yonghegong Temple** 200
    By: 宗喀·益西丹佛 Zongka Yixidanfo
    With: Madelyn Bjork

Index 212

List of Figures

Photography by Bob Blanchard, unless otherwise noted.

Introduction
1. 本书作者民大-德雷克师生集体照 4
   Group photo of the teams from Minzu and Drake

Baiyunguan Temple
2. 白云观山门入口 8
   Mountain Gate entrance of Baiyunguan
3. 窝风桥下的好运钟 11
   Good-luck bell beneath Wofeng Bridge
4. 道士敬香 11
   Daoist priest offering incense *(photo by He Yinglong)*
5. 碧霞元君造像 12
   Statue of Bixia Yuanjun, Goddess of Sunlight
6. 斗姆元君殿内的神仙们 13
   Statue of Doumu Yuanjun, Mother Goddess of the Big Dipper, in front of immortals
7. 静心燃香 14
   Lighting incense as an offering
8. 为神仙齐声唱诵的道士们 16
   Daoist priests praising the immortals
   (photo by He Yinglong)

Beiding Niangniang Temple
9. 象征凡间与圣所之分界的山门 22
   Mountain Gate of Beiding Niangniang Temple
10. 院落布局错落有致 23
    Temple of the Heavenly Kings
11. 四大天王之一 24
    One of the Four Heavenly Kings
12. 长眠香即道教的福牌 27
    Long-Lasting Incense
13. 被鲜花和香果环绕的主神碧霞元君 28
    Statue of Bixia Yuanjun, Goddess of Sunlight

Changping Mosque
14. 昌平清真寺的礼拜大殿 32
    Prayer hall of Changping Mosque
15. 昌平城区的穆斯林墓地 35
    Muslim graveyard of Changping District
16. 国旗和新月，昌平清真寺会在每年的开斋节和古尔邦节举行升国旗仪式 37
    Chinese flag and crescent moon of Islam

17. 清真寺的门卫老马正在礼拜 38
    Gatekeeper of Changping Mosque praying
18. 清真寺门楣上精美的伊斯兰装饰 40
    Islamic inscriptions above gateways
19. 阅读古兰经的克什米尔留学生 41
    International student from Kashmir reading the Qur'an
20. 穆斯林在做晌礼拜 43
    Muslims during the *Dhuhr* prayer

Chongwenmen Church
21. 崇文门教堂大门 47
    Gate of Chongwenmen Church
22. 崇文门教堂内景 48
    Worship hall of Chongwenmen Church
23. 崇文门教堂讲台 50
    Pulpit of Chongwenmen Church
24. 崇文门教堂青年诗班 51
    Youth choir of Chongwenmen Church
25. 受访者徐玉发 52
    Xu Yufa, member of Chongwenmen Church
26. 崇文门教堂复活节受难日教堂外景 53
    Good Friday cross in courtyard of Chongwenmen Church *(photo by He Yinglong)*

Confucius Temple and Imperial College
27. 孔子雕像 57
    Statue of Confucius
28. 孔庙核心建筑大成殿 58
    Dacheng Hall, the main building of the Confucian Temple
29. "十二哲"之一卜子配祀牌位 61
    Memorial tablet for Confucian sage Bu
30. 上书"圜桥教泽"琉璃牌坊 62
    Paifang with the inscription "Education endowed by the love of the emperor is endless like running water"
31. 国子监核心建筑辟雍殿 63
    Piyong Hall, the main building of the Imperial College
32. 十三经刻石 64
    Stelae garden of thirteen Confucian classics

Dongsi Mosque
33. 坐在清真寺内的信徒 69
    Member of Dongsi Mosque sitting in the prayer hall

34. 东四清真寺小净室 70
    Ablution (*wudu*) room at Dongsi Mosque
35. 银杏树遮掩的望月楼 73
    Moon-watching tower at Dongsi Mosque
36. 东四清真寺的礼拜大殿 75
    Prayer hall at Dongsi Mosque
37. 何阿訇 76
    Imam He
38. 伊玛目在敏拜尔作呼图白 78
    Imam He giving a sermon (*khutbah*) in the prayer hall

Dongyue Temple
39. "秩祀岱宗" 牌楼 81
    Ornamental gate with the inscription "Worshipping Mount Tai deity according to the royal rites"
40. 通往岱岳殿的福路 82
    Fu Road leading to Daiyue Hall
41. 文昌帝的坐骑 85
    Riding horses of the Wenchang Emperor
42. 御碑亭 86
    Royal Stelae Pavilion
43. 燃香处 89
    Incense lighter
44. 记录愿望和许愿者名字的祈福红布 90
    Prayer wheels at Dongyue Temple
45. 东岳庙的猫 91
    One of the many cats of Dongyue Temple

Guangji Temple
46. 康熙皇帝御笔亲书的石门金字 "敕建弘慈广济寺" . . 94
    Emperor Kangxi's inscription on the main gate of Guangji Temple
47. 大雄宝殿里的罗汉像 95
    Buddhist *arhat* in Daxiong Hall
48. 天王殿内景之弥勒像与天王像 97
    Statues of Maitreya and the Heavenly King in Tianwang Hall
49. 过去佛像 98
    Statue of the Past Buddha (Kaśyapa)
50. 胜果妙音图 100
    Qing Dynasty mural "Fruit of Realization and Sound of Emptiness" in Daxiong Hall
51. 跪拜在大雄殿前的信众 102
    Visitor worshipping in front of Daxiong Hall
52. 圆通殿前诵读佛经的信众 103
    Visitors reading Buddhist scriptures in front of Yuantong Hall

Haidian Church
53. 现代教堂风格，像一本打开的圣经 107
    Front of Haidian Christian Church
54. 肖恩服侍于教会青年诗班 108
    Sean, who serves in the youth choir (*photo by He Yinglong*)
55. 海淀教堂的聚会 110
    Worship service at Haidian Christian Church
56. 海淀堂的领祷员 111
    Minister leading prayers at Haidian Christian Church
57. 圣经与十字架 113
    Bible and cross

Housangyu Church
58. 后桑峪村全貌 117
    Village of Housangyu
59. 礼敬圣母处 118
    Place of prayer in front of a statue of the Virgin Mary
60. 教堂院子里的圣母像 120
    Statue of the Virgin Mary in the church courtyard
61. 神父祝圣圣餐 121
    Priest serving Eucharist (*photo by He Yinglong*)
62. 后桑峪乐队 122
    Housangyu church band
63. 怀抱耶稣的圣若瑟 125
    Statue of St. Joseph with baby Jesus
64. 在耶稣圣心堂祈祷的信徒 127
    Parishioner praying at the Church of the Sacred Heart of Jesus

Huode Zhenjun Temple
65. 火神庙的前院 128
    Front courtyard of Huode Zhenjun
66. 王灵官:道教护法神之一,在火神庙中为镇守山门之神 130
    Wang Lingguan, guardian deity at the gate of Huode Zhenjun
67. 祈福法会 130
    Daoist priest leading prayer ritual
68. 在财神殿担任义工的王居士 134
    Mr. Wang, on duty at the Wealth God Hall (*photo by He Yinglong*)
69. 在月老殿供奉的化妆品 137
    Cosmetics left as offerings in Moon Elderly Immortal Hall (*photo by He Yinglong*)
70. 火神像以及信众送来的锦旗 138
    Statue of Fire God and banners
71. 正在烧香的香客 139
    Believer worshipping with incense

Tanzhe Temple

72. 天王殿 141
    Hall of the Heavenly Kings
73. 透过香炉看到的转经筒 142
    Tibetan prayer wheel as seen through incense burner
74. 龙王殿前石鱼 143
    Stone fish in front of Dragon King Temple
75. 玉兰茶楼 144
    Yulan Tea House
76. 帝王树 146
    The Imperial Trees
77. 莲灯 147
    Lotus candle
78. 观音菩萨 149
    Statue of Avalokiteśvara

Tianning Temple

79. 山门殿拱门下的天宁寺和佛塔 ... 153
    Main temple and stupa of Tianning Temple
80. 天宁寺里的佛塔底座 154
    Base of stupa at Tianning Temple
81. 药师殿内的墙壁上挂满了写着生者姓名的小牌子 . 157
    Plaques for the living on the walls of Pharmacist Buddha Temple
82. 弥陀殿里的亡灵牌位 158
    Statue of Amitābha with plaques for the deceased
83. 天宁寺里的香火 161
    Burning incense at Tianning Temple
84. 药师佛像下方摆放着举行仪式时候尼姑使用的颂词 162
    Statue of Śākyamuni Buddha with eulogy used by nuns during ceremony

Tongzhou Mosque

85. 清真寺正门 165
    Main gate of Tongzhou Mosque
86. 重修清真寺的碑文 166
    Stone tablet commemorating the reconstruction of Tongzhou Mosque
87. 穆斯林小帽与念珠 168
    Table with Muslim hat and prayer beads (photo by He Yinglong)
88. 女寺里的信徒 171
    Women in women's prayer hall
89. 礼拜殿大全景 172
    Exterior of the prayer hall
90. 礼拜殿内部 173
    Interior of the prayer hall
91. 净室外晾晒的手巾 175
    Ablution (wudu) towels hanging to dry in the sun

Xishiku Church

92. 哥特式的教堂和堂外的中式黄亭 177
    Gothic Cathedral and Chinese yellow pavilion
93. 西什库堂内景 178
    Interior of Xishiku Catholic Church
94. 堂内举行主日弥撒 180
    Procession at end of Mass
95. 讲述了中国教会史的玻璃彩窗 ... 183
    Stained-glass history of the Chinese Church
96. 在西什库教堂祈祷的女信徒 184
    Woman praying at Xishiku Catholic Church

Xizhimen Church

97. 教友们聆听张神父讲道 189
    Father Zhang preaching at Xizhimen Catholic Church
98. 教堂八角形洗礼池 190
    Baptism font at Xizhimen Catholic Church
99. 弥撒圣祭中张神父 诵念感恩经文 ... 193
    Father Zhang saying the Eucharistic prayer
100. 祝圣圣体的神父 194
    Priest holding sacraments (photo by He Yinglong)
101. 弥撒圣祭中教友领受圣体 197
    Receiving the Eucharist in Mass

Yonghegong Temple

102. 雍和宫的外部景观 201
    Exterior view of Yonghegong (Lama) Temple
103. 戒台楼里的乾隆皇帝像 202
    Statue of Emperor Qianlong in Jetai Building
104. 雍和门殿与拜佛的信众 204
    Worship of statues of Buddhas in Yonghegong Hall
105. 法轮殿里的宗喀巴大师像 206
    Statue of Tsongkhapa in Falun Hall
106. 万福阁内供奉的一尊高18米的弥勒佛像 208
    Eighteen-meter statue of Maitreya Buddha in Wanfuge Pavilion
107. 持香拜佛的人 209
    Woman worshipping with incense
108. 释迦牟尼的壁画 211
    Fresco of Śākyamuni (photo by He Yinglong)

介绍：北京的宗教

游斌

一个宗教就是一个故事。这个故事在人群中行走，进入人们的生活，便成为千万人的故事。

北京的宗教也是一个个这样悠远而多彩的故事。从中华文明起源伊始，北京就处于多种古代文化的交汇处，带有中华文明自古以来的多样性。随着丝绸之路的开通和延伸，域外宗教的传播亦进入北京地区。源于古印度恒河流域的佛教于公元300年左右来到北京，始建于公元307年的潭柘寺可视为佛教在北京地区最初传播的物化迹象。伴随着中亚各种信仰人群进入中国，伊斯兰教也来到北京。牛街礼拜寺建成于公元996年左右，至今已逾千年。而早在马可·波罗的游记中，就谈到在北京有基督徒、穆斯林等。公元1294年，受罗马教宗差遣，孟高维诺到达元大都，向忽必烈汗提出传教的请求，并得到允许。同一时期藏传佛教也开始传入，受元朝皇帝尊崇而享有显著地位。北京城内现存年代最早、规模最大的藏式佛塔妙应寺白塔，于元朝初期（公元1271年）即已建造。

自元朝之后，明、清两朝也先后定都北京。北京，地处农耕文明与游牧文明的交接地带，位于丝绸之路的东端，其宗教多样性的程度进一步加深。中国本土的道教在此开坛设观，新的民间信仰也不断涌现。佛教的中国化程度不断加深，在北京传播发展的过程中，汉、藏佛教更吸收融合京城的文化，北京佛教逐渐具备了鲜明的帝都特色。以利玛窦为代表的耶稣会士在北京的活动，带来中西文明交流的黄金时代，并在北京建立东堂、西堂、南堂、北堂等基督教堂，进一步丰富并充实着北京的宗教多样性。当中国历史进入近代，基督教新教也来到北京，星星点点的新教教堂，开始散布于北京各地。这些宗教在北京大地上留下它们的印记，也进入北京人的心灵和生活世界，在互鉴互学中形成丰富多彩的北京宗教文化。

北京的这种宗教多样性，在我2017年受 Timothy Knepper 教授邀请访问德雷克大学时，激活于我的脑海之中。 Timothy Knepper 主编了一本"美国腹地的宗教多样性"（A Spectrum of Faith: Religions of the World in America's Heartland），图画精美，文字精练，对于美国的宗教多样性及其内在形成机理做了细致而准确地描绘。这本书是他指导德雷克大学宗教学本科同学的结晶。他带领同学们走遍得梅因的宗教场所，记述各宗教之信仰者的心灵故事。这诚然是培养人才的一个绝佳途径。同学们的研究、写作和组织能力在这一项目中得到了极大的提升。纸上学千遍，不如动手做一件。想到我们哲学与宗教学学院的那些优秀学子，我便与 Timothy Knepper 教授商议，由中央民族大学哲学与宗教学学院的同学们对北京的宗教多样性来做一深描，以此向国际学术界讲述北京宗教的悠远故事，分析中国人的宗教心灵，探究中国文化的宗教性格，阐发多元宗教在中国文化处境内形成的互鉴通和宗教关系模式。为此，我们采取中央民族大学与德雷克大学合作的方式，由中国学生首先写出中文文章，翻译成英文后再由美国同学进行提问、评论，并在2019年美国同学来访北京时，与中国同学共访这些宗教场所之后，共同完成中英文文稿的写作。之后，2020年1月游斌与Timothy Knepper教授一起对这些文稿逐篇进行细致讨论，才完成最后的书稿。

Introduction: Religions in Beijing

You Bin

Religion is a story. It walks through the crowd, enters people's life, and becomes the story of thousands.

Religions in Beijing are long and colorful stories. Ever since the beginning of Chinese civilization, Beijing has been at the intersection of cultures, preserving diversity, the hallmark of Chinese civilization, throughout history. Foreign religions started to enter Beijing with the opening and extension of the Silk Road. With origins in the Ganges valley of India, Buddhism was introduced to Beijing around 300 CE. Its initial spread is evidenced by the Tanzhe Temple, which was built in 307. As various faith groups from Central Asia arrived in China, Islam was also introduced to Beijing. The Niujie Mosque was built around 996, surviving for more than a thousand years. Both Muslims and Christians were documented in Beijing as early as the travel logs of Marco Polo. In 1294, at the request and dispatch of the Pope, Giovanni da Montecorvino arrived at the capital of the Yuan Dynasty. He requested permission from Kublai Khan to preach, which was granted. At the same period of time, Tibetan Buddhism also arrived in Beijing, where it enjoyed a prominent position, revered by the emperors of the Yuan Dynasty. The earliest and largest extant Tibetan-style pagoda in Beijing, the white pagoda of Miaoying Temple, was built in the early Yuan Dynasty (1271 CE).

After the Yuan Dynasty, the Ming and Qing Dynasties established their capitals in Beijing. Located at the eastern tip of the Silk Road during a time of transition between agricultural and nomadic civilizations, Beijing began witnessing even more religious diversity. Daoism, a native Chinese religion, set foot in Beijing by building temples and altars. New folk beliefs continuously sprung up. Expressions of Buddhism became more localized; in Beijing, Han and Tibetan Buddhism absorbed the culture of the capital city, picking up distinctive imperial-capital characteristics. The activities of the Jesuits in Beijing, as represented by Matteo Ricci, took the cultural exchange between East and West to a golden era. East Church, West Church, South Church, and North Church were built, adding more richness to the religious life of Beijing. Protestantism landed in Beijing late in Chinese history. Not long afterwards, a scattering of Protestant churches was seen across the city. All these religions not only left their footprints in Beijing but also entered the souls and lives of the people of Beijing. Through mutual exchange, interaction, and learning, these different religions collectively created a colorful culture of religion in Beijing.

However, had I not made the trip to Drake University in Des Moines, Iowa, in 2017 at the invitation of Professor Timothy Knepper, religious diversity in Beijing would have remained a mere idea in my mind. At that time, Dr. Knepper had published *A Spectrum of Faith: Religions of the World in America's Heartland*. With exquisite photographs and polished words, the book gives a detailed and vivid account of religious diversity, its formation, and its function in America. As chief editor, Dr. Knepper walked his undergraduate students through all the religious sites in Des Moines, documenting stories of the hearts and souls of the religious followers. The book is a collective effort under the guidance of Dr. Knepper. I could not have imagined a better venue for developing and improving the many different talents and skills of students: researching, writing, and organizing. Inspired by *A Spectrum of Faith* and informed by our own pool of talent back home at Minzu University of China, I came to the idea of

1. 本书作者民大-德雷克师生集体照 Group photo of the teams from Minzu and Drake universities

　　我们相信，宗教是活在文化与心灵中的故事。为说明这一点，我们努力对北京17个宗教场所进行深度描写。对每一个宗教场所，我们试图从三个方面进行讲述：一个宗教空间的故事、一个宗教教职人员的故事、一个信众的故事。将这三个方面的故事综合在一起，我们希望呈现出不同宗教是如何在漫长的历史岁月中将自己烙印在北京这座城市的建筑与空间之上，它们具有怎样的深入人心的力量，如何吸引人为其奉献一生，如何渗透生活而又转化生活，又怎样以不同方式将人们整合为一个群体。

　　在中国，包括佛教、道教、伊斯兰教、天主教与基督教在内的五大宗教享有完全相同的法律地位。但是，中国宗教的复杂性、多层次性、多面性却使我们不能不对儒家和民间信仰加以关注。儒家的宗教性还在争议之中，但儒家无疑是各宗教在中国都要与之进行对话，进而互学互通的对象。而民间信仰由于它的变易性、草根性而难以从严格的法律意义上界定其身份，但它却是中国人宗教性格的真实反映。因此，本书也包含了儒家与民间信仰的内容。

　　在此书完成之际，我们特别感谢中央民族大学和德雷克大学的行政团队对此项目的支持。本项目得到中央民族大学创新引智基地"一带一路宗教研究"的支持，属于"一带一路宗教文明史专题"（KC2037）的教学成果。中央民族大学的宋敏、胡华征、刘成有、蓝慧文对国际学术合作始终热心支持，为宗教学在中央民族大学的发展提供了优良的国际合作环境；潘少铎、范小青、田世珠、邝全、谭泽民为此项目做出大量的组织、培训和后勤工作；中美两位摄影师 Robert Blanchard 与和映龙精彩地将北京的宗教影像呈现给读者。中央民族大学张筱嘉、梁卫国对本书文字做了一些编校工作。北京这些宗教场所的各界人士，为我们的调研和座谈提供了诸多便利，我们对他们表示衷心感谢，他们才是北京宗教的真正主角。

developing our own version of religious diversity. After some discussion with Dr. Knepper, the two of us decided to have philosophy and religion students from Minzu University of China offer an in-depth depiction of Beijing's religious diversity. Through them, we wish to tell an extended story to the international academic world, investigating the religious souls of Chinese people, exploring the religious aspects of Chinese culture, and interpreting the co-existence and co-learning between different Chinese religions. This was a collaborative project: first, Chinese students produced an initial draft of each chapter; next, after translation, American students raised questions and comments about these chapters; then, during a summer 2019 visit to Beijing, the American students visited each of the religious sites with the Chinese students and worked with the Chinese students to produce a final draft of each chapter; finally Timothy Knepper and I worked together in January 2020 to review all the chapters, address lingering issues, and finalize the entire book.

We believe that religions are stories in the minds and souls of people, as well as in the culture of a society. To illustrate this point, we strive to offer an in-depth account of each of the seventeen religious sites in Beijing. For each place of worship, there are stories of its religious space, of its religious leaders, and of its practitioners. We strive to illustrate how each religion transcends time, leaving behind clear marks in the space and architecture of Beijing; what great power religion has to call people to a lifetime of devotion; and how religions penetrate into and become part of ordinary people's lives, eventually integrating individuals into one community.

In China, all five major religions—Buddhism, Daoism, Islam, Catholicism, and Christianity—enjoy equal legal status. However, we did not exclude Confucianism and "folk religions" in our research, as the nature of Chinese religion is complex and multi-dimensional. Although the religious identity of Confucianism is still controversial, it is undoubtedly a partner in dialogue, learning, and integration to every other Chinese religion. To legally define the identity of "folk religions" can be challenging due to its grassroots nature and tendency to generate derivatives. However, folk beliefs reflect the real religious characters of the Chinese people. This book therefore also contains chapters about Confucianism and "folk religion."

Upon completion of this book, we would like to express our gratitude to the administrative teams of Minzu University of China and Drake University for their efforts in this project. *Religions of Beijing* is supported by the "Research Center of the Religions of the Belt and Road Initiative." Song Min, Hu Huazheng, Liu Chengyou, and Lan Huiwen from Minzu University of China have been forever enthusiastic and supportive of international collaboration, without which an excellent environment for international cooperation in the development of religious studies at Minzu would not have been achieved; Pan Shaoduo, Fan Xiaoqing, Tian Shizhu, Kuang Quan, and Tan Zemin, made a great effort to provide training and logistics for this project; two photographers, Robert Blanchard and He Yinglong, presented to readers and audiences fabulous pictures and images of Beijing religions; and Zhang Xiaojia and Liang Weiguo from Minzu University of China offered text-editing help for this book. We also express our sincere gratitude to the people of all the religious sites in Beijing. They provided many conveniences for our research. They are the real protagonists of religions in Beijing.

Timothy Knepper

It would seem futile to identify a point of origin for a publication project as expansive and ambitious as *Religions of Beijing*: The op-ed that I wrote for the *Des Moines Register* in 2015 about a local Vietnamese temple's dedication of a Quan Âm statue? My first meeting with Bob Blanchard, the photographer who

介绍

蒂莫西·耐普

要为像《北京的宗教》这样庞大而富有心愿的出版项目找到一个出发点，似乎颇不容易。是2015年那篇我给《得梅因纪事报》(Des Moines Register)所写有关越南裔佛教寺庙的观音塑像落成典礼的评论文章吗？或是我第一次与摄影师鲍勃·布兰查德的会见？正是他阅读了专栏，给专栏拍照，后来同意与我共同开启一段旅程。这段旅程孕育了由学生撰写、图片叙述爱荷华州得梅因宗教《信仰的光谱》(得梅因：德雷克社区出版社，2017年)的出版。亦或是2015年我第一次见到游斌博士？他被德雷克大学中国文化交流项目前主任柯克·马丁(Kirk Martin)邀请到德雷克大学(Drake University)，了解我们的"比较项目"（Comparison Project），并参与其中一场跨宗教的对话。游斌博士后来提议，由他与我以北京为对象再做一遍"信仰的光谱"研究，作为中央民族大学和德雷克大学的一次合作。

如果说这些事件中没有一件具有特别的决定性意义，但每一件又都是形成要件，比如德雷克大学国际项目主管安妮克·基尔（Annique Kiel）给我的鼓励；这个项目获得了德雷克大学纳尔逊研究所(Drake University's Nelson Institute)颁发的奖项；布卢姆斯伯里出版社（Bloomsbury）的卡米拉·厄斯金对这个项目的支持；2018年6月，达里亚·特伦蒂尼（Daria Trentini）陪同我前往北京，对民大同学们进行民族志研究的"培训"；鲍勃·布兰查德（Bob Blanchard）再次参与拍摄宗教场所和宗教活动的照片，而这次是在地球的另一端；约翰·芬达（John Fender）设计并编辑了这些照片，这次不仅有英文，还有中文；梁兆枫罗（Phoebe Liang D'Alessandro）将中国学生的作品初步翻译成英文；我开设"北京的宗教"一课的同学们在2019年上半年的修改和编辑；以及布卢姆斯伯里出版社的拉里·佩斯格劳娃（Lalle Pursglove）灵巧的能力来完成这个项目。要全面认识和充分感谢所有为这个项目作出贡献的人，是难以做到的。

为了记录起见，我在此对我的那些学生们表示赞赏，他们一直坚持到最后，为无数的查证和翻译问题费尽心力。他们是玛德琳·比约克、萨拉·费尔德曼、爱尔兰娜·拉尔森、妮可·玛格琳、凯尔西·里克和卡默隆·托马斯。我也谢谢那些只参加了春季2109课程和/或2019年5月"北京的宗教"旅行研讨会的学生：卢克·布兰瑟沃、罗莎琳·凯里、达娜·康尼根、蕾切尔·菲舍尔、珍妮·福格莱松、肖恩·格里芬、乔希·拉迪霍夫、亨利·穆里洛、迈克·奥沙利文、约翰·大卫·奥滕巴赫、娜塔丽·谢尔曼、科林·斯蒂芬斯和安娜·安赛瑟克。我非常感谢德雷克大学罗兰和玛丽·纳尔逊外交与国际事务研究所授予的"紧迫全球问题研究基金"，和德雷克大学国际中心向我提供的国际伙伴关系研究经费。

最重要的是，我想感谢与我共事的那些学生——游斌博士的19位学生，他们不仅富于创造性地、出色地描写并研究他们的社区，而且在2019年5月我们为期两周的北京访问中慷慨和不辞辛苦地招待、友好地对待美国同学和我自己。正如在我们离开北京前，由于大雨而航班推迟一天，雨夜中他们一个同学发微信说："一定是上帝（或天、道、法、上帝、太极）在阻止你们这么快就离开，因为他知道我们已经变得如此亲近"。

最后，因为总有一些事情比"最重要的"更重要，那就是，我要感谢游斌博士，与他的友谊，是我在过去的四年里最珍视的。

read that op-ed, took photos at that dedication, and later agreed to begin a journey with me that culminated in the publication of a student-written, photo-narrative about religion in Des Moines, Iowa: *A Spectrum of Faith* (Drake Community Press, 2017)? My first introduction to Dr. You Bin, who was invited to Drake University in 2015 by our former director of the Chinese Cultural Exchange Program, Kirk Martin, to learn about The Comparison Project and participate in one of its interfaith dialogues? Dr. You's later proposal that he and I replicate *Spectrum* in Beijing as a collaboration between Minzu University of China and Drake University?

If none of these events were singularly decisive, all were significantly formative, as were the encouraging support from Annique Kiel, the director of Drake International; the award from Drake University's Nelson Institute that I later received for the project; the nurturing support of the project by Bloomsbury's Camilla Erskine; Daria Trentini's ready willingness to accompany me to Beijing in June 2018 to train the Minzu students in ethnographic research; Bob Blanchard's rivaled willingness to take photos of religious sites and practices yet again, this time on the other side of the globe; John Fender's design and layout of those photos, this time alongside not only English words but also Mandarin characters; Phoebe Liang D'Alessandro's translation of those characters into words; the developmental and copy editing, respectively, of my Spring 2019 and May 2019 "Religions of Beijing" students; and the deft competence of Bloomsbury's Lalle Pursglove to see the project through to completion. It is just as futile to comprehensively recognize and adequately thank all those who contributed to this project.

For the sake of record, I recognize here those students of mine who stayed on board until the final end, laboring over countless factual and translation queries: Madelyn Bjork, Sara Feldman, Ireland Larsen, Nicole Margheim, Kelsey Rick, and Kameron Tomes. I also thank those students who were only involved in the Spring 2019 course and/or May 2019 travel-seminar on "Religions of Beijing": Luke Branthaver, Rosalind Carey, Danae Conigan, Rachel Fischer, Jennie Foglesong, Sean Griffin, Josh Ladehoff, Henry Murillo, Mike O'Sullivan, Jondavid Ottenbacher, Natalie Sherman, Collin Stephens, and Anna Wondrasek. I am very grateful for the "Pressing Global Issues Grant" awarded by Drake University's Rolland and Mary Nelson Institute for Diplomacy and International Affairs, as well as for the International Partnership Grants that I received from Drake International.

Above all, I want to thank those students with whom I worked least—the nineteen students of Dr. You's who not only creatively and competently researched and wrote about their communities but also graciously and tirelessly hosted and befriended my students and me for our two-week visit to Beijing in May 2019. As one of you "WeChatted" on the rainy evening before our departure, God (or Tian, Dao, Dharma, Shangdi, Taiji) must have been preventing us from departing so soon, knowing how close we all had grown.

Finally, since there is always something above what is "above all," I thank "Ben" (Dr. You Bin), whose friendship, above all, I have cherished over the last four years.

白云观

陈 睿

京城繁花似锦,熙熙攘攘,却也不乏世外桃源之地。北倚西护城河,南接莲花池东路,月坛街道所辖之地,老幼妇孺大都知道有一世外桃源——全真道重镇白云观。

"白云",总使人联想到宏大、浪漫的画面,譬如唐代崔颢的《黄鹤楼》诗句"黄鹤一去不复返,白云千载空悠悠",又如唐王之涣《凉州词》的"黄河远上白云间,一片孤城万仞山。"道教白云观在唐代曾被称作"天长观"。无论"白云",抑或"天长",恍惚间皆暗指大道之绵延流动和长久永恒。白云观的建筑形制,很是端正。山门将世俗世界与神圣空间大致分离开来。山门上一横额"琼林阆苑"四字极尽人间笔墨之精,一念间,恣肆纷扰等皆如行云流水般游向天际。

时空:圣与俗的相遇

由山门向北进,红墙青拱之间,历经风霜的"敕建白云观"匾额,昭示着白云观曾作为皇帝御令建筑的烟云过往,默默吟唱李唐王朝的盛世与悲歌。有趣的是,由匾额所在的第一道正门进入,一道窝风桥打破平坦路径,桥下的钟声清脆悦耳,先声夺人,即所谓"钟声福兆"。声音是宗教仪式过程中的标记性要素之一。道教充分发挥

2. 白云观山门入口 Mountain Gate entrance of Baiyunguan

Baiyunguan Temple

Chen Rui, with Nicole Margheim, editor

As bustling and flowery as it appears to be, the capital city of Beijing never lacks for paradise-like escapes. One such escape, known to old and young, men and women, is called Baiyunguan ("White Cloud Temple"). Situated on Yuetan Street in Beijing's Xicheng District, Baiyunguan is bounded on its north by the West Moat and connected by Lianhuachi East Road in the south.

People always associate "baiyun"—white clouds—with grand and romantic scenes, as illustrated in the Tang Dynasty poem "Yellow Crane Tower" by Cui Hao (704–754):

The yellow cranes would never return,
leaving the white clouds drifting idly by for thousands of years.

Or the Tang Dynasty poem "One Song of Liangzhou Ci" by Wang Zhihuan (688–742):

The Yellow River vanishes into the far white clouds,
one lone town lies among towering mountain ranges.

In the Tang Dynasty, the Daoist Temple Baiyunguan was called Tianchangguan ("Temple of Heavenly Perpetuity"). Both "white clouds" and "heavenly perpetuity" connote the great Dao winding through to eternity.

The Temple features a symmetric architectural style. The temple's Mountain Gate separates the secular world from the holy space. At the sight of the four characters 琼林阆苑 ("Fine Jade and Lofty Park") inscribed on the top of the Mountain Gate, which exemplifies the best of paint and brush art in the human world, one instantly feels their chaotic secular thoughts turned to floating clouds running towards the edge of heaven.

Time and Space: Where the Holy and the Secular Meet

North of the Mountain Gate, between the red walls and the green arches, there is a plaque reading 敕建白云观 ("Royal Edict to Build the Baiyun Temple"), stating the imperial order to build the temple. It serves as a reminder of the initial prosperity and later decline of the Tang Dynasty (618–907), a long gone past vanished like smoke. After the first main gate, the flat path is broken by "Wofeng Bridge." One's attention is immediately caught by the pleasant tinkling sound of the bell beneath the bridge. This is what is called "bell sound, good luck." Sound is one important hallmark of religious ritual, with the sound of the bell creating a solemn Daoist ritual atmosphere, mentally preparing practitioners to enter the supernatural world. A popular activity called "Hitting the Golden Eye" was even developed, according to which if one hits the "golden eye" (bell) with a coin, one will have good luck. This is a timeless ritual that visitors can perform without the need for a ceremony master.

From here, one can see the basic architectural layout of the temple. Along the central axis, from south to north, are Lingguan Hall, Yühuang Hall, Laolü Hall, Patriarch Qiu Hall, and Siyü Hall. The latter four halls are larger than the first one. Yühuang Hall is flanked by two halls that face inward to each other: Caishen ("Money Deities") Hall on the east, and Sanguan ("Three Officer Great Deities") Hall on

了此要素在塑造仪式意义和调整信徒对超自然世界的理解等方面的作用，甚至发展出全部由民众参与和主持的无时间规定性的仪式，即被称作"打金钱眼"的民俗活动。

行至此处，已基本窥观内的建筑风格。中轴殿宇整体为南北走向，依次为灵官殿、玉皇殿、老律堂、邱祖殿、四御殿，且后四者规模更大。玉皇殿的东西侧面，是财神殿与三官殿相向而立。钟楼与鼓楼则各居于财神殿和三官殿两侧。钟鼓二楼前各植两株翠松，终年苍绿，只是不同季节有不同景致，仿佛四神立于中道两侧，沉默中迎来送往。

由灵官殿穿过后，常见人们举香朝玉皇殿、财神殿、三官殿方向敬拜，是否进殿再拜，则取决于个人的心理需求，即体现其对宗教的功利性追求。这种选择动机与游人或信徒当下的生活境遇有极大关联。玉皇大帝、财神、三官信仰集中体现了以道教为代表的中国传统宗教与西方宗教的极大不同——道教的崇拜体系是多神的，道教的神灵功能与大众人生观念紧密结合，所以极大影响中国人看待俗世的方式。道教认为，玉皇大帝创生万物、分辨是非，总管三界、十方、四生、六道的一切祸福。中国千年封建王朝，人间历史更迭，或合或分，政权始终由至高帝王执掌。在中国人心目中，神仙佛菩萨世界中至高者应当是玉皇大帝，却常忽视在道教内部尊崇三清（元始天尊、灵宝天尊、道德天尊）应甚于玉皇崇拜的事实。

宗教解决人间问题首推生死与命运。道教倡导长生成仙，与佛教对来世的设想乐此不疲相比，则更重视今生的所作所为。"三官"的内涵为天官赐福，地官赦罪，水官解厄。前往三官殿朝拜与参观的人数众多，并且常有中年人与本殿道长交流关于如何摆脱厄运的问题。个中原由，一方面在于该殿所供奉天、地和水三官能在一定程度上满足人对平安康泰的内心祈愿，另一个深层的原因则与儒家的矛盾思想有关，即儒家一面强调"敬鬼神而远之"，另一面倡导"事死如事生，事亡如事存"。在这种看似矛盾的态度中，却体现出中国人对祖先崇拜的深厚情感。中国民众对先祖的祭祀与追思在中元节（农历七月十五日）纪念中鲜活地体现出来。例如在以烧纸钱等方式祭奠去世亲人的行为背后包含了两种复杂的心理：一面是寄托思念；一面是希望亡灵能保佑在世家庭成员的平安，而不是搅扰。到了宋代，道教的三官信仰与三元日（农历正月十五称为上元，农历七月十五称为中元，农历十月十五称为下元）逐渐靠近，并最终实现了神灵崇拜与节日庆典的融合。换个角度来讲，由于三元日在民间的影响极为深远，三官信仰也使得道教神灵在民间信仰体系中获得新的生命，并体现儒道精神在民间的下移和延伸。

日常：内修与敬神

玉皇殿后，药王殿、救苦殿分立于老律堂两侧，但依旧处于中路位置。往日，除了道士们日常诵经以外，每逢道教神灵和祖师圣诞日，老律堂便成为观内更重要的处所。此殿亦称"七真殿"（始建于公元1228年），殿内供奉丘处机等七位道教全真派祖师。历史上，丘处机与成吉思汗雪山会面，使全真道达到极盛，所以他对于全真道的勃兴和发展意义重大。全真道在教义与修持方面标榜儒释道"三教圆融"。其反对外丹修炼而强调内丹的重要性，重视识心见性和清修自苦。宫观道士的日常维持，可分为规范性的日常功课以及文化知识生活方面的自习自修两方面。前者是最为常规的活动。早坛和晚坛功课的时间，经文是必不可少的，多为四字一句，且多以精气神之内修内炼为本。同时，唱和要与经文相结合。

3. 窝风桥下的好运钟 Good-luck bell beneath Wofeng Bridge

4. 道士敬香 Daoist priest offering incense *(photo by He Yinglong)*

the west. These two halls are themselves flanked by a clock tower and drum tower. Two evergreen pines guard these towers, silently greeting people passing by, offering different sights in different seasons.

After passing through Lingguan Hall, one often sees people worshipping while facing Yühuang Hall, Caishen Hall, and Sanguan Hall. The decision to enter these halls to worship is entirely up to the individual, subject to each person's own life situation. Here, there is a big difference between Chinese religions, as represented by Daoism, and Western religions. Daoism is polytheistic, at least to some extent. The functions of Daoist deities are closely related to people's views towards life, which in turn impact people's views towards the secular world.

According to Daoism, an immortal called Yuhuang ("Jade Emperor") creates all beings, distinguishes right from wrong, oversees yin and yang, and manages the fortunes and mishaps of all three realms, ten directions, four life-forms, and six worlds. Through thousands of years of Chinese history, with one dynasty continually replacing another and the country perpetually passing from division to reunion, one constant fact was the control of the regime by the emperors. Chinese people consider the supreme governing God among immortals, Buddhas, and bodhisattvas to be the Jade Emperor, neglecting the fact that Daoists should hold the highest esteem for the Three Purities (Yuanshi Tianzun, Lingbao Tianzun, Daode Tianzun).

5. 碧霞元君造像 Statue of Bixia Yuanjun, Goddess of Sunlight from the East

  以老律堂为中心，分为三个方向：向北行是邱祖殿、四御殿等；向东则分布有雷祖殿、真武殿等；西面则是元君殿、元辰殿等。

  东进路途中，题有"抱元洞府"四字的门洞将中轴建筑与偏殿区巧妙、含蓄地分离开来。东路真武殿主神号称"玄天上帝金阙化身荡魔天尊"，造型魁梧，高额，目光迥然有力，被赋予护佑群生、协衡天道的职责。殿内供奉天蓬、天佑二天将。"玄天上帝"原为民间宗教体系的真武神，他对中国文化影响极深。道教产生后，其将民间玄武信仰吸纳进来。玄武在宋代改名为真武，并一直沿用到今天。建于明英宗正统三年（公元1438年）的雷祖殿，供奉雷祖及风雨雷电四位自然天神。之所以供奉多位神而非一位神，是由于在雷神人格化过程中，神灵职能逐渐丰富，身份也渐渐多元。雷神"头如猕猴"，电母神手中造雷电所用的法器，恍惚间将人带入中国古典巨著《西游记》中对雷公电母及其风雷滚动、电雨将倾的形象描绘于其中。

  出"抱元洞府"向西行，面前是"会仙福地"。道观普遍不如佛寺那样恢弘，但外观精致、朴素，砖瓦与外墙色彩深重，含蓄内敛。其内部构造简约，主神和辅神有序分列，绕以仙鹤踱步与蛟龙飞腾的主题，俨然一副天界福景。

  西路的元君殿，有一点与其他殿宇不同——主神碧霞元君背靠南而面向北，所以该殿入口在北方。殿内所供碧霞元君，有五位化身，其总体功能为赐福赐子、护佑婚姻。五位性别皆为女性，为观者传递强烈的亲和力。这一点也成为其被民间亲切称为"泰山老奶奶"之香火绵延的一个原因。只是这位白云观内的碧霞元君同其他四位奶奶，相比在泰山供奉的奶奶，却少了很多风光。

6. 斗姆元君殿内的神仙们 Statue of Doumu Yuanjun, Mother Goddess of the Big Dipper, in front of immortals

Religions solve human problems, primarily life, death, and destiny. Daoism advocates becoming immortal. Compared with Buddhism's vision of the afterlife, Daoism pays more attention to what has been done in the current life. Belief in the immortals called Sanguan includes blessings by Heaven, pardons by Earth, and relief of misfortune by Water. Daoist worshippers and visitors flood to Sanguan Hall. Many middle-aged people often talk to the Daoist priest on duty, inquiring how to be relieved from misfortunes. The three immortals offered here—Heaven, Earth, and Water—satisfy people's wishes for peace, safety, and health. This reflects the spiritual nature of the Chinese people; for example, Confucianism emphasizes "respecting spirits but staying away from them" and advocates "serving the dead as if they were alive; serving the departed as if they were still around." This seemingly contradictory attitude reveals the Chinese people's strong sentimental attachment to ancestors. The commemoration ceremony at the Zhong Yuan Festival (Ghost Festival) most vividly exemplifies this tradition. For example, there are two complicated reasons behind the burning of paper money for the ancestors at these memorial services: cherishing the thoughts of the deceased relatives, and preventing the celestial spirits of the dead from disturbing the living. After the Song Dynasty (960–1279), the Daoist belief in the Sanguan was increasingly linked with the Sanyuan Festivals (on the fifteenth day of the first, seventh, and tenth lunar months), eventually merging, the result of which was the integration of the worship of heavenly spirits and the celebration of festivals. From a different perspective, Sanguan belief enabled the rebirth of Daoist spirits in folk religions, thanks to the profound influence of the Sanyuan Festivals on ordinary peoples' lives. This also shows that the spirit of combining Confucianism and Daoism extends into folk religions and communities.

7. 静心燃香 Lighting incense as an offering

相比之下，西路殿宇的尽头有元辰殿，香火始终旺盛。这里供奉斗姥元君与六十太岁神。拜斗姥，即拜掌管凡人薄籍的神；拜太岁，即叩拜各人出生之年的保护神。静心向他们供香，能够消灾延寿，或许能够满足人基本的心愿，即对平安的期待。

灵性的表达：认同与实践

恍惚之间，不远处似有乐声响起，张弛有度，其间夹有人的唱诵之声。随声所至，只见殿外经幡飘扬，殿的里外几乎都站满了人，原是恰逢文昌帝君圣诞日（农历二月初三）法会庆典。就白云观而言，道众群体的规模并不小，或许与其十方常住制度有关——虽不能私收弟子，却可以接受道众留居，但是组织管理十分有序。门庭内的多数信众双手呈现抱拳样式，左手叠在右手上，对向合并在胸前。这种拜神灵的方式连同其他日常礼貌性礼仪在《周礼》和《礼记》中都有出处。中国道教学院C道长讲到，"作为一般游客信众，了解道教礼拜仪式和基本知识的并不是很多，大家只不过是延续了民俗传统，带着向往幸福美好的心情来拜神，真正深入学习道教常识的不多"。C道长接着说，"手势不是最重要的，而庄严仪式之内的存心最为重要,如果把精力放在研究仪式而不是探究仪式要解决的问题，恐怕要多研究五百年，也不一定能弄明白"。

Routine: Internal Cultivation and Immortal Worshipping

The Medicine King Temple and Temple of Salvation from Suffering both stand behind Yühuang Hall, on either side of the Laolü Hall. Laolü Hall is not only where Daoist priests chant daily but also the most important temple in Baiyunguan on the birthdays of the deities and founders of Daoism. Laolü Hall is also called the "Temple of Seven Immortals." Built in 1228, the temple is dedicated to the seven founders of Quanzhen Daoism. The development of Quanzhen Daoism culminated with Patriarch Qiu Chuji's meeting with Genghis Khan at Snow Mountain (in the 1220s). Thus Qiu Chuji is of great significance to the development and prosperity of Quanzhen Daoism. In terms of doctrine and practice, Quanzhen advocates integration of the three religions: Confucianism, Buddhism, and Daoism. It opposes the practice of external alchemy, instead advocating alchemy within the body, which attaches great importance to discovering one's true nature and cultivating a non-attached mind.

The daily activity of the Daoist priests at the temple can be divided into two spheres: on the one hand, religious practices; on the other hand, self-learning, self-cultivation, cultural knowledge, and daily life. The former is mostly routine. Reciting or chanting scriptures is necessary in the morning and evening. These scriptures mostly involve four-character sentences that are focused on internal training and cultivation of *jing* (essence), *qi* (vital energy), and *shen* (spirit).

From Laolü Hall, the buildings expand in three directions: to the north they include the Patriarch Qiu Hall and the Siyü Hall; to the east, the Temple of Leizu and the Temple of Zhenwu; and to the west, the Temple of Yuanjun and the Temple of Yuanchen. Walking to the east, the arched gate with the inscription 抱元洞府 ("Baoyuan Cave") tactfully separates the central-axis area from the peripheral halls. The immortal worshipped at Zhenwu Hall on the East Road has the title "Xuantian Shangdi Jinque Huashen Dangmo Tianzun" ("immortal in charge of getting rid of the devil"). The statue has a strong build, wide forehead, and bold eyebrows. The eyes project clear light and firm power, as the immortal is empowered to protect earthly lives and coordinate heavenly tasks. Tianpeng General and Tianyou General are also worshipped here.

"Xuantian Shangdi" was originally the immortal called Zhenwu in folk religions. He had a strong impact on Chinese culture. When Daoism was adopted, it enlisted Zhenwu as one of its deities. Zhenwu was renamed Xuanwu in the Song Dynasty, and this name continues to today. Leizu Hall, built in the third year of the Yingzong regime (1438) during the Ming Dynasty, is dedicated to Leizu and the four nature-immortals: wind, rain, thunder, and lightning. The reason why many immortals are worshipped instead of one is that in the process of personalizing thunder, the functions of the immortals were gradually enriched and their identities were slowly diversified. The Thunder immortal has a head like a macaque. The magical tool held by the Lightning Mother reminds people of the relationship between Thunder Father and Lightning Mother—the alternating of thunder and lightning before heavy rain—characters and scenes from the *Journey to the West* (sixteenth century), a classic of Chinese literature.

Passing underneath an archway with a plaque that reads 抱元洞府 ("A Celestial Place to Embrace Oneness") and walking to the west, one arrives at "Fortune Land of Meeting Immortals" (会仙福地). Daoist temples are usually not as striking as Buddhist temples; rather they are simple and exquisite. The darker and heavier colored bricks and tiles give Baiyunguan a reserved and restrained architectural style. The internal structure is simple. The main immortal and auxiliary immortals are lined up in an orderly manner, with the theme of the background composed of cranes leisurely striding

8. 为神仙齐声唱诵的道士们 Daoist priests praising the immortals *(photo by He Yinglong)*

and dragons soaring to the sky. One could mistake this as paradise.

The Yuanjun Hall on the West Road has one unique feature: the Goddess of Sunlight from the East (Bixia Yuanjun) faces north; thus the entrance to the hall is located on the north side. Five incarnations of the Goddess of Sunlight from the East are worshipped here. In general they bless people with good marriages and childbirth. All five incarnations are female, which instantly closes the psychological distance between the immortals and their worshippers. This might explain why the Old Grandma at Mount Tai (a nickname of Bixia Yuanjun) sees constant streams of pilgrims. By comparison, the offerings received at Baiyunguan are considerably less.

In contrast, the Yuanchen Temple at the end of the West Road appears always to be flourishing. Here the Mother Goddess of the Big Dipper (Doumu Yuanjun) is in charge of recording the moral deeds of people, while the sixty immortals take turns safeguarding people's birth years over a sixty-year cycle. By bringing a calm mind and offering joss sticks, supplicants hope to be relieved of all disasters, live a long life, and ultimately attain peace.

Expression of Spirituality: Recognition and Practice

In a moment of trance, one hears the sound of music close by, blended with singing and chanting. Following the sound, one sees prayer flags fluttering in the air. Laolü Hall is filled with people both inside and out. It turns out to be the Wenchang Emperor's birthday ceremony (on the third day of the second lunar month). The number of Daoist participants is considerable, especially as far as Baiyunguan is concerned. This is possibly due to the uniquely Daoist "Ten-Direction Residence System," which means that Daoist temples are owned by the public and therefore Daoists of any school can take residence in them. Most of the believers in the court present "holding-fist style," with their left hands stacked on top of their right hands, both placed in front of their chests. This way of worshipping, along with other daily rituals, are recorded in both the *Rites of Zhou* and the *Book of Rites* (two Confucian classics). According to Daoist priest C, a teacher at the Chinese Daoist College that is located in Baiyunguan, "Ordinary visitors don't have much knowledge about Daoism or its rituals. They simply come to worship, bringing a good mood and good wishes, a traditional practice in folk traditions."

He then continued, "Gestures are not the most important thing, but rather the true heart you bring to attend the solemn ceremony. If one's effort is focused on researching rituals rather than the issues that the rituals try to solve, one would take an extra 500 years to practice."

"Objectively speaking, we see more people on ordinary days," continued Daoist priest C. "Baiyunguan is one of a few big Daoist temples in Beijing given the city's population of twenty million. However, there are many historical sites in Beijing. Baiyunguan isn't the primary choice for outside visitors. Some travel agencies even proposed to collaborate with us and share the profit, but the proposal was declined by our Daoist priests. For years, the price of entrance tickets has been kept at 10 Yuan. Revenue from tourism is not our goal."

On the outer circle of the massive crowd of lay practitioners and tourists, we met Ms. Guo from this neighborhood. She happened to visit the temple today and was attracted by the beautiful music. She is not unfamiliar with the ceremonial activities; still she was curious about what was going on. "Ceremonies and temple fairs here are very interesting," she said. "I am not a believer, and I don't have neighbor friends who visit here often. Still, I try to come here myself whenever there are activities. I have met a number of believers. Many come from the suburbs. I have learned a lot by chatting with them."

客观地讲，"平日来白云观的信徒更多"，C道长说，"白云观是两千万人口的北京城为数不多的大道观之一，但北京古迹众多，作为古迹，白云观并不是外地游客的首选。曾经有旅行社与白云观联系，提出要合作分成，白云观的道长们没理会他们。白云观的门票二十多年来一直是十元，可见，旅游收益并不是白云观的目标"。

俗众外围巧遇一位郭女士，她住在附近，恰好经过道观，也被悠扬的曲调吸引过来。虽然对观内的法事活动并不陌生，但她还是想看一看。"这里的法事和庙会活动很有意思"，她说，"我虽然不是信徒，身边也没有很多常来道观的邻居，可有活动的时候，能来就来。在信众里也认识了不少人。他们很多从郊区赶过来，和他们聊天，收获不小呢！"

由拥挤的俗众中远望，见三位道长身着华丽法衣作为主礼者平行横列于供桌前。法衣蓝青白黄紫五色相间，八卦图式以金丝线绣于袖口。其余道士为辅礼者，横向分列于主礼区两侧。供桌摆设几乎都是圆形的水果供物。主礼人念诵并吟唱经文时，一般背向信徒们。此三人作揖、叩首朝拜的同时，俗众无一不跟随、效仿。实际上，在站立观望道士们举行礼仪的过程中，一部分信徒并不太明白道士们说辞的内容和意义。而道士的礼仪行动，更多的是代表不能直接与神灵交流的信众，向所供奉祖师，向被纪念的神仙，向唱诵的祈祷文中涉及的诸多神灵表达敬礼，并诚惶诚恐地祈求神灵将俗众所求心愿赐予他们。

作为科名举子信奉的文昌帝君在当下的道教、民间宗教中依然具有强大的生命力。在明代的文昌信仰高峰时，文昌帝君甚至取代了孔子之地位受到崇奉。大致看来，现今的北京白云观庆贺文昌圣诞法会仪式有如下显著的特征：1.道士团体与信众保持一定的距离，各自保证在所属——神圣空间与世俗空间中。2.唱诵祷词更多以赞颂的形式，对道教主要神灵、祖师及其功绩进行回顾，且反复体现强烈的儒释道三教圆融精神。3.铃铛作为主要法器，伴随仪式的起止，以及节奏的需要，具有一定的仪式功能。4.仪式中有香供养。C道长提到，香供养的目的是通过香，使主礼者存想诸神诸灵。5.主礼的三位道长在叩首、用香、唱诵之中穿插禹步来实现位置的变换。正如C道长所说："仪式的关键在凝神定气，还有阴阳五行生克的理念，亦有礼乐文化包含其中。任何宗教都有仪式，非宗教也有，如人民英雄纪念碑的祭典、天安门广场阅兵。仪式贵在存心，离开心谈仪式，就是演戏，就没有效果。"

道教在发展过程中，与其他宗教之神灵的互渗现象相对显著。在一般情况下，中国人有针对性地选择神灵并朝拜。而在很多情况下，随意求一位神灵即可满足人所有的心愿，只求灵验、有效即可，这反映了中国人的一种宗教特征。

随着时代的发展，宗教场所日益承担越来越多的社会功能。白云观在21世纪以来也对周围民众社区作了不少贡献。C道长说："道观不是一个钱箱子，只会收钱。近年白云观公益支出有近两千万。"C道长接着说，"除了慈善捐助之外，白云观的公益讲堂、公益太极拳班、经书赠送、网站、微博和微信等宣传也是一种公益。白云观现在每周有公益讲堂，有几十人参加；有公益太极拳班，每期也有几十个学员。总的说来，居士教育规模不大。"但道教的神灵观、处世观等内容对中国社会的影响早已深入每个中国人的骨髓之中。当代大作家鲁迅毕竟曾以一言以蔽之："中国的根柢全在道教。"

From the far end of the crowd, three ceremony masters in sumptuous vestments stand parallel to the table of offerings. The vestments have five interwound colors: blue, green, white, yellow, and purple. Eight trigrams are embroidered with golden threads on the cuffs. The rest of the Daoist priests are ancillary to the celebration, and therefore line up horizontally on both sides of the main ceremony area. The offerings are mostly round-shaped fruits. When the ceremony masters recite the scriptures and sing, they usually turn their backs to the crowd. When they bow, kowtow, and worship, the crowd follows suit. Not everyone understands what the masters are singing or chanting, let alone its significance. The Daoist masters, therefore, express reverence to the deities for those who are not able to communicate with them directly. With great caution and awe, they request the deities to grant the crowd's wishes.

The immortal called the Wenchang Emperor, who was much respected by ancient scholars, still maintains powerful influence in Daoism and folk religions today. At the peak of belief in the Wenchang Emperor during the Ming Dynasty, even Confucius' status was challenged by the Wenchang Emperor. The ceremonial ritual for celebrating the Wenchang Emperor's birthday at Baiyunguan is a holy stage-show. Daoists maintain a certain distance from lay people and tourists since the two groups belong to different realms: sacred and secular. The prayers chanted by the Daoists consist mostly of praises of the main Daoist deities and founders, as well as of the integration of Daoism, Confucianism, and Buddhism. The bell is the main ceremonial instrument, accompanying the beginning and end of the ceremony, and offering rhythm for the ceremony itself. During the ceremony, incense is lit to help create a holy atmosphere. The goal of using incense, as explained by Daoist priest C, is to lead people to their memories of the immortals. The three ceremony masters constantly switch their positions by maneuvering their steps while kowtowing, waving incense, and chanting. Daoist priest C said, "The key to the ceremony is to collect one's spirit and stabilize *qi*. The concepts of yin/yang and the Five Elements, music, and the culture of rituals are all embedded in the ceremony. Every religion involves rituals, so do non-religious events like the memorial of the national heroes or military parades at Tiananmen Square. The most precious element for a ritual is a solemn heart. Without the heart, rituals are merely acting and achieve no results."

Exchanging divinities with other religions is one prominent feature of Daoism. Ordinarily, the Chinese select their target divinity to worship freely. On many occasions, however, they randomly request a god to grant all their wishes, as long as their prayers can be answered. This reveals one of the religious characteristics of the Chinese people.

As time passes, religious sites increasingly undertake more social functions. Since the twenty-first century, Baiyunguan has made numerous contributions to the neighboring community. Daoist priest C pointed out, "The Daoist temple is not a money box concerned only for profit. In recent years, Baiyunguan has spent nearly 20-million Yuan on public charities. In addition to donations, we also hold lectures, *taiji* classes, and offer free scriptures. Our websites, Weibo and WeChat all serve as platforms for public wellness. Our weekly lectures and *taiji* class attract a few dozen participants, but the scale of lay education is not big." Nevertheless, the influence of Daoist immortals and worldviews on Chinese society is deeply embedded in the heart of every Chinese person. As the great contemporary writer Lu Xun (1881–1936) once remarked, "The roots of China are all in Daoism." That says it all.

北顶娘娘庙

郑幼敏

历史

民间宗教构成了千千万万底层群众的笃诚信仰，对中国北方地区的汉族文化产生了深远的影响。中国民间有"北元君，南妈祖"之说，与南方地区广为人知的妈祖一样，碧霞元君是北方地区闻名于世的女神，因其道场在泰山，便有"泰山圣母碧霞元君"的尊称，俗称泰山娘娘。"碧霞"意指东方的日光之霞，"元君"则带有浓重的道教色彩，是道教女神的尊称。至于民众俗称的"娘娘"，是汉语里面对女性的尊称，民间把神话传说或道教中修炼成仙的女性也称作"娘娘"。碧霞元君最初是一位民间神，以"泰山玉女"的形象在汉唐时期出现，元代被纳入道教的祭祀范围，到明代"碧霞元君"的神号问世，民间的祭祀活动愈加繁盛，后来演变成一种皇家祭祀，到清代甚至被归入国家祀典。

供奉碧霞元君的北顶娘娘庙，恍如住于水立方和鸟巢之间的隐士，兜兜转转终得寻见它的踪迹。经过修葺，尽管后两进院落还未动工，朱红色的外墙与黄绿色的瓦片已然流露出新意，不会使人联想到这座庙肇始于明朝，以及几百年来的风风雨雨。一位自称"上知天文、下知地理"的导游谈到，这里原本是一座残破的土地庙，在明朝宣德皇帝（1425–1435）年间被敕建成北顶娘娘庙。当年宣德皇帝的母亲去泰山顶上向碧霞元君求子，随后便生了宣德皇帝。民间信仰讲求祈愿与还愿，可古代交通不便，于是北京就出现了娘娘庙，北顶娘娘庙便是其中之一。但"庙"何以称为"顶"？难道是由于北方多山，庙建在山顶的缘故吗？事实上，"五顶"都在城里，这种称谓实源于泰山。碧霞元君的本庙在泰山顶上，即"碧霞元君祠"。为了使碧霞元君"感觉"自己仍住在泰山顶上，便把庙称作"顶"，故称"北顶"。

到了清代，统治者广泛地修建碧霞元君庙，北顶娘娘庙就在乾隆年间经历了一次官方重修，山门上依旧可见"敕建北顶娘娘庙"的字样。民国时期却逐渐衰败，只遗存山门、二进殿和钟楼。1976 年，后殿因地震坍塌，先后被翻盖为北顶小学和工厂，只有山门和前殿保持原样。2003年，北顶娘娘庙被列为北京市文物保护单位。2008年北京奥运会前，北顶娘娘庙原本在奥运会主场馆的最初规划中，市政府为保护北顶娘娘庙，不但将国家游泳中心的选址北移，还根据考古发掘成果修复北顶娘娘庙，冠之以"北京民俗博物馆分馆"之名，成为奥林匹克公园的一部分。北顶娘娘庙受一家政府文物机构管辖，日常的安保、卫生、售香、旅游接待、供品管理等内容则由物业公司和公园分派的工作人员负责。

空间

仲春时节的北京，白日已有些微热。国家倡导文明敬拜，寺庙便少了烟火的气息，殿前的香炉紧闭，唯有一绺绺的红色祈福牌在风中来回碰撞，发出清脆鸣响。

北顶娘娘庙与国家体育场、国家游泳中心毗邻。庙宇完全采用道观的建筑形制，四进纵向的院落呈方形延伸，沿中轴线依次排列的主体建筑有山门殿、天王殿、娘

Beiding Niangniang Temple

Zheng Youmin, with Nicole Margheim, editor

History

Folk religions constitute the devout faith of thousands of ordinary people and exert great influence on Han culture in northern China. In the Chinese folk world, the saying goes, "Northern Yuanjun and Southern Mazu." Like the popular goddess Mazu of the south, Bixia Yuanjun (the Goddess of Sunlight from the East) is the favored goddess of northern China. Since her rite is at Tai Mountain (in Shandong Province), Bixia Yuanjun was given the honored name "Tai Mountain Madonna Bixia Yuanjun," or more commonly "Tai Mountain Niangniang." "Bixia" means "sunray from the east"; "Yuanjun" is a Daoist title for goddesses; and "Niangniang" is a term of respect to address females, especially in Chinese mythology and among Daoist immortals. Bixia Yuanjun was originally a folk goddess. She emerged as Tai Mountain Jade Maiden in the Han and Tang Dynasties (206 BCE – 220 CE, 618–907). In the Yuan Dynasty (1271–1368), Daoism included her in its list of deities to worship. But it was not until the Ming Dynasty (1368–1644) that the holy title Bixia Yuanjun was given to her, augmenting her worship in the folk world. This worship later evolved into a royal rite, becoming classified as a national ritual during the Qing Dynasty (1644–1912).

The Beiding ("Northern Top") Niangniang Temple dedicated to Bixia Yuanjun now lies hidden between Beijing's Ice Cube and Bird's Nest. I had to search carefully to find a trace of its location. At that time, the temple was undergoing renovation. Although work on the two rear courtyards had not yet started, a new vermilion façade and yellow-green tiles had already given the temple a fresh look. Who would associate this temple with one that was built during the Ming Dynasty and had weathered hundreds of years of rain and storm?

A tour guide who claimed to be immensely knowledgeable said that this site once contained a Land God temple, which over time had fallen into disrepair. During the era of Emperor Xuande (r. 1425–1435), an imperial order was given to build a Beiding Niangniang Temple on the site. Legend has it that the mother of Emperor Xuande had made her way to the top of Tai Mountain and prayed to Bixia Yuanjun for a son. Later, she gave birth to Emperor Xuande. Folk traditions attach great importance to expressing thanks to the gods if one's request is fulfilled; however, transportation conditions were poor at the time. So, the emperor decided to build Niangniang temples in Beijing, one of which was Beiding Niangniang Temple. But where does the name *"ding"* (top) come from? Are these temples built on mountain tops as is common in northern China? As a matter of fact, all the Five *"ding*s" are located in the city (where there are no mountains). Instead, the name *"ding"* relates to Mount Tai, the top of which is where the original temple of Bixia Yuanjun is located. To provide Yuanjun "top-of-the-mountain" status, the temple was therefore named *"ding."*

Numerous Bixia Yuanjun temples were built across the country during the Qing Dynasty. At that time, under the reign of Emperor Qianlong (r. 1735–1796), Beiding Niangniang Temple underwent official reconstruction. The inscription 敕建北顶娘娘庙 ("Royal Edict to Build the Temple") is still visible on the Mountain Gate. During the period of the Republic of China (1912–1949), many of the temple's structures fell into ruin, leaving only the Mountain Gate, Erjin Hall, and the bell tower. The back hall collapsed due

北顶娘娘庙

9. 象征凡间与圣所之分界的山门 Mountain Gate of Beiding Niangniang Temple

10. 院落布局错落有致 **Temple of the Heavenly Kings**

to the earthquake in 1976; afterwards, it was replaced first by the Beiding Elementary School, then by a factory. The Mountain Gate and the front hall were the only structures that remained intact. In 2003, Beiding Niangniang Temple was listed as a Cultural Relic Protection Unit in Beijing. In its initial planning, however, the 2008 Olympics designated the temple as the site of one of the main stadiums. The Beijing municipal government successfully fought to keep the temple, and the site for the National Swimming Center was moved to the north. The government then decided to renovate the temple to its original look, using clues from archeological excavations, and naming it "Beijing Folk Museum Branch," as part of Olympic Park. At present, the Beiding Niangniang Temple is owned by the Beijing Municipal Administration of Cultural Heritage. Its daily maintenance, including security, sanitation, sales, tourism, and management of offerings are handled by a property management company and staff from the park.

Space

These days, the state advocates "civil" worship. The temple therefore does not permit smoke and fire, and has closed the incense burner. Instead, one must buy and offer red praying-cards, which are afterwards hung on the fences of the temple. In the wind, they strike one another, giving off tinkling sounds.

Construction of the temple follows Daoist temple architectural style. The four rows of longitudinal courtyards form a square. The main structures lining the central axis are: Mountain Gate Hall; Tianwang Hall for the Four Heavenly Kings; Niangniang Temple for the Goddess of the Sunlight from the East (Bixia Yuanjun), Eyesight Goddess (Mingmu

北顶娘娘庙

11. 四大天王之一 One of the Four Heavenly Kings

Yuanjun), and Children-Sending Goddess (Guangsi Yuanjun); Mount Tai (Dongyue) Hall; and Jade Emperor Temple (with the last two currently under repair). This is a convenient arrangement for the worshippers. Although the temple adopts the appearance of a Daoist temple, is devoted to Daoist deities, and has historically invited Daoists to reside there, Beiding Niangniang Temple is not a Daoist temple. Although Daoism is a native religion that actively interacts with and integrates folk religions, the central themes of Daoism involve the Dao and the Immortals. No Daoist temples can do without a space dedicated to the Three Purities; however, there is no such space at Beiding Niangniang Temple.

Mountain Gate Hall is located at the temple entrance, with the Bell Tower and Drum Tower standing on either side. The "Mountain Gate" is considered the front portal in Daoist architecture. The ancient Daoist temples were usually built in mountains and hills; therefore the gate was called "Mountain Gate," separating the secular world of the mountains from the immortal world of the temple. Bells and drums were used mostly to tell time. For Daoist temples, they are also ritual instruments, provided with the power to communicate with the gods and drive away evil spirits. They can also be used to call Daoist gatherings. Since there are no Daoists in Beiding Niangniang Temple, however, the gates of the bell and drum towers are locked. These buildings now serve only to provide shade for visitors on sizzling hot days.

Walking straight to the north, one arrives at the Temple of the Heavenly Kings. It was empty before being converted to a school shop during the Cultural Revolution. In recent renovation, however, the Four Heavenly Kings were added—Moliqing, Molihong, Molihai, and Molishou, all of whom come from the novel *Investiture of the Gods* (*Fengshen Yanyi*), which was written by Xu Zhonglin in the late sixteenth century. Their prototypes are the famous ritual-guarding generals of Buddhism, who rule the affairs of the human world. Temples for the Heavenly Kings often exist only in Buddhist temples. But these four statues were undoubtedly a creation from the folk world. As the tour guide explained, "Whoever has read the novel *Journey to the West* [written by Wu Cheng'en in the sixteenth century] understands that the Four Heavenly Kings were borrowed by the Jade Emperor from Tathagata Buddha and then dispatched to guard the Heavenly Gate." At the corner behind the temple, a product called "Long-Lasting Incense" is sold. All tourists will be led here after visiting the temple.

After passing the Heavenly Kings Hall, one can dimly see the statues of the three goddesses at Niangniang Temple. Bixia Yuanjun, often called Tianxian Niangniang ("Goddess of Heavenly Immortals"), is in the middle. She blesses visitors with fertility and good life. On her west stands Mingmu Yuanjun ("Eyesight Goddess"), who is in charge of wisdom. On Bixia Yuanjun's east is Guangsi Yuanjun (commonly called "Children-Sending Goddess"), who is in charge of fertility. Some say these latter two goddesses are maids of Bixia Yuanjun; others, that they are incarnations of Yuanjun. Canopies and curtains are used around the statues. Canopies were originally placed on the thrones of emperors. Here they signify the honor and majesty of the goddesses. White clouds and heavenly cranes were embroidered on the front side of the hanging curtains. At the back of the hall, there are exquisite frescos, which visitors are unfortunately not allowed to enter to see. Instead, cultural relics from the Han and Tang Dynasties are exhibited in the East and West Halls. Outside the Temple there is a section of red fence, with prayer cards hanging all over it.

Practice

According to Daoist rituals, people are supposed to kowtow to show special respect to gods and immortals. Tour guides usually offer a simplified demonstration of how to kowtow, highlighting the

娘殿、东岳殿、玉皇殿（东岳殿和玉皇殿仍在修复当中），原供奉碧霞元君、明目元君、广嗣元君、东岳大帝、关帝、药王等神祇。便于引导香客循着次序参神进香。即便建筑形制与道观相同，并且供奉道教神灵，甚至历史上还有道士入驻，目前北顶娘娘庙仍然不是一座道教寺庙。道教是中国的本土宗教，与民间信仰相互影响、相互吸收，但道教的根本信仰不离道与神仙，因此道观必定供奉道教的至高神——"三清"。

庙宇的入口是山门殿，钟楼与鼓楼伫立于两侧。山门是道教建筑的正面门户，古代道观多筑于山林之间，故有"山门"之称，象征凡间与仙境的分界。钟和鼓是庙宇中用于报时的工具，道观内的钟和鼓还是道教的法器，具有通神驱魔的神力，在日常的道事活动中，主要用于报时和召集道众。如今没有道士在庙里活动，钟楼和鼓楼只是紧闭着，在烈日当空的时日里制造两抹余阴。

径直往北到达天王殿，殿内原没有神像，在"文革"后还被改成学校的小商店，如今供奉的四大天王是修复时添加的。四大天王即魔礼青、魔礼红、魔礼海、魔礼寿，是中国长篇小说《封神演义》中的角色，原型是佛教中著名的四位护法神将，司掌人间的风调雨顺。天王殿通常只在佛寺中出现，北顶娘娘庙内的四大天王无疑来自民间的创作。一名导游解释道："看过《西游记》就知道，四大天王是玉皇大帝向如来佛祖借去守天门的。"天王殿后的转角处是售卖"长眠香"的场所，香客参观完天王殿便会被引到此处。

穿过天王殿，隐隐可以瞥见娘娘殿内的三位神像。手持令牌的碧霞元君居于正中，俗称"天仙娘娘"，具有送生保育、造福众生、护国佑民等职能。西侧为明目元君，俗称"眼光娘娘"，主管智慧；东侧为广嗣元君，俗称"送子娘娘"，司掌生育。两位嗣神一说为碧霞元君的侍女，也有碧霞元君化身之说。神像周围装饰着华盖与幔帐，华盖原置于天子的宝座之上，悬挂在神像头顶则象征神的尊贵与威严；幔帐，悬挂于神像前，绣有白云与仙鹤。神像背后有精美的壁画，但普通人被无情地拒绝进入。东西配殿正展出中国汉唐时期的文物，妙趣横生。娘娘殿外侧是一排红色的栅栏，垂满香客的祈福牌。

实践

按道教礼仪，人应对神和仙行叩拜礼，以示特别尊敬。导游们在接待旅游团体时，会示范简化版的道教叩拜礼，还特意与佛教区分开来。先以左手抱右手，因有"左手为善，右手为恶"之说，意为扬善隐恶。随后俯伏叩首，头磕在双手背上，心中存想神容并诚心祈祷。如此重复三次即可。有趣的是，可能佛教的影响过于强大，经常来参拜的或零星的香客，大多采用佛教的方式，双手合十，双膝跪地，俯伏参拜。问其缘由，得到的是"佛道不分家"的答案。如此看来，导游和香客几乎只知佛道，并无民间信仰的概念。

此外，庙内供奉的神像被视为神的灵身，应时时予以供养，常设的供品包括香、花、灯、水、果。敬神最常见的方式莫过于敬香，世人多称"烧香"，旨在"以香达信"，即人的诚心通过香烟达于神明，获得神的降福。但庙内禁止燃香，于是一种新型的"长眠香"应时而生，即道教的福牌，涵盖财运、事业、健康、教育等内容。关于禁止燃香，北京其他寺庙也有类似的状况，但不如北顶娘娘庙这般彻底。工作人员的解释是政府规定，也许还有文物保护、商业操作等考量，具体原因不得而知。买福牌的活动被称为"请福牌"，还会附上一块经过开光的、刻有"娘娘"二字的朱砂。

difference between Daoist and Buddhist versions. Left hands are said to represent good; right, evil. Therefore, left hands should embrace the right ones, meaning advocating the good and suppressing the evil. One begins by placing the right hand into the palm of the left hand, then kneels and kowtows, resting the stacked hands on the ground, palms up, then "knocking" one's head against them. While "knocking," one should quietly say prayers, bearing in mind the image of the god or goddess. Repeating these steps three times, the kowtow is complete. Interestingly, most visitors appear to be more influenced by Buddhism, performing the Buddhist style of kowtow, where hands begin in a "praying hand" position, and hands are later placed on the floor on either side of where the head "knocks" the ground. According to these people, there should not be a distinction between Buddhist and Daoist rituals. This is evidence that most people do not actually have any concept of "folk religions," but only of Buddhism or Daoism.

Statues inside temples are regarded as the bodies of heavenly spirits. Therefore, offerings should be provided regularly. Standard offerings include incense, flowers, lamps, water, and fruit, with incense as the most common. People hope to obtain trust from the god or goddess through fragrance, presenting their sincere mind in return for blessings. However, lighting incense is now forbidden inside the temple. Thus a new "Long-Lasting Incense," which is actually just Daoist blessing cards, was developed instead. Different cards pertain to different issues—marriage, wealth, career, health, education, and so on. Although other temples also implement an incense ban, none enforces it as strictly as Beiding Niangniang Temple. Buying blessing cards is nicknamed "Inviting Blessing Cards." Included in the package is a consecrated cinnabar with the two characters 娘娘 ("Niang Niang") engraved on it. Visitors usually choose to hang the blessing cards in the temple and take the cinnabar home, thereby "praying for blessings and taking

12. 长眠香即道教的福牌 Long-Lasting Incense

home bliss." These blessing cards remain at the temple permanently. That is why the name "Long-Lasting Incense" is used. Each card costs 100 Yuan. According to a cleaning lady, the price was 20 Yuan a couple of years ago. The increase, however, has not slowed sales, as Beiding Niangniang is known to work miracles. Every day, people bring in fresh bouquets and fruit to the Heavenly Kings Temple and Niangniang Temple.

The birthday of Bixia Yuanjun is on the eighteenth day of the fourth month of the lunar calendar, though there is also a custom of celebrating it on the fifteenth day of the third month of the lunar calendar, which is the Robe Changing Day of Bixia Yuanjun. The former birthday was exclusively celebrated by emperors; thus ordinary people had no choice but to choose a different date. People

13. 被鲜花和香果环绕的主神碧霞元君 Statue of Bixia Yuanjun, Goddess of Sunlight from the East

香客可将福牌悬于神殿内，朱砂则带回家，寓意"祈福迎祥，戴福还家"。这种福牌因能一直悬于庙内而被称作"长眠香"，单价为100元/幅，保洁阿姨向我透露，前几年的单价是20元。但涨价了也不会影响它的销量，北顶娘娘庙可是出了名的灵验。天王殿和娘娘殿几乎每天都有新鲜的花束和水果，香客会特意带来一些。

碧霞元君的生日为农历的四月十八，不过也有农历三月十五的说法。三月十五本是元君"换袍日"，由于"四月十八"的庆贺已为皇家垄断，进香的普通民众无奈望祠兴叹，只能另选时日。于是借元君"换袍日"，信众聚会行香，久而久之，便将其传说成元君的生日，反映皇家与汉族民间对碧霞元君主祀权的争夺。碧霞元君的神诞日会举行盛大的庙会，百姓云集，烧香奉祀，祈祷许愿。北顶娘娘庙的庙会还出售农具，一直持续到新中国成立初期才中断。如今每逢农历的四月十八，虽然不再有过去那种盛大的庆祝活动，但北顶娘娘庙依然游客云集、人山人海。

人物

碧霞元君信仰的核心是主生。碧霞元君的道场在泰山，"泰"意为"天地交而万物通"，加之泰山位于东方，为太阳初升之地，按五行属木，意指天地万物的生长，便自然而然地承载着主生之说。前来参拜的香客以女性居多，怀着求子的心愿。然而，碧霞元君的职能不仅限于生育，她是民众心中有求必应、无所不能的圣母。明万历二十一年（1593年）间的《东岳碧霞宫碑》记载："元君能为众生造福如其愿，贫者愿富，疾者愿安，耕者愿岁，贾者愿息，祈生者愿年，未子者愿嗣，子为亲愿，弟

therefore borrowed the date of Robe Changing Day, a time when believers traditionally gathered to light incense. Over time, the latter date (the fifteenth day of the third month of the lunar calendar) was simply said to be Yuanjun's birthday, revealing an underlying tension between the emperors and the ordinary Han people over the power of worshipping gods. On this latter date, temple fairs were held, with crowds of people flooding in, burning incense, praying, and worshipping. Some agricultural tools were sold at the fair. This tradition lasted until the beginning of the People's Republic of China (1949). Currently, no celebrations are held on the eighteenth day of the fourth month of the lunar calendar, though the temple is still crowded then with tourists.

People

The core of belief in Bixia Yuanjun is life. Her holy site is on Mount Tai, which is named after the "*Tai*" hexagram in the *Yijing* that represents when Heaven and Earth intersect and the myriad things connect. Mount Tai is in the east where the sun rises. According to the "Five Elements" theory, east corresponds to wood, controlling the growth of everything in nature. Most of the visitors are therefore women wishing for a child. But Bixia Yuanjun is not just in charge of fertility; she is also an omnipotent holy mother who answers all requests from all people. As was recorded on the "Dongyue Bixia Palace Monument" in the twenty-first year of the Ming Wanli Era (1593), "Yuanjun brings happiness to people and grants every person's wishes: the poor be rich, the sick be peaceful, farmers see a harvest; those wishing for long life enjoy longevity; those without children carry on the family generations; children live up to the wishes of the family; younger brothers live up to the expectations of older ones; relatives get along, isolating no one; God answers prayers from all sincere minds."

An old, gray-haired man visits Beiding Niangniang Temple on the first and fifteenth day of each month. When asked, he says his wife had been in the late stage of cancer three years earlier. He heard that the temple worked miracles and thus made numerous trips asking for Niangniang's blessing. His wife's health slowly recovered. "She now eats more than I do, thanks to Niangniang," he chimes, now as happy as a child. People usually visit the temple to pray for relief from illness, tragedy, poverty, or infertility for themselves or their relatives. No one knows whether their wishes will be granted, but the action itself brings great confidence and comfort, relieving stress and sadness. "Take blessings home" is a promise the temple makes, offering assurance. For the majority of the working class, nothing is as comforting as divine power.

The Beiding Niangniang Temple is a sanctuary for souls. People who are exhausted by daily troubles often come here for a "recharge." I once met a visitor from Shanghai who wished to feel the aura of the temple. He talked about his stress from job promotion, marriage, and buying a house. Visiting the temple, according to him, was the highest level of "recharging." When I met him, he was struggling about whether to make wishes. Although his opportunity to visit the dignified Niangniang was rare, he worried that he did not have enough time to return later to redeem his vows. I tried to comfort him, "Feel free to make your wishes. As long as the grace of Niangniang is in your mind, the date of redeeming [your vows] is no longer important." He waved his hands. "It is never good to owe gods." He entered the hall, pulled a 10 Yuan note from his pocket, and gently placed it on the offering table. He bowed down, kowtowed a few times, took in the scene for a few moments, then left. Many career seekers like him come to the temple seeking smooth paths.

Because of Beiding Niangniang Temple, some people are able to preserve their beliefs and

为兄愿，亲戚交厚，靡不相交愿，而神亦靡诚弗应。"

有一位头发花白的老人，每月初一和十五定会来到北顶娘娘庙。问其缘由，才知他的老伴三年前已是癌症晚期，听说这里的庙十分灵验，便勤耕不辍地求娘娘护佑。如今老伴的身体逐渐恢复，他乐得像个孩子似得说道："现在比我还能吃呢！多亏了娘娘啊！"人们大多为着自己或亲属的疾病、灾难、贫穷、无子，不辞远道进庙祈祷，难以断定他们是否能够如愿以偿，但这种行为本身就可以催生信心和安慰，暂时减轻心灵的忧虑与悲戚。"带福还家"，就是种种希望实现的保证，在劳苦大众那里，没有比神力的安慰更胜一筹的了。

北顶娘娘庙是心灵的庇护所，为世俗琐事耗尽心神的人时常来这里"充电"。偶遇一位上海游人，来此沾沾庙宇的灵气。他向我吐露升职、结婚、买房的压力，调侃似得说这是"充电"的最高级形式。他纠结着是否应该许愿，毕竟难得一见"娘娘的威严"，又担心无法及时还愿。他的犹豫使我发笑，我试图安慰他，"只管许愿便是，心里惦念'娘娘'的恩德，不必拘泥于还愿的时日。"他摆了摆手说道："不好欠神仙的债。"随后走进娘娘殿，小心翼翼地掏出一张10元的人民币，轻轻地堆到供桌上，俯身拜了又拜，观望良久才转身离开。还有很多像他这样初入职场的迷茫青年，来此祈求事业顺遂。

北顶娘娘庙是一部分人信仰的延续。有一群信仰泰山神的山东汉族，已在北京定居十余载，无法返回家乡敬拜。恰好北顶娘娘庙也供奉泰山的神灵，于是每逢重大庆典，庙内都有他们的身影。还有一位年近八十的老奶奶，是佛教居士，遗憾自己腿脚不灵光，周围又无佛寺，只好选择就近的北顶娘娘庙参拜。当她盘问起自己贡献的纯大理石花瓶的去处，并一再强调那是从敦煌买来的，我便饶有兴致地看着她。庙内的主管翻腾了许久，终于在里屋找到两个黑色的瓶子。她面露苦色，责备主管的草率，原本还想送来一个布满佛像的盘子，见此光景只好作罢。起初我难以理解为何她如此执着于送来佛教的物品，难道不担心得罪道教的神灵吗？在随后的交谈中，她解释道："这是女儿和女婿的定情物，从敦煌带过来的。现在我是马上就要死的人了，拿这么好的东西来也没用，给娘娘多好啊！"这位积极勇敢的老太太，年轻时奔波于大学、佛教寺院、佛学院听课，虽然多次感叹自身的衰老，但依旧执着地寻找信仰的依靠。

无论娘娘是否有求必应，人们对神灵无上权力的想象与推崇始终存在。虽说目前只修复了天王殿和娘娘殿，但香火真是旺极了。即便是工作日，也有来来往往的香客，不难想象节假日的盛况。一是借助了奥林匹克公园的名气，二是因为网络上一度疯传的"2004年娘娘显灵"事件所传达的神灵的"怒气"，这怒气也着实来自那些被迫搬迁的人。从几位保洁人员那里得知，北顶娘娘庙所在的村子叫"北顶村"，他们是原北顶村的村民。由于奥林匹克公园建设的需要，北顶村被全部列入征地范围，村民全部搬迁。由此，北顶村这个地名便从北京的行政区划上消失。留下来的唯一痕迹，是被修缮一新的北顶娘娘庙。事实上，最初的规划是将北顶娘娘庙拆掉。讲解员会玩笑似得问："你们知道号称'最强钉子户'的是谁吗？"随即把当年拆庙的情形描述得绘声绘色。大致情节是，工人在拆庙门时，一场罕见的大风席卷而来并造成人员伤亡等等。由此，人们慕名而来，许多民众为娘娘的神威而欢欣鼓舞，痛斥那些"干犯神灵"的人。

无论被赋予何种地位，北顶娘娘庙始终承载着民众古朴率真、直发胸臆的信仰。就像在古代，贫困的下层民众只有在帝王将相、神仙佛祖俯视的茫茫人寰中劳作与奉献，但他们亦有所思所欲，所喜所惧，建构着自己的此岸与彼岸。

practices. A group of people from Shandong Province (where Mount Tai is located) are believers of the God of Mount Tai. They have been settled in Beijing for more than a decade. Since they are not able to return home to worship regularly, they come here because all the gods of Mount Tai are present at this temple. They never miss any big celebrations or rituals here. A nearly eighty-year-old lady who happens to be a lay Buddhist visits here too. She has physical difficulty travelling far, and there are no Buddhist temples nearby. She inquired about a pure marble vase that she offered earlier, repeatedly saying that it was acquired at the Dunhuang Grottoes. The staff searched for a long time, eventually uncovering only two black bottles. A bit disappointed, she blamed the temple staff for not looking hard enough. She had originally planned to offer a plate of Buddha images. This caused me to wonder why she would present Buddhists offerings that might offend Daoist deities. She said, "These are the love tokens of my daughter and son-in-law from the Dunhuang Grottoes. My days are numbered. What do I need these things for? How wonderful if I can offer them to Niangniang?" In her youth, this courageous lady used to frequent Buddhist temples, universities, and institutions to attend lectures on Buddhism. Although she now laments about her age, she is not prepared to give up the pursuit of her belief.

Regardless of whether Niangniang answers their prayers, people never stop believing in and admiring her power. Although only two buildings have been restored so far—Tianwang Temple and Niangniang Hall—many people nevertheless come to worship. Perhaps this is due to the fame of the nearby Olympic Park. One can only imagine how busy the temple is on weekends and holidays given that streams of visitors come even on weekdays.

According to a few of the cleaning staff, the village here used to be called Beiding Village. To build Olympic Park, the entire village was designated for land acquisition, and all villagers were forced to move. Henceforth, the name "Beiding Village" disappeared from the Beijing Administrative Map. The only trace of its existence now is Beiding Niangniang Temple. In fact, the initial plan was to tear down this temple too. A tour guide jokingly asked, "Does anyone know who the toughest "nail-house" [unmovable object] is?" He then told some peculiar stories that occurred as they were attempting to tear down the temple—for example, how an unusual gust of wind whipped through the complex as they were trying to remove the gate, causing several casualties. As a result of these strange incidents, many people became encouraged by the power of Niangniang and came to the temple to condemn those who would try to offend her.

Throughout history, Beijing Niangniang Temple has carried on a simple and straightforward ancient belief of the ordinary people. In the ancient past, the emperors and deities remained far above, leaving the bottom poor laboring and sacrificing. But these plain folks have their own feelings and desires, joys and fears. They never waste a moment to weave their own dreams.

昌平清真寺

马文

历史

昌平清真寺位于北京市昌平区城北街道三官庙胡同向东200米处，由于地处昌平县城五街，故又被称为五街清真寺。根据昌平文史资料记载，昌平清真寺始建于元代(1271–1368)末期，明代(1368–1644)中期迁于现址，距今已有 500 余年历史，现为是北京市重点文物保护单位，也是昌平及其周边近 8000 多名穆斯林重要的宗教活动场所。

昌平城内的穆斯林迁居较早，故有"先有清真寺，后有永安城（昌平旧城）"的说法。最早定居昌平的是元朝军队中的屯田戍边外籍穆斯林士兵，其后，又有明朝大将常遇春(1330–1369)北伐期间随军来此落户的"回回人"，永乐(1402–1424)年间明朝迁都北京，为修建皇陵、永安城，穆斯林移民随之而来并定居于此，逐渐奠定了昌平早期穆斯林聚居区的人口基础。昌平伊斯兰教的历史可以从城东的一块外籍穆斯林墓地——伯哈智（哈智即哈吉，意为完成朝觐麦加之人）墓得到印证。伯哈智，又被当地穆斯林称为"筛海巴巴"（筛海为阿拉伯语，巴巴为波斯语，均表示对于年长、资深宗教人士的尊称），据墓志记载，此人为阿拉伯人，明朝洪武(1368–1398)初年来到中国传教，晚年寓居昌平，期间昌平城东山口出现一只巨蟒，祸害百姓无数，伯哈智舍身除害，但身中剧毒于农历3月24日在清真寺去世，当地穆斯林厚葬其于蟒山

14. 昌平清真寺的礼拜大殿 Prayer hall of Changping Mosque

Changping Mosque

Ma Wen, with Ireland Larsen, editor

History

Changping Mosque is located 200 meters east of Sanguanmiao Hutong on Chengbei Street in the Changping District of Beijing. It is also known as the "Fifth Street Mosque," due to its location on Fifth Street. According to local historical records, the Changping Mosque was first built in the late Yuan Dynasty (1271–1368) and later relocated to its current site about 500 years ago during the middle of the Ming Dynasty (1368–1644). Currently, the Changping Mosque is a Major Historical and Cultural Site Protected by Beijing, as well as an important religious site for the some 8000 Muslims nearby.

Muslims were among the first settlers of what is now Changping. As the old saying goes, "First came the mosque, then came the city of Changping." The earliest Muslim settlers were foreign soldiers of the Yuan Dynasty, who guarded the border and opened up this former wasteland for farming. Later in the Ming Dynasty some Muslims living in China who had served the famous Muslim general Yuchun Chang (1330–1369) in his northern military expedition chose to stay in Changping. When the capital was moved to Beijing during the reign of Emperor Yongle (r. 1402–1424), some Muslim immigrants settled in the area to help build the imperial tomb and Yong'an City (the predecessor of Changping). The tomb of Ber Haji on the east side of Changping offers witness to this early immigration. Also called Sheikh Baba by local Muslims, Ber Haji's epitaph indicates that he was an Arab who came to China to preach during the reign of Emperor Hongwu (r. 1368–1398) of the Ming Dynasty. Legend has it that when Ber Haji heard about a giant python that was terrorizing people in the east mountain pass, he killed the snake, though he was seriously injured in doing so, later dying at the mosque. Local Muslims gave him an elaborate funeral, burying him in front of Mangshan ("Python") Mountain. This story of "killing the python and chasing away demons for the local people" is still told today.

Where there are Muslims, there must be mosques; Changping is no exception. The Changping Mosque has gone through four large-scale constructions and repairs throughout its history. In the middle of the Ming Dynasty, the mosque was relocated to its current site in order to make way for the government office. In the late Ming Dynasty, a new gate for the mosque was built. In the middle of the Qing Dynasty (1644–1912), the grand hall for worship was renovated and a new festoon gate was added. And at the end of the twentieth century, the grand hall was restored. In the last ten years, more repairs were undertaken and new facilities added, gradually shaping the mosque we see today. Additionally, an independent women's mosque was established in the 1920s in Changping, with a female imam from northwest China appointed to preach there. The mosque however closed in the mid-1950s.

Like the other seventy mosques in Beijing, the Changping Mosque belongs to the earliest and largest school of Islam in China: *Qadim*. Of the twenty imams who have preached at the Changping Mosque over time, three (including the current imam) have also come from the Sufi order *Jahriyya*. Nevertheless, the religious tradition of the Changping Mosque has not changed much over time, maintaining the characteristics of both Qadim and Jahriyya. Throughout the history of the mosque, there have been three prominent imams: Jin Zichang

昌平清真寺

前。至今民间还流传着他"舍身杀蟒，为民除害"的故事。

由于履行宗教功课的需要，有穆斯林居住的地方必然会有清真寺，旧时被称为永安城的昌平也不例外。昌平清真寺历史上共经历四次较大规模的修整。明朝中期迁址重建，后期重修了清真寺大门，清代(1616–1912)中叶礼拜大殿进行了修缮，新建了垂花门。20世纪末，又对清真寺的大殿进行了修复。此后的十多年里，又先后对清真寺的局部进行了多次修整，增加了基础设施，逐渐形成了清真寺现在的形制。此外，20 世纪 20 年代，昌平穆斯林群众还成立了清真女寺，专门聘请西北女阿訇任教，但维持的时间并不长，20世纪50年代中期因礼拜人数锐减及国内政治形势的原因而停办。

同北京的其他70座清真寺一样，昌平清真寺属于中国伊斯兰教历史上最早、信众最多的教派：格底目（Qadim，阿拉伯语，意为古老的），它是一种遵循哈乃斐教法学派的不同于苏非的逊尼派传统。其信众以本地的独立的清真寺为中心，组织较为松散。值得注意的是，历史上有据可考的在昌平清真寺任教的20名阿訇中，有包括现任阿訇在内的3位来自中国的纳格什班迪（Naqshbandi）苏非教团哲合林耶（Jahriyya）。哲合林耶这一名称来源于阿拉伯语"jahr，意为公开的，高声的"，引申为"高声诵念迪克尔（Dhikr，记念、赞颂真主，也称记主词）"，故有"高念派"之称，与默念记主词的其他的纳格什班迪苏非派相区别。尽管如此，昌平清真寺的宗教传统并没有发生较大的转变，只是在一些个别宗教仪式中兼具格底目和哲合林耶两派的特点。清真寺历史上著名的阿訇主要有3位，分别是曾留学爱资哈尔大学的金子常(1902–1961)、翻译《古兰经》的杨品三(1921–1983)，以及曾于2000年至2016年担任中国伊斯兰教协会会长的陈广元(1932–)。

空间与形制

历史上的昌平清真寺东与裕陵卫隔街相望，南与白公祠、陈公祠隔胡同相邻，西与香火寺隔小道相对，北与州府衙门之间隔东、西帽儿胡同，如今昌平清真寺所在的街道被称为三官庙胡同。

早期的清真寺大门为传统的中国寺庙建筑风格，沿袭了中国佛教寺院"三门"的形制，除了正门弧形拱顶石刻的阿拉伯语"麦斯知德"（masjid，清真寺），其他元素基本与佛教寺院的山门别无二致。传统的清真寺大门于文革期间被毁，上个世纪90年代重建后的大门为中阿结合式混凝土建筑，大门整体呈绿色，继续沿用了中国传统寺院建筑的三门形制，大门顶端有三个阿拉伯特色的绿色圆顶和新月，中间大门门楣上有中国伊协前任会长陈广元(1932–)阿訇书写的"清真寺"三个楷书大字。通过大门，清真寺的院落被迎面的垂花门分隔为前后两进院落。过垂花门为二进院落，迎面是雄伟高大的礼拜大殿，大殿南北两侧分别为图书室和女礼拜殿。大殿为三开间，门楣上各有一块木匾，正中"开天古教"，意在表明伊斯兰教悠久的历史，据传为清朝著名穆斯林将领闪殿魁(?–1903)所写，左侧为"泽被群生"，是抗日战争时期昌平五街汉族民众为感谢当地穆斯林和清真寺庇护之恩所赠，也从侧面反映了当地和谐的民族关系，右侧为"独一无贰"，表达的是伊斯兰教核心的"认主独一"信仰，是为纪念1996年清真寺重修而作。

礼拜大殿使用面积近300平方米，能容纳300多人礼拜。大殿最里边是三间窑殿（mihrab），北侧窑殿内有木制宣教台（minbar），台旁立一枣木手杖。周五主麻

15. 昌平城区的穆斯林墓地 Muslim graveyard of Changping District

(1902–1961), otherwise known as Mohamed Nasulundin, who studied at Al-Azhar University in the 1930s, was proficient in Chinese, Arabic, and English, and was also accomplished at Arabic calligraphy; Yang Pinsan (1921–1983), otherwise known as Nurhaq, whose translation of the Qur'an into Chinese is titled *Selected Translation of the Qur'an Classification*; and Chen Guangyuan (b. 1932), otherwise known as Hillalundin, the former president of the Chinese Islamic Association from 2000 to 2016.

Space, Form, and Style

Historically, Changping Mosque faced the Yü Royal Mausoleum to the east, was situated next to the Bai and Chen ancestral temples to the south, and faced Xianghuo Daoist Temple to the west. To the north, the Dong Mao'er and Xi Mao'er Hutongs lie between the mosque and the Prefecture Government Office. The street on which Changping Mosque is located today is therefore called "Three Official Temples Hutong."

The original gate of the mosque adopted traditional Chinese-temple architectural style, following the "three gateways" employed in Buddhist temples. With the exception of a stone carving of the Arabic word *masjid* on the middle arch, the architecture of the mosque was no different from that of Buddhist temples. This original gate was destroyed in the 1950s, later to be replaced in the 1990s by a new one that utilized the green-colored steel and concrete structure of Chinese–Arabic hybrid style, while continuing the traditional form of the "three gates." On top of the gate, there are three Arabic-style green domes and a crescent moon. On the

拜前，阿訇站在此挂杖宣教、演讲，意在仿效先知穆罕默德当年在麦加的椰枣树下的宣教，这也是中国穆斯林用智慧缅怀先知的方式。从外部看，大殿正中窑殿上方为六角形望月楼，意喻伊斯兰教的六大信仰。昌平清真寺布局严谨有序，给人以典雅古朴庄严肃穆之感，是广大穆斯林的精神家园。

宗教实践

穆斯林日常最主要的宗教活动即礼拜。平日在清真寺礼拜的穆斯林仅有十多人，而且以居住在本地的中老年人为主。每周五的主麻人数可达到300多人，以年轻人居多，他们大多是来自周边高校的大学生，以及在昌平周边工作和做生意的流动穆斯林。每年的开斋节和古尔邦节是昌平清真寺最热闹的日子，这两天前来清真寺参加礼拜穆斯林人数将达到近 2000 人。节日会礼一般会在九点正式开始，首先由集体升国旗仪式拉开序幕，接着阿訇诵念赞圣词进入大殿，随后开始宣讲卧尔兹（al-Wa'z, 汉语宣教性演讲），内容以信仰为出发点，多结合国家政策、法律、社会现实等问题展开，号召穆斯林大众在坚守信仰的同时，做一个合格的国家公民。演讲结束之后便开始礼拜，节日会礼共两拜，随后，阿訇登上敏拜尔（minbar）持杖用阿拉伯语发表呼图白（khutbah, 阿拉伯语宣教）演讲，内容以颂主赞圣、劝善戒恶等内容为主。之后，节日会礼结束，大家互道节日问候，昌平区清真寺也为所有前来礼拜的穆斯林免费发放事先准备的肉粥和油香等食物。

除了礼拜，穆斯林对于每年的斋月十分重视。伊斯兰教认为，这个月是真主降示《古兰经》的月份，所以，也是一年中最尊贵的月份。作为穆斯林最基本的五项宗教功课之一，《古兰经》规定，符合条件的穆斯林必须在此月守斋戒，每天从日出到日落期间停止饮食、房事等活动。夏天的斋戒时间可长达18小时，对于穆斯林来说是一个不小的考验，特别是身在大城市工作压力更大的流动穆斯林群体，所以，一顿可口的开斋饭（iftar）不仅能缓解每天十多个小时的饥渴，而且更能从心理上给予穆斯林以慰藉。昌平清真寺从 2010 年起就开始为前来清真寺开斋的穆斯林免费准备开斋饭，这个传统已经持续了 8 年。来清真寺开斋的人主要由本地穆斯林、周边高校的穆斯林大学生以及在昌平务工和经商的流动穆斯林组成，其中也不乏外籍穆斯林，平均每天接近百人。

开斋时间一到，大家 8 到 10 人围坐在一张圆桌前分享由清真寺后厨准备的美食，即便互不相识，一句"色俩目"（salam, 阿拉伯语，祝你平安）的问候会迅速拉近之间的距离。虽然来自不同的地域、说着不同的方言，但这丝毫不影响席间欢乐融洽的氛围。开斋饭结束后，年轻人们纷纷挽起袖子，开始收拾餐桌碗筷，帮助志愿者打扫卫生，清洗餐具。而年长的穆斯林纷纷端着志愿者准备好的茶水，坐在回廊上谈笑风生，等待下一个礼拜的到来。

在斋月里，举办学习班也是昌平清真寺的惯例，这一传统始于 2002 年。学习班的内容丰富，包括有关信仰基础知识、宗教功修、礼仪，以及基础阿拉伯语和书法等，授课形式也多种多样，除了清真寺的学习班，还包括网络课堂以及外出参观交流活动，每年斋月学习班学员人数达到近百人。学习班除了针对穆斯林群体，同时也为对伊斯兰文化感兴趣的非穆斯林开放。正是在这种包容精神的感染下，每年都有学习班的非穆斯林皈依，截止 2018 年年底，在昌平清真寺皈依的新穆斯林人数已达到 205 人。

16. 国旗和新月，昌平清真寺会在每年的开斋节和古尔邦节举行升国旗仪式 Chinese flag and crescent moon of Islam

lintel of the middle gate, there is an inscription of three Chinese characters, 清真寺 ("mosque"), by Chen Guangyuan (b. 1932), the former president of the Chinese Islamic Association. The courtyard itself is divided into front and back halves by a festoon gate. On the back half is the grand, awe-inspiring main prayer hall. The entrance to the hall also contains "three gateways," each of which has a door plaque on the lintel. The middle one reads 开天古教 ("The Faith Since the Beginning of Heaven"), in recognition of the long history of Islam. This is said to be the calligraphy work of San Diankui (d. 1903), a Muslim general of the Qing Dynasty. On the left plaque is inscribed 泽被群生 ("Kindness Extends to All"); this plaque was a gift from the Fifth Street Han people in Changping as a token of their gratitude for the protection that local Muslims and the mosque provided during the Second Sino-Japanese War (1937–1945), a warm memory of harmonious Han–Muslim relationships in the past. The plaque on the right says 独一无贰 ("*Tawhid*, The Unity and Uniqueness of God"), delivering the central doctrine of Islam—the oneness of God—to commemorate the reconstruction of the mosque in 1996. The north and south sides of the main worship hall are the library and the women's worship hall, respectively.

The prayer hall occupies an area of nearly 300 square meters and can accommodate more than 300 people. At the far end of the main hall there are three *mihrab* niches. The northern one has a wooden platform for preaching (*minbar*), with a jujube cane resting on the side. Before Jumu'ah prayers on Fridays, the imam preaches and speaks here, modeling how Prophet Muhammad used to preach under the date palm tree in Mecca. Above the middle niche, there is a hexagonal moon-watching tower, the six sides of which represent

昌平清真寺

17. 清真寺的门卫老马正在礼拜 Gatekeeper of Changping Mosque praying

the six beliefs of Islam. The layout of the Changping Mosque is neat and orderly, giving people a sense of elegance, simplicity, and solemnity. It is the spiritual home of the Muslim people.

Religious Practice

Salat (prayer) is the most important daily activity of Islam. Only a dozen Muslims pray at the mosque on ordinary days, most of them middle-aged and elderly local residents. On Fridays, as many as 300 people may attend Jumu'ah. Most of them are young people from neighboring universities, working-class residents, or business people from the Changping area. The mosque is the busiest on *Eid al-Fitr* and *Eid al-Adha*, each of which attracts nearly 2000 people in celebration. These festival ceremonies usually start at 9:00 a.m. with the raising of the national flag. The imam will then enter the hall while chanting the Qur'an. He will then give an *al-wa'z*, sermonizing about religion in combination with national policy, law, and social issues. The goal is to appeal to faithful followers as well as good citizens. Prayer starts after *al-wa'z*, with two units of prayer (*raka'āt*) for festival ceremonies. Then, the imam ascends the *minbar*, holds the jujube cane with one hand, and gives the *khutbah* speech in Arabic. The content consists mostly of praising Allah, advocating good, and refraining from evil. The speech ends the festival ceremony. People then walk around and exchange holiday greetings. The Changping Mosque additionally provides free meat porridge and snacks for all Muslims who come to the ceremony.

In addition to prayer, Muslims attach great importance to the annual observance of Ramadan, believing it to be the month when Allah revealed the Qur'an. Therefore, Ramadan is considered the most prestigious month of the year. According to the Qur'an, one of the five pillars of Islam is that all eligible Muslims must fast this month, with no food, drink, sex, and other activities from sunrise to sunset daily. Fasting during summer can be a big challenge for Muslims, especially those working in the big cities, due to the pace of work and life. Therefore, a delicious *iftar* feast breaks the fast, not only relieving the followers of over ten hours of hunger and thirst but also offering mental comfort. Since 2010, Changping Mosque has been providing free *iftar* meals for all visiting Muslims. The mosque serves *iftar* for nearly 100 people daily during the month of Ramadan—mostly local residents but also Muslim students from neighboring universities, as well as those who work or do business in Changping, and even some foreign Muslims.

After the breaking of the fast, everyone sits in round tables of eight to ten people, enjoying the delicacies prepared by the kitchen of the mosque. A simple greeting of *salam* closes the distance between people, even those who have never met. Although people might speak different dialects and come from different regions, the atmosphere is always filled with joy and harmony. When the *iftar* finishes, young people roll up their sleeves and voluntarily help to clean the tables. Senior Muslims take their tea, which is prepared by volunteers, to the porch where they chat, waiting for the next prayer (*isha*, the nighttime prayer).

Another common practice of the Changping Mosque during Ramadan is to host classes, a tradition dating back to 2002. A variety of topics are taught at the classes: basic knowledge about faith, religious practice, etiquette, Arabic, and calligraphy. The classes are conducted in various forms: in-person lectures, online classes, and site visits. Each year, the Ramadan class attracts nearly 100 students, open to both Muslims and non-Muslims. It is with this all-inclusive spirit that some non-Muslim students convert to Islam every year. Through 2018, Changping Mosque has converted 205 people to Islam.

18. 清真寺门楣上精美的伊斯兰装饰 Islamic inscriptions above gateways

19. 阅读古兰经的克什米尔留学生 International student from Kashmir reading the Qur'an

Recognition and Integration

The imam of Changping Mosque, Ma Yanhu, also named Isma'il, came from Xiji County in Ningxia Hui Autonomous Region, a settlement of 300,000 Hui Muslims in northwest China. Natural conditions in the region are very harsh. In 1972, the United Nations Food Development Agency included it as one of the least suitable areas for human survival. Due to poverty, Isma'il did not go to regular schools like other children did. Instead, he studied religion at tuition-free mosques. Ten years of systematic religious study changed him into an accomplished young man who would eventually become the imam of Changping Mosque. Isma'il's effort won him wide recognition and affection from Muslim communities in Beijing. Although he has established his residency in Beijing, he has not forgotten those in his hometown who still live in poor conditions.

Since 1998, he has helped the Muslim youth from his hometown to relocate to Beijing and find employment in areas such as security, property management, and the *halal* catering industry. Many of them are young women, who warmly refer to Isma'il as "a maternal relative in Beijing." Isma'il never feels that helping those from his hometown conflicts with his daily work. Doing good is a basic requirement of Islam. With the help of local Muslim people and some businesses, the living conditions of the young people from the northwest have dramatically improved. Most importantly, their views towards life and the world have changed, especially those of the young women. They are no longer bound by the obstacles and restrictions of the old traditions, which required them to remain at home, cook three meals a day, and take care of

昌平清真寺

认同与融入

　　昌平清真寺的阿訇伊斯玛仪勒（Isma'il）来自中国西北一个有着 30 万回族穆斯林的聚居区——宁夏西吉县，由于这里自然条件恶劣，1972 年曾被联合国粮食开发署认定为最不适合人类生存的地区之一。家庭贫困导致年幼的伊斯玛仪勒并没有跟大城市同龄孩子一样走进学校，而是进入了不收学费的清真寺学习宗教知识。接受了十多年的系统的经堂(清真寺)教育，伊斯玛仪勒终有所成，于 1992 年开始在北京市昌平清真寺担任阿訇，通过个人的努力，这个来自西北贫困地区的年轻人也逐渐赢得了北京本地穆斯林群众的认可和爱戴。居安则思危，身处首都的伊斯玛仪勒虽然获得了北京城市居民身份，但他始终没有忘记地处西北贫困地区的父老乡亲。从 1998 年开始，他想方设法介绍家乡的穆斯林青年到北京务工，从事保安、物业、清真肉食品加工和清真餐饮等工作，其中女工占了很大比例。这些来京的青年穆斯林形象的称呼伊斯玛仪勒为"北京城里的娘家人"。在伊斯玛仪勒看来，对于家乡人民的帮助与他日常教务工作并不矛盾，这也是伊斯兰关于善功的基本要求。在本地穆斯林和企业的帮助下，这些来自西北的穆斯林青年的生活得到了改善，个人观念也发生了变化，特别是他们当中的女性，逐渐摆脱掉了传统观念的束缚，走出家门，进入城市，既挣了票子又换了脑子，积极融入城市生活，期待通过自己勤劳的双手创造更加美好的明天。

　　与之形成鲜明对比的是，来京20多年，伊斯玛仪勒自己的生活并没有多大改变，他们一家4口还暂住在清真寺的东院的两间平房里。作为清真寺的寺产，东院临街的商铺对外出租，收取租金以维持清真寺的日常开销，出租对象也都是本地或者外地的穆斯林，主要经营清真牛羊肉、熟食和日用品等，东南角是一家馒头店，老板来自伊斯玛仪勒的家乡。店里主营馒头、花卷，除了能看到老北京的牛肉饼，油饼外，还能看到在宁夏西吉十分受欢迎的烤馍、糖酥饼等面点。

　　伊斯玛仪勒的家十分局促，但被妻子收拾的温馨、整洁，一切都错落有致。一进门就是电视、茶几和沙发，门口的柜子还扮演着厨房案板的功能，客厅的最里面摆着两张床，一大一小。最先进入视野的是两张床上叠好的被子，这是只会在宁夏南部山区的回族家庭看到的场景：被子被叠得整整齐齐，两两摞在一起，上面盖着绘有牡丹等花卉的手工刺绣，简单大气，与整洁的床铺相得益彰。

　　到了午饭时间，家里来了客人，他是伊斯玛仪勒阿訇众多老北京的回族朋友之一，祖祖辈辈都生活在清真寺周围，如今在清真寺门口经营清真牛羊肉生意。伊斯玛仪勒泡上了地道的八宝茶，妻子很快端上来了两盘爆炒羊羔肉，同时上桌的还有在羊肉上蒸的饼子以及杂粮馒头。无论是茶，还是羊肉以及饼子、馒头，这都是地道的西吉吃法。杂粮面食是上个世纪七八十年代宁夏西海固人"最好"的主食，伊斯玛仪勒的妻子不禁感慨，"那个时候吃这些杂粮都吃吐了，现在却卖得比白面贵好几倍，真是时代变了！"由于说的是方言，餐桌一头的老北京朋友一脸茫然，伊斯玛仪勒又用夹杂着方言的普通话翻译了一遍，之后一桌人哈哈大笑。与父母的完全不同的是，伊斯玛仪勒的两个的孩子都是在北京出生和长大，操着一口浓重的北京腔，他们身边的朋友都是北京本地孩子，他们俨然已将自己当成了北京人的一分子，虽然他们的户籍还在老家西吉。

　　吃完午饭，隔壁的邻居——伊斯玛仪勒的助理，同样来自宁夏西吉县的伊布拉欣（Ibrahim），领来自己两个十来岁的孩子，要求他们为今天的客人表演节目，兄妹俩用陶笛演奏了日本导演宫崎骏的动画片《天空之城》的同名主题曲。伊布拉欣和伊

RELIGIONS OF BEIJING

20. 穆斯林在做响礼拜 Muslims during the *Dhuhr* prayer

children and elderly. Instead, they work hard to make money, integrate into city life, and create beautiful lives.

In stark contrast, Isma'il's own life has not improved much since he came to Beijing twenty years ago. The four members of his family still live in the two rooms in the east courtyard of the mosque. Shops along this courtyard are owned by the mosque, contributing rental income for its daily operation. The tenants are mostly Muslims, who sell *halal* beef, mutton, other ready-to-eat foods, and daily necessities. The shop at the southeast corner is a steamed-bun shop, whose owner is from Isma'il's hometown. Many food products are available at his store, such as steamed buns, steamed rolls, the old Beijing beef patties, and deep-fried pancakes. Even roast clams and sugar cakes—popular food in Xiji, Ningxia—can be found at his shop.

Although Isma'il's home is very humble, his wife keeps it clean, neat, and cozy. Next to the door is a TV, tea table, and sofa. The cabinet at the door also functions as a kitchen chopping-board. The innermost part of the living room is set up with two beds, one big and one small. Two quilts stacked neatly on the bed immediately catch the eyes, a scene that only appears in Hui homes in Xiji, Ningxia. The quilts are evenly folded and stacked, covered by a sheet of hand-embroidered peony flowers, simple and elegant, enhancing the appearance of the neatly made bed.

Ali, Isma'il's neighbor, visited at lunch time. He is one of the many native Beijing Hui friends whom Isma'il has made. Ali's ancestors all live in the neighborhood of the mosque. He has a shop at the gate of the mosque, where he sells *halal* beef and mutton. Isma'il made authentic "Eight Treasure Tea" for the guest, while his wife quickly brought in two plates of

斯玛仪勒夫妇并不知道两个孩子吹奏的是什么曲目，但他们只是觉得好听，期间还不时的微笑和鼓掌。老北京客人起身要离开了，伊斯玛仪勒的妻子急忙从厨房里端出了一大碗爆炒羊羔肉叫他捎带回去给妻子和孩子，老北京客人反复推辞，怎奈何根本抵挡不住西北回族人的热情。

下午黄昏时分，又到了礼拜的时间，伊斯玛仪勒和伊布拉欣二人戴上了哲合林耶标志性的六角帽，起身前往清真寺。虽然北京的伊斯兰教没有所谓新、老教派之分，但昌平清真寺在一些宗教符号和仪式上具有明显的苏非门宦特征。除了像陈列在清真寺展览室的《穆罕麦斯》和《曼达伊哈》等经典，六角号帽，是中国最大的苏非教团哲合林耶最显著的标志。哲合林耶穆斯林认为，六角号帽的六角分别代表着伊斯兰的六大信仰：信真主、信使者、信经典、信天使、信末日、信前定，而中心的凸起的一角则表示认主独一，在外在形式上，哲合林耶通过六角号帽与其他苏非门宦和教派相区别。

前来参加礼拜的人并不多，伊斯玛仪勒阿訇在领拜时会刻意放慢节奏，以照顾到几位北京本地老人。昏礼（maghrib）的时间不长，总共五拜，前三拜是主命拜（必须的），后两拜是圣行（嘉许的），本来礼拜完成后，整个仪式就结束了，但参加礼拜的几位本地年长的穆斯林同伊斯玛仪勒和伊布拉欣二位阿訇跪坐在了一起，围成了一个圈子——"打伊热"（dayr，阿拉伯语，意为圈子），开始高声念诵赞美先知生平的抒情诗《穆罕麦斯》，这是270多年前哲合林耶领袖马明心(1718-1781)从也门回国后赋予穆斯林的一种独特的宗教仪式，"打伊热"的圈子也强烈地暗示着哲合林耶信众对于信仰的保护。虽然，参与礼拜的人数不多，但赞圣的声音在空旷的礼拜大殿悠扬回荡，给人的感觉是仿佛又回到了大西北。

fried lamb meat. Sitting on the lunch table were also coarse-grain buns and cakes steamed on top of lamb meat, all authentic Xiji cuisine. Coarse grains were the "best" staple food for Xihaigu people in Ningxia in the 1970s and 1980s. Isma'il's wife couldn't help but comment, "Eating too much coarse grain at the time made us sick. Now, the price of it is a few times higher than refined wheat. What a different time it is now." She said this in her hometown dialect, leaving the Beijing guest totally confused. Isma'il repeated it in Mandarin, though blended with his hometown accent. The whole table laughed and laughed. In contrast to Isma'il and his wife, their two children were both born and raised in Beijing. They speak with a heavy Beijing accent, and their friends are all native Beijing children. Although their resident accounts are still in Xiji, they consider themselves Beijing people.

After lunch, Ibrahim, Isma'il's neighbor and assistant, who is also from Xiji, came to visit with his two children. When requested to play music for the guests, the children played on the *ocarina* the theme song of the famous Japanese director Hayao Miyazaki's animated film *The City of the Sky*. The adults had no clue what the children were playing, still they appeared to enjoy it, smiling and applauding. When Ali was ready to leave, Isma'ils' wife hurriedly fetched a big bowl of fried lamb from the kitchen, asking Ali to bring it home to his wife and children. Although Ali politely declined several times, he was no match for the extremely hospitable Muslim from northwest China.

When the time for *maghrib* prayer came at dusk, Isma'il and Ibrahim put on their iconic hexagonal cap of the Jahriyya Sufi order, got up, and left for the mosque. Although Islam in Beijing does not make distinctions between old and new sects, the religious symbols and ceremonies of Changping Mosque show its Sufi characteristics. Besides Jahriyya classics such as *Mukhammas* (Chinese version of *Qasīdat al-Burda,* "Ode of the Mantle," a lyrical poem praising the Prophet) and *Madayah* (another poem praising the virtue of the Prophet), both of which are displayed in the mosque's exhibition hall, the hexagonal cap is the most prominent feature of Jahriyya, China's largest Sufi sect. According to Jahriyya Sufis, the six edges represent the six major beliefs of Islam—belief in Allah, prophets, revealed books, angels, the day of judgment, and predestination—with the center point indicating the oneness of God. Jahriyya distinguish themselves from other Sufi sects by the hexagonal cap.

Not many came to the prayer. Although Isma'il intentionally slowed down so the few elderly people could follow, the prayer still did not last long—just a total of five units of prayer (*raka'āt*), the first three of which are obligatory (*wajib*), the last two, recommended (*sunnah*). The prayer was supposed to end there, but a few elderly Muslims decided to sit with the two imams, Isma'il and Ibrahim. They formed a circle (*dayr*) chanting *Mukhammas*. This is a unique religious ritual created by Mingxin Ma (1718–1781), the leader of Jahriyya, more than 270 years ago. It demonstrates that followers of Jahriyya guard their faith. Although not many were present, the chanting reverberated throughout the grand hall, as if taking people back to the northwest of China.

崇文门教堂

陈景枢

北京基督教会崇文门堂,是一座历史悠久的基督教教堂,在北京地区享有盛名;同时也是一所涉外的教堂,在国外享有一定声誉。教会已经接待了英国坎特伯雷大主教乔治·凯里博士,以及两位美国前总统比尔·克林顿和乔治·布什。著名的福音派基督徒威廉·富兰克林·格雷厄姆,在他有生之年也多次拜访此教堂。每个主日都有外国使馆的官员、国外信徒来此做礼拜,此外,教堂还经常与国内外其他教会举行交流活动。

人群中的教堂

崇文门教堂始建于1870年,是美国卫理公会(美以美会)在北京乃至华北地区所建立的第一座基督新教教堂。当时的教堂被命名为亚斯立堂,这个名字就是为了纪念美国卫理公会(美以美会)的第一位主教:弗兰西斯·亚斯立。

在信众看来,教会一百多年来的变迁,仿佛是上帝在呼召他们来到崇文门,建立这样一座教堂。早在教堂刚刚建立的时候,仅仅能容纳四五百人。但很快随着信徒的不断增加,人们不得不在原址重建了亚斯立教堂,将其规模扩大。在义和团运动中,亚斯立教堂葬身于一场大火之中。几年后清政府拨款再次重建了亚斯立教堂,并延续至今,这就是今天的崇文门堂。以前,亚斯立堂的主任牧师基本上都由外国传教士担任,直到1904年新堂建成后,才开始有华人担任主任牧师。1982年,教堂正式更名为北京基督教会崇文门堂,由此而新生。

北京基督教会崇文门堂自建成之日起,其交通一直十分便利,位于北京崇文门地区,在旧时与东交民巷使馆区距离不远,方便使馆信徒的礼拜活动。而在现在,崇文门堂的位置,更是身处于北京的中心区域,交通便利的同时又保留着教堂的静谧氛围。

崇文门堂建筑风格别具特色。1904年重建的教堂造型为近代折衷主义风格,正立面由三组不同风格的部分组成,砖木结构,灰砖清水墙面,铁皮屋顶,呈现古老、简约和优雅的感觉。这使得崇文门教堂有别于其他基督教堂,更为古朴肃穆。一进入崇文门教堂的正堂,最引人注目的就是独特的伞形屋顶,不同于其他教堂的穹顶,崇文门的木质伞形屋顶给人一种安全可靠之感。处于教堂之中仿佛确实处于上帝的庇护之下,仿佛可以感受到上帝的呼召一般。同时教堂的院落中还有其他的建筑分布在其中,主要包括办公区、售书处,最为突出的是供儿童活动的活动房,和迎接慕道人士的多媒体室,使他们感受到教会的温暖。

不过,早期的亚斯立教堂可不仅仅是一座教堂,它还包括了美以美会的一系列的附属建筑,譬如牧师住宅和其他的一些房产,其中甚至还有三块墓地;除了这些以外,还有教会所建立的医院和学校,如同仁医院、妇婴医院、汇文幼儿园、汇文小学、汇文中学、慕贞女中、护士学校以及汇文大学、汇文神学院等。这些医院和教会今天虽已不再属于教会,但它们中的一部分仍然发挥着原本的作用。

Chongwenmen Church

Chen Jingshu, with Madelyn Bjork, editor

Chongwenmen Church of Beijing Christian Council is a well-known and long-established Christian church. It is an internationally oriented church, focused on establishing networks with believers from other countries, which brings high prestige from abroad. The church has received Dr. George Carey, the British Archbishop of Canterbury, as well as two former U.S. presidents, Bill Clinton and George W. Bush. The prominent evangelical Christian William ("Billy") Franklin Graham, Jr. also made several visits to the church throughout his lifetime. Staff from foreign embassies and Christians from overseas attend worship services at Chongwenmen. The church also frequently holds exchange activities with other churches at home and abroad.

A Church in a Crowded Area

Founded in 1870 by the Methodist Episcopal Church in America, Chongwenmen Church was the first Protestant church not just in Beijing but in all of northern China. The church was initially named Asbury Church, after Bishop Francis Asbury (1745–1816), one of the first two Methodist Episcopal bishops. Although the church has undergone many trials and tribulations over the past 150 years, its members consider them all part of God's "calling."

Over its 150-year history, Chongwenmen Church has faced many challenges and weathered many storms; nevertheless, its members have stood firm and strong. Although many different staff have served the church over this time, each has been fully devoted to God's call. At its beginning, Chongwenmen Church (which was then "Asbury Church") was not as big as it is now, seating only 400–500 people. As the number of members increased, the church was expanded. This expansion ended when the church was burned down during the Boxer Rebellion in 1900. Several years later, the Qing government paid for the rebuilding of the church, which was completed in 1904. Soon thereafter, the first Chinese pastor was appointed. Later, the church was repaired in the 1980s. At that time, it was renamed the

21. 崇文门教堂大门 **Gate of Chongwenmen Church**

22. 崇文门教堂内景 Worship hall of Chongwenmen Church

教堂中的信众

新生的崇文门教堂面临着许多的问题，其中最为突出的是信徒的问题。曾经，崇文门青年聚会多是五六十岁的老年人，连中年人都少之又少；而且多是家族式的信徒。这样的教会活力不足，长此以往没有新鲜血液的补充，教会也就得不到发展。教会当时的主堂牧师决定扩大青年会的规模和影响，将更多的人吸引进来，让他们感受到福音与呼召。

但在这种情况下，谁都没有一个明确的方案来解决这个问题，这时有一位从缸瓦市堂的青年会回到崇文门堂的青年学生，提出了一个方案，仿照缸瓦市堂的模式，组建青年诗班，以此来吸引年轻人加入。

这个想法产生后，却缺少一个重要的因素——指挥。青年诗班的排练、献诗无不需要一名优秀的指挥来居中协调。幸运的是，一位专业的指挥加入进来，这位指挥在俄罗斯留学时曾接触过东正教，回国后也想继续从事侍奉工作，但是一直没有找到合适的地点，直到有一天无意间来到崇文门堂，听闻这里的青年诗班恰巧缺少一位指挥，便投身于此，直至身体不允许继续工作为止。尽管在发展过程中，有更多的新人，包括更专业的音乐人加入进来，他依然坚守在青年诗班的岗位上，从指挥到伴奏，再到排练室的指导，他不求回报地持之以恒地做着力所能及的事。受他的影响，他的家人也纷纷投身于教会工作中来，为青年诗班的发展贡献出自己的力量。也正是因为有这样的专业人士的坚守与奉献，崇文门堂青年诗班的专业性日益增强、远近闻

Chongwenmen Church of the Beijing Christian Council and began a new life.

From its beginning, Chongwenmen Church has been easily accessible. In the past, it was near the Dongjiaominxiang Embassy Zone, a convenient location for the embassy staff to attend worship services. Today the church is even more advantageously located, as it sits in the central district of Beijing, enjoying easy access without losing its appeal of peace and tranquility.

Chongwenmen Church adopts a unique modern-eclectic style. The façade is composed of three different styles—bricks and wood, gray brick walls, and an iron roof—bestowing the church with a sense of antiquity, simplicity, and grace. Stepping into the worship hall, one's attention is immediately caught by the wooden umbrella-shaped roof, which offers a sense of safety and protection. Sitting inside the hall, one feels as if one is in a shelter provided by God.

In addition to the church, there are other buildings in the courtyard, including an office and a bookstore. There are also activity rooms for children and a multimedia room for the catechumens. These facilities help create a welcoming atmosphere.

Even at its beginning, Asbury Church was not just a church. It also included other properties of the Methodist Church, such as the priest's house and three cemeteries. The church also established hospitals and schools such as Tongren Hospital, Maternal and Child Hospital, Huiwen Kindergarten, Huiwen Primary School, Huiwen Middle School, Muzhen Middle School for Girls, Nursing School, Huiwen University, and Huiwen Institute of Theology. Although these hospitals and schools are no longer the property of the church, some still function as originally planned.

The Church's Followers

The newly established "Chongwenmen Church" faced many problems in the 1980s, the most serious of which was the age of its believers. Most of the members who attended the "Youth Assembly" were older than fifty, many of whom were related. If the church could not attract new, younger members, it would soon lose its vitality and existence. The chief pastor therefore decided to enlarge the scale and extend the influence of the Youth Assembly so that more people could hear the Gospel and God's call.

No one had a solution, at least not until a young student happened to return to Chongwenmen Church from the Youth Assembly of Gangwashi Church, another church in Beijing. He proposed to imitate Gangwashi Church by establishing a youth choir that would appeal to young people.

The idea was a good one, though lacked one important element—a conductor for the choir. People began praying for such a conductor, soon after which one just happened to join the church. He had been studying music in Russia, where he learned about the Christian faith from the Russian Orthodox Church. Now that he was back in Beijing, he wished to be involved in serving the Church. It took him a long time to find a suitable church. When he visited Chongwenmen Church and learned that they were looking for a choir conductor, he decided to apply for the position. He has been fully devoted to the choir ever since.

Over time, some young professional musicians joined the choir. All the while, the conductor has been untiring in his job—directing, accompanying, rehearsing—never asking for anything in return. Under his influence, his family joined the church in service and practice, also contributing to the youth choir. His persistence and devotion has drawn young people to the choir, which now enjoys a good reputation far and near.

Some members joined the choir out of their love for music. Over time, however, they heard the call to

23. 崇文门教堂讲台 Pulpit of Chongwenmen Church

24. 崇文门教堂青年诗班 Youth choir of Chongwenmen Church

join Christianity, believing that God not only led them to serve the church but also called them to entrust their lives to God. In serving the Lord, they found peace and happiness of mind.

Mr. Guo is a native Beijing resident, born and raised in the neighborhood of the church. He is very familiar with the people and events of the Chongwenmen area. When Mr. Guo learned that the church had a new choral program with a professional conductor, he eagerly signed up. As time went by, he found life dramatically changed. The social activities he used to attend became meaningless, while choir rehearsal grew into an indispensable part of his life. There were days when he felt tired from work and wanted a break, but there was always a voice directing him to come back to the group for rehearsal. Although he felt exhausted after each rehearsal, he was also spiritually enriched. Now he is very committed to attending the practices and gatherings. Over time, he found his circle of friends renewed, his social life simplified, and his interaction with people easier. The choir are like "family members" to him. They offer each other help and support. His life is now more fulfilled. He is continually guided by the lyric "entrusting yourself to the Lord," able to handle difficulties and hardships with a peaceful mind, knowing that he is no longer alone, for God is always there with him.

Another choir member, Xu Yufa, has had similar experiences. As an immigrant to Beijing, he was a total stranger to the city when he first arrived. He heard that the youth choir of Chongwenmen Church was well known for its professionalism and quality, so he decided to join. At the time, the choir was relatively new, welcoming even non-Christian members. By participating in the choir activities, he heard the calling of God and felt destined to draw close to God. He was later baptized at Chongwenmen Church.

25. 受访者徐玉发 Xu Yufa, member of Chongwenmen Church

名，吸引了不少人的加入。

在加入青年诗班的人中，有一部分最初是怀着对音乐的喜好而接近的，却在参与活动的过程中，逐渐感受到了一种声音，仿佛冥冥之中有一个力量使得他们最终皈依。如他们所信仰的那样，仿佛是上帝引导他们到崇文门堂侍奉，又仿佛是受到呼召，他们逐渐地将自己交托给了上帝，在侍奉上帝的过程中获得内心的平稳与喜乐。

郭先生是北京本地居民，自小就生活在崇文门地区，对这里人和事都是那样熟悉。当听说熟悉的教堂新增了一个"唱歌的地方"，而且还有专业的人士来指挥，他欣然加入其中。随着时间的流逝，他逐渐感觉到了生活不断地发生着变化。往日参加的活动似乎总与现在的自己格格不入，平日里的各种社会聚会索然无味，相反，教堂聚会和排练变得越来越必不可少。对他来说，最初不是没想过偷懒，毕竟每天的工作十分辛苦，还要抽出大量时间去排练，这就使得每天更加劳累。但他说，每当想偷懒不去参加聚会的时候，总有一个声音在呼唤他重新回到聚会和排练中，虽然每次排完练身体疲惫，但是精神却感到充实。久而久之也就习惯了定期去参加排练和聚会，随着时间的推移，身边的朋友和圈子得到了净化，人际关系也越来越简单，人与人之间的交往也变得更加得顺畅，每天都过得很充实。在这个过程中，他获得了许多"家人"，在这些家人的支持和陪伴下，简单的生活、简单的交际，带来的却是真切而充实的生活。遇到事情的时候，他都有依靠，不仅来自那群教会中的家人，更来自一种

26. 崇文门教堂复活节受难日教堂外景 Good Friday cross in courtyard of Chongwenmen Church *(photo by He Yinglong)*

更高的依托，"就仿佛可以将自己完全交托于祂"。在这种声音的指引下，他无所畏惧，生活中所面临的一切艰难困苦，都可以平静地面对。

来自外地的教友徐玉发有着相似的经历。初来乍到，他人生地不熟，急需找一个可以依靠的地方。他听说，崇文门堂的青年诗班具有较高的音乐水准，便想加入其中。那时正值青年诗班初创的时期，人员不多，因此即使不是基督徒，也可以加入。据他说，在参加活动的过程中，他逐渐感受到一种冥冥之中的呼召，仿佛就注定应在这里与上帝相遇，于是，他在崇文门堂受洗。受洗之后，他的人生看似没有变化，但心中却有了一种依靠。虽然，在日复一日的排练与侍奉中，他很难保持恒一的坚持，常觉得排练很耽误时间，有时去的就少了。即便如此，青年诗班的弟兄姐妹也没有弃他远去，而是不断的关心他、帮助他，使得他重新感受到上帝的呼召，回归到青年诗班的侍奉之中。后来，虽为生计而辗转多地，但他依旧不忘青年诗班的侍奉，最终家人也大多受洗，加入崇文门堂这个大家庭之中。这样的生活，使他与另一位本地的信徒产生了交集。

徐玉发认识的这位信徒——陈斌也是一位北京的本地人，不过与其他人不同，是一个更加偶然的因素导致他接触到基督教。自小就生活在崇文门地区的他，虽然早已熟知身边就有一座崇文门教堂，却似乎从未认为这座教堂与他有什么关系。随着时间的变迁，他搬离了崇文门地区，却在大学的学习过程中接触到了基督教。当时的他正在北京师范大学读文学，有一门外国文学需要阅读原著，其中就有圣经的选段，因此他就去缸瓦市堂买书，正赶上礼拜，进去感受了一下，仿佛有一种不同的，闻所未闻的感觉扑面而来。从此，他便参与其中，虽然一开始的目的是要学好西方文学，但在这个过程中，他逐渐地感受到了一种呼召。两年后，他便受洗成为一名基督徒。这时，恰逢崇文门堂青年聚会遇到瓶颈，因为当时信徒多是中老年人，为了吸引更多年轻人的参与，时任主堂牧师征集建议如何提高教会的吸引力，最终决定组建青年诗班，于是将他从缸瓦市堂找来一起组建青年诗班。逐渐地，青年诗班有了发展的雏形，找到了专业的指挥和伴奏，慢慢地成为在北京小有名气的专业诗班。陈斌与徐玉发逐渐熟悉起来，最后与他的妹妹成为夫妻，一同在青年诗班进行侍奉。

虽然人们的经历各不相同，但他们都相信，蒙受着上帝的呼召，他们在偌大的人群中汇聚到一起，在崇文门堂一起服侍着上帝。在呼召之下，他们成为比家人还亲密的兄弟姐妹。

Although some aspects of his life after baptism did not change, he had found a place that he could count on, a harbor to anchor his mind. Nevertheless, the agenda of the youth choir was demanding, requiring great commitment. Soon, Xu Yufa felt he did not have time for its many rehearsals and his attendance began to wane. The choir, however, never abandoned him. They constantly helped him and showed him care. Xu Yufa heard God's calling again and returned to the choir. Even while his work took him to different cities, he remained involved in the choir. Under his influence, most of his family were eventually baptized, joining the big Chongwenmen family. Chongwenmen also connected his life to that of another church member.

This church member is Chen Bin, a Beijing native. Unlike many others, Chen Bin's encounter with Christianity was accidental. Although he grew up in the Chongwenmen area and knew about the church as a child, he never felt any connection with it. Later, he later moved out of Chongwenmen, studying literature at Beijing Normal University. Learning foreign literature requires a lot of reading, including the Bible. One day, Chen Bin went to Gangwashi Church to buy some Christian books. Worship happened to be going on at the time. Chen Bin stepped in, immediately experiencing something he had never before seen or felt. He attended the worship and started to get involved with the church. Although his initial intention was simply to learn literature, he felt a calling from God. Two years later, he was baptized and became a Christian. At the time, Chongwenmen Church was planning to set up a youth choir. Chen Bin was asked by the chief pastor to join the preparation committee, which was tasked with finding a conductor and founding the choir. It was through this process that Chen Bin met Xu Yufa, eventually marrying Xu Yufa's sister. Together, all of them serve the choir and the church.

Although each member of Chongwenmen has his or her unique path, together they gather in response to God's call to serve the Lord. In answering this call, they form a family, becoming brothers and sisters.

孔庙与国子监

谭泽民

早春的北京有着一份独特的暖意，春天的气息，从一草一木一砖一瓦中渗出来。在北京东城区安定门内，有一条东西向的古老街道，傲然屹立的国槐和古色古香的飞檐牌匾，笼罩在孟春织就的生机勃勃之中，巍然、肃穆，似在共同诉说着属于这里隽永的记忆。在日益繁华的大都市中，这条街道似是卓然出世，一派春意盎然中，保持着自身的一份古朴素雅。国子监街，正是因为大街中部北侧的北京孔庙和国子监而得名。

历史

北京孔庙和国子监的旧址可以追溯到元朝。元世祖忽必烈（1215-1294年）建都北京后，修建"大都"时便规划好了"庙学"所在地，就是现在的孔庙和国子监。从此这里就成为元、明、清三朝国家最高学府和教育管理机构。

孔子（前551-前479年）是儒家学说的开创者，享有"万世师表"的独尊地位。在古代中国，儒家学说成为正统教育的主要教学内容，取得国学的地位。在礼乐上，它也发展出一套严格的祭祀体制。当古代教育与礼乐文化结合时，就形成了中国古代独特的学校建制：庙学一体。北京孔庙和国子监则为左庙右学。

孔庙是为祭祀先师孔子而修建，是祭奠大圣人的重要场所。由于中国古代社会极力推崇儒家思想，并以儒家思想为治理国家的理念，因此，自汉代以来的统治者十分重视对孔庙的控制，只有封建帝王才能举行最高规格的祭孔仪式。故此，中国古代围绕孔庙发展出了一系列严格的祭祀活动。

据记载，孔庙的祭祀活动最初起源于孔子的后裔，属于一般的家祭。公众祭祀则始于西汉。汉高祖（前256年-前195年）十二年十二月，刘邦从沛县回长安，路过曲阜以"太牢"祭祀孔子，从而开了帝王祭祀孔子的先河。自汉代以后，祭孔活动得以延续，规模逐步提升，明清时期达到顶峰，被称为"国之大典"。清代，顺治皇帝（1638-1661年）定都北京，在北京孔庙专门举行一年一度的祭孔大典，并尊孔子为"大成至圣文宣先师"。随着清王朝的灭亡，祭孔活动有所减少。民国时期，虽然仍然举行祭孔活动，但活动规模和意义已发生变化。新中国成立后，官方和民间基本上取消了祭孔活动，甚至在文化大革命期间，大搞"批林批孔"运动，祭孔被视为封建迷信。到上世纪70年代末，祭孔活动才逐渐恢复。

两千多年的祭孔活动的背后暗含的是儒家学说的发展历程。从西汉到清朝，祭孔活动不断增多，规模逐步提升，礼仪规格不断上升，而这段时间的儒学也处于上升的阶段。西汉时期，儒家与政治结合使得儒家开始成为中国封建社会的国学。而到了东汉时期，儒家与政治的结合落实到礼乐上，客观上促使儒家思想国学的地位更加稳固。到了宋朝，朱熹回归儒家的经典，但将四书置于五经之前，发展出内在化的新儒学，在更广泛的民间及地方层面，则出现了较独立的教化机构——书院，儒家的国学地位达到顶峰。从两汉到清末，儒学成为统治地位的学说延续了2000多年的时间。

Confucius Temple and Imperial College

Tan Zemin, with Sara Feldman and Rosalind Carey, editors

The air of Beijing in early spring has a unique warmth permeated with the aroma of every tree and blade of grass, every brick and tile. Inside Anding Gate in the Dongcheng District of Beijing, an ancient street runs from east to west. Chinese national pagoda trees stand still. Flying eaves and building plaques bestow a feeling of antiquity, creating a solemn and peaceful scene removed from the dense centers of modern urban prosperity, recounting tales of the area's storied history. Imperial College Street derives its name from the Confucius Temple and Imperial College located halfway down the street on the northern side.

History

The Confucius Temple and Imperial College can be traced to the Yuan Dynasty (1271–1368), when Kublai Khan (1215–1294), the first emperor of the Yuan Dynasty, established the capital in Beijing and began building the new Great Capital. The "temple school" was part of the construction plan. It is where the Confucian Temple and Imperial College is located today. It was the highest-level education institution for the Yuan, Ming (1368–1644), and Qing (1644–1912) Dynasties.

Confucius (551–479 BCE), popularly regarded as the founder of "Confucianism," enjoys the status of "Pre-eminent Manifestation of the Great Educator for Generations." Confucian teachings were the main subject of learning in ancient China, enjoying lasting national prestige. By combining education with ritual and music, Confucianism developed a comprehensive and rigid system of rites and worship. This dual system of education combined with rituals and music dictated the unique layout of schools in ancient China—the union of school and temple. At the Confucian Temple and Imperial College, therefore, the temple lies on one side (east), the college on the other (west).

The Confucius Temple is dedicated to Confucius, the great ancestor of educators. Because the feudal

27. 孔子雕像 **Statue of Confucius**

孔庙与国子监

28. 孔庙核心建筑大成殿 Dacheng Hall, the main building of the Confucian Temple

rulers of China highly respected Confucianism and took it as a governing philosophy, they attached great importance to the Confucius Temple. Only these rulers could hold the highest-level worship ceremony for Confucius there. A regimen of strict sacrificial activities at the Confucius Temple was therefore developed in pre-Qing China.

Historical records indicate that the earliest worship of Confucius began with his descendants as a form of family worship. Later, public worship of Confucius commenced on the twelfth month of the twelfth year of the Western Han Dynasty (195 BCE), when Emperor Liu Bang stopped at Confucius' hometown of Qufu (enroute from his home county of Pei to the capital in Chang'an) to worship Confucius with an imperial sacrifice called *tailao*, thereby beginning the tradition of imperial worship of Confucius. The tradition continued over time, with the number of worshippers continually growing, reaching its peak in the Ming and Qing Dynasties as the "National Grand Ceremony." When Emperor Shunzhi (r. 1644–1661) began Qing Dynasty rule in Beijing, he adhered to the tradition of annual worship for Confucius, honoring Confucius as "The Greatly Accomplished, Ultimate Sage, Master of Culture, and Most Ancient Educator" (大成至圣文宣先师).

Worship of Confucius decreased with the demise of the Qing Dynasty. During the Republic of China (1912–1949), Confucius worship continued, though on a much smaller scale and with much less significance. When the People's Republic of China was founded (1949), memorialization of Confucius at the public and official level stopped entirely. During the Cultural Revolution (1966–1976), the campaign of "Attacking Lin Biao and Attacking Confucius" was launched and worship of Confucius was considered superstition. It was not until the late 1970s that Confucian ceremonies resumed.

The over-2000-year-old tradition of Confucius worship mirrors the rise and fall of Confucian teachings. As Confucian rituals became increasingly formal, solemn, and popular, Confucian teachings grew in importance for imperial rule. In the Western Han Dynasty (206 BCE – 9 CE), Confucian teachings were adopted by Han rulers, who used them to establish the platform for national education (*guoxue*). In the Eastern Han Dynasty (25–220), Confucian teachings were implemented in rituals and music, further solidifying its position as *guoxue*. In the Song Dynasty (960–1279), the Confucian scholar Zhu Xi (1130–1200) began to spiritualize Confucianism, attaching more importance to the "Four Books" of Confucianism—Confucius' *Analects*, as well as *Mencius, Great Learning*, and *Doctrine of the Mean*—than to the older "Five Classics." At roughly the same time, independent educational schools (*shuyuan*) were established to promote Confucianism among the common people.

This is just part of China's long history of education. The Five Emperor Era of ancient times (2697–2597 BCE) saw the establishment of education sites called *chengjun* ("cultivating and formalizing"). During the two Han Dynasties a "Highest-level School" (*Taixue*) was instituted. Education was further formalized during the Western Jin Dynasty (266–316) through an "Imperial School" (*Guozixue*), which was later converted into an "Imperial College" (*Guozijian*) during the rule of Emperor Sui Yang Di (r. 604–618) of the Northern Qi Dynasty. At that time, the *Guozixue* was also empowered to administer national education affairs, and the position of *jijiu* (the most senior scholar who proposed the toast to ancestors) was set up. Since then, the Imperial College has played this double role, serving as both the highest-level school and the ministry of national education. This double-role lasted up until the end of the imperial dynasties. In 1905, the Qing Dynasty reformed education, and the Imperial College was included in the Education Department, thus ending its former prestige. From 1956 to 2005, the Imperial College served as the Capital Library of Beijing. In 2006, it was finally converted into a museum, becoming a historical and cultural tourist site.

从清朝末年到上世纪70年代末，祭孔活动越来越少，渐渐淡化，而这段时间的儒学总体来说逐渐式微。经历了从太平天国、洋务运动中的"中体西用"到新文化运动前后"打倒孔家店"的过程，一直到文化大革命时期"批林批孔运动"。20世纪80年代以后，祭孔活动在全国范围内恢复，这一时期的儒学也逐渐复兴。

中国有着悠久的教育历史，是世界上古代最为重视教育和教育最发达的国家之一。据古代文献记载，早在原始社会的五帝时期，就有了名为"成均"的教育活动场所，两汉时期，设立最高学府"太学"，西晋时期，晋武帝初立国子学。隋朝开皇初年，建立国子寺统辖国子学、太学，到了隋炀帝（569-618年）大业三年，将国子寺改称国子监，由此开始，国子监便成为历代国家最高学府和教育管理机构，并一直延续至清朝末年。到了1905年清末改革学制，国子监的教育和行政功能并入学部，国子监作为古代国家最高学府和教育管理机构的历史使命便宣告结束。1956年至2005年，国子监作为北京首都图书馆而存在，2006年，北京市设立国子监博物馆，国子监成为历史文化类旅游景区。

作为最高学府，国子监是人才汇集之地，贵族子弟和各地方官员推荐的优秀人才在国子监学习儒家经典和传统礼乐，接受古代最高规格的教育。作为国家层面的教育管理机构，国子监源源不断为中央集权统治提供优秀毕业生参与国家管理，并通过制定统一教材等方式扮演着统一古代国家意识形态的角色。因此，围绕国子监的教育实践活动具有隆厚的政治色彩和独特的特征。无论是日常教育活动、礼仪活动，还是君王"临雍讲学"，都有严格的规定和程序。

国子监具有严格的教育形式。在入学选拔、课程设置、考试制度等方面，国子监都有严格的规定。首先，国子监的入学选拔一般采用推荐加入学考试的形式。各地方的秀才需要得到地方官的推荐才能报名参加国子监的入学考试。入学考试成绩合格才能进入国子监学习。其次，国子监的课程设置具有很强的政治倾向。国子监的学生主要学习八股文、四书五经、通鉴、书法、皇帝的诰表等。教材统称为"监本"，除了供国子监学生学习外，还发到全国各地其他学校。在众多教材中最为特殊和重要的是"儒家十三经"，由乾隆皇帝亲自颁布并以石碑的形式保存至今。再次，国子监有严格的考试制度和学制。在国子监读书，每月一小考，三月一大考，如果有三次考试不及格，就会被淘汰。国子监的学制一般为三年，考试实行积分制，需要达到一定的积分才能毕业，如果积分不够就需要继续坐堂。国子监也有班主任和上课老师，班主任被称呼为助教，老师被称为"博士"，著名政治家张居正（1525-1582年），戏曲家孔尚任（1648-1718年）等都在国子监当过老师。最后，历代国子监都有严格的校规。如明太祖朱元璋（1328-1398年）在位时，亲自为国子监制定了严格的规章制度，如禁止学生进厨房，禁止在宿舍唱歌、喝酒，禁止对人对事批评议论等。学生一旦违反这些规定，轻则遭到杖责，重则充军，甚至直接被处死。

国子监具有严格的礼仪活动。作为中国古代社会设立的最高学府，在日常教育活动中国子监兼具礼仪的教育内容，其目的是使得学生在学习过程中能学礼、知礼、懂礼、讲礼、行礼。除了讲授礼仪，学校自身也以礼致学，从而形成了学校的礼仪制度。国子监作为国家最高学府，礼仪制度上十分严格。国子监的礼仪包括释奠礼、束脩礼以及日常学习生活中的礼仪活动。释奠礼一般指陈列酒和食物祭奠先师先贤；束脩礼，即拜师礼是古代学生和老师初次见面时的一种礼节。国子监的礼仪教育并不限于仪式本身，国子监作为教育习礼的场所，其一切活动都必须遵循礼仪制度的规定，其目的是为了使学生的一切活动都能内化为自觉的行为。

In feudal society, children of aristocrats and other gifted children recommended by local officials gathered at the Imperial College to receive education in the Confucian classics, traditional etiquette, and royal rites. Those who graduated entered civil service, providing support for the imperial regime. The college also produced textbooks to unify education and thought across the country. All these educational activities were imbued with political prestige, enjoying distinctive royal characteristics. They also followed formal rules and regulations.

The policies of the Imperial College were strict from admission to graduation. Only those recommended by local officials were permitted to enroll in the college entrance exam, and only those who successfully passed the exams were admitted. Most of the courses in the curriculum involved the Confucian classics (with calligraphy being one of the additional subjects). A rigid examination system was employed. A minor exam was held monthly; a major one, quarterly. If a student failed three exams cumulatively, he was required to drop out. Students could graduate in three years on the condition that they accumulated the total number of required credits. Otherwise, the student had to make up courses. There were other strict campus rules and disciplines. While Emperor Zhu Yuanzhang (r. 1368–1398) of the Ming Dynasty was on the throne, there were regulations that forbade entry to the kitchens, singing in the dorms, consumption of alcohol, feigned illness, attire other than uniforms, and criticizing and commenting on people and issues. The Imperial College offered clear paths of employment, allowing students either to take the imperial exam and become government officials or to seek apprenticeships in the government network.

One of the most important subjects for the Imperial College was etiquette and rites, which stressed their understanding, articulation, and practice. As

29. "十二哲"之一卜子配祀牌位 Memorial tablet for Confucian sage Bu

the highest-level institution of the country, the college had a rigid and comprehensive system of etiquettes and rites. These included the rites of *Shidian* and *Shuxiu* (as well as other daily etiquettes and rituals). The former, *Shidian*, is a ritual of worship for deceased educators and scholars that involves offerings of wine and food. The latter, *Shuxiu*, is an ancient ceremony for the first meeting between a master and his pupils. Through education and practice, students at the *Guozijian* gradually embraced these etiquettes and rites as integral parts of their life.

30. 上书"圜桥教泽"琉璃牌坊 Paifang with the inscription "Education endowed by the love of the emperor is endless like running water"

空间格局

  古代学校建制为庙学一体，北京孔庙和国子监为左庙右学。二者既为一体，又相互分离，整体建筑都坐北朝南，沿两条中轴线对称分布。

  在孔庙院落的中轴线上，由南向北依次坐落着先师门、大成门、大成殿、崇圣祠。先师门是孔庙的大门，面阔三间，基本保留了元代的建筑风格。走进先师门，最吸引眼球的是一尊伟岸的雕像，惟妙惟肖，这是至圣先师孔子的雕像。在孔子雕像的后面，迎面看到的便是大成门，面阔五间，坐落在高大的砖石台基上，中间的御路石上高浮雕海水龙纹图样，五龙戏珠，栩栩如生。步入大成门，映入眼帘的是孔庙的中心建筑大成殿，是孔庙内最神圣的殿宇。殿内金砖铺地，其规制是我国封建社会的最高建筑等级，能与故宫太和殿媲美。殿中供奉"孔子至圣先师"牌位，神位两边设有配享的"二十四哲"牌位。神位前置祭案，上设尊、爵、卣、笾、豆等祭器均为清乾隆时的御制真品。大殿内外高悬清康熙至宣统九位皇帝的御匾，均是皇帝亲书的对孔子的赞语，是珍贵的文物。每逢祭孔大典，大成殿所在的院落钟鼓齐鸣，乐舞生平，仪仗威严。

  在国子监中，从南向北依次排列着集贤门、太学门、琉璃牌坊、辟雍殿、彝伦堂、敬一亭等建筑，且沿中轴线呈左右对称的方式排列。国子监的第一道大门名为

31. 国子监核心建筑群辟雍殿 Piyong Hall, the main building of the Imperial College

Space

Ancient school construction was characterized by the union of temple and school. Thus Beijing's Confucius Temple and the Imperial College are located next to one another, two parts of one whole, even though there is a clear division between them. The entire complex "sits in the north and faces the south," with a symmetric layout along the central axis.

Along the central axis of the Confucian Temple, from south to north, stand Xianshi Gate, Dacheng Gate, Dacheng Hall, and Chongsheng Temple. Xianshi Gate is the main gateway of the temple. It has three wide arches, retaining the Yuan Dynasty architectural style. Upon entering the gate, the first thing that catches the eye is the exquisitely crafted statue of Confucius. Behind the statue is Dacheng Gate, which contains five wide arches. It sits high on a stone and brick base. After the gate, one enters Dacheng Hall, the central structure of the Confucius Temple. The floor is paved with gold bricks, the highest construction standard in Imperial China, comparable with Taihe Hall of the Forbidden City. The memorial tablet of Confucius, the greatest sage and educator, is enshrined in the hall, along with twenty-four other Confucian scholars. The worship table in front of the shrine displays the authentic votive objects manufactured according to imperial orders during the Qianlong Era (r. 1735–1796) of the Qing Dynasty. Plaques of praise for Confucius, endowed by nine emperors from Kangxi (r. 1661–1722) to Xuantong (r. 1908–1912), hang inside and outside the hall. When the grand memorial ceremony for Confucius is held, the drums and bells in

32. 十三经刻石 Stelea garden of thirteen Confucian classics

集贤门，有"集聚贤人"之意。越过集贤门是国子监的第二道大门太学门，太学门门阔三间，门上悬挂"太学"匾额。穿越太学门映入眼帘的是一座三间四柱七楼琉璃牌坊。作为皇家专用的牌坊形式，国子监中的琉璃牌坊建于乾隆四十九年，是当时全国唯一一座专为教育设立的牌坊。正面题有"寰桥教泽"四字，具有赞颂皇帝的教化恩泽泽被学子之意，具有道德教化的功能。琉璃牌坊后面是国子监的中心建筑辟雍殿。《礼记·王制》有云："大学在郊，天子曰辟雍，诸侯曰泮宫"。

辟雍本为周天子为教育贵族子弟设立的大学，取四周有水，环形如璧为名。国子监中的辟雍是清乾隆四十八年兴建，作为国子监的中央建筑，建于中轴线中心一座圆形水池中央的四方高台上，是一座方型重檐攒尖顶殿宇。辟雍殿主要是古代皇帝讲学的地方，乾隆皇帝之后，每逢新帝即位都会来辟雍殿讲学，史称"临雍讲学"。从琉璃牌坊到辟雍殿的东西两侧为六堂，六堂名称都取自儒家经典，东侧北起依次为率性堂、诚心堂、崇志堂，西侧北起依次为修道堂、正义堂、广业堂。六堂最初是国子监的教室，每十一间成为一堂，共六十六间。辟雍殿的北侧是彝伦堂，现在国子监的彝伦堂为明代永乐年间重建，在辟雍殿修建之前，皇帝则在彝伦堂讲学。辟雍殿建成后，彝伦堂成为国子监举行重大活动的场所，同时兼具藏书的功能。

在孔庙与国子监之间的夹道内，现今保存着北京最大的碑林，包括著名的"十三经刻石"，以及诸多的皇家御制的石碑，"十三经刻石"共计189座，上面篆刻着《周易》《尚书》《诗经》《周礼》《仪礼》《礼记》《春秋左传》《春秋公羊传》

the courtyard are sounded, music rises, and dances are performed, presenting a magnificent scene.

The central buildings of the Imperial College are also symmetrically arranged on its central axis from south to north. First come three separate gates: Jixian Gate, Taixue Gate, and a special, ornamental gate called a "Paifang." Taixue Gate bears a plaque reading 太学 ("The Imperial College"), whereas the Paifang—a glazed gate with three arches, four columns, and seven levels—contains a plaque with the characters 圜桥教泽 ("School surrounded by a circular pool connected outside by bridges"), implying that the education endowed by the love of "Tianzi" (the emperor, a.k.a. the "son of Heaven") is endless like running water. The Paifang was built in the forty-ninth year of the rule of Qianlong; it is the only Paifang in the country dedicated to education.

Piyong Hall, the central structure of the Imperial College, is directly behind the Paifang. "Piyong" was the name given to the school established by the rulers of the Zhou Dynasty (1046–256 BCE) for the children of aristocrats. *Pi* refers to a circular and flat piece of jade with a hole in the middle; *yong*, a flowing river. Therefore, Piyong Hall consists of a square building that sits in the middle of a circular pool of water (as was also likely the case for the original Piyong school of the Zhou Dynasty).

Piyong Hall was built in the forty-eighth year of the Qianlong Era of the Qing Dynasty. As the central building of the Imperial College, it sits squarely in the middle of the central axis. The hall is a square building with a pointed roof with heavy flying eaves. It used to be the site where ancient emperors taught. Every subsequent emperor after Qianlong would come to Piyong Hall to give a lecture, which was called "Teaching in Piyong."

Lining both sides of the central axis between the Paifang and Piyong Hall are the Six Halls. On the east, they are Shuaixing Hall, Chengxin Hall, Chongzhi Hall; on the west, Xiudao Hall, Zhengyi Hall, and Guangye Hall. These halls used to be the classrooms of the college. To the north of Piyong Hall is Yilun Hall, which was built during the Yongle Era (r. 1402–1424) of the Ming Dynasty. Before the construction of Piyong Hall, Yilun Hall was the lecture hall for the emperors. Afterwards, it was used as a library and a center for important events.

The largest collection of stelae in Beijing is preserved in the corridor between the Confucius Temple and the Imperial College. These include the famous Thirteen Classics stelae and many royal stone monuments. There are 189 stelae that collectively contain the Thirteen Classics of Confucianism: *Classic of Changes, Classic of Documents, Classic of Poetry, Rites of Zhou, Ceremonies and Rites, Book of Rites, Commentary of Zou on the Spring and Autumn Annals, Commentary of Gongyang on the Spring and Autumn Annals, Commentary of Guliang on the Spring and Autumn Annals, Analects of Confucius, Classic of Filial Piety, Mencius,* and *Erya*. The original texts were hand-written by Jiang Heng (1642–1742), a student from the Imperial College. It took him twelve years to finish the whole work. In the fifty-sixth year of the rule of Qianlong (1791), an imperial order was given to carve these writings by Jiang Heng onto the stones. It was an enormous project that involved the carving of 620,000 individual characters. The carvings were orderly, and the content was precise. This is the most complete stone version of the Confucian classics.

Revival of Confucianism

The end of the 1970s witnessed an unexpected revival of Confucianism. The Cultural Revolution had just ended, communism enjoyed less favor, and the world was more stable and peaceful. Meanwhile, there was a vacuum of faith in the people. Out of a need for social and cultural reconstruction, Confucianism resurged, aided by the cultural self-consciousness of the intellectual elite.

《春秋谷梁传》《论语》《孝经》《孟子》《尔雅》共十三部儒家经典，整部石经的蓝本是雍正年间的江苏金坛贡生蒋衡（1672-1742年），历时12年写成的楷体手书，乾隆五十六年（1791年）下旨刻石立碑，全部石经共计62万余字，规模宏大、刻法工整、内容准确，是最为完整的一部石刻儒家典籍。

儒学复苏视野下的孔庙和国子监

近些年以来，儒学在经受了几次冲击后开始复兴。20世纪70年代末文化大革命结束，人们的价值出现真空，这为儒学复兴创造了有利条件。除此之外，积极稳定的外部环境、社会文化的重建和知识群体的文化自觉都为儒学的复兴奠定了基础。因此，70年代末以来，官方、学者、民间等都积极致力于儒学在当代的发展。一方面，人们尝试在儒家思想传统中寻求符合现代社会发展的内在价值，重建中国人的伦理道德；另一方面，重视儒家经典，重视挖掘宋代以来儒学的心灵性，将儒家的政治理念融入当代社会。在国学复苏的背景中，孔庙和国子监正扮演着全新的角色。首先，恢复为礼仪场所。每逢孔子诞辰日，孔庙常常会举行规模宏大的祭孔活动，目的在于弘扬中华传统文化。国子监博物馆成为青少年成人礼的举办场所，如今北京市多所高中都来此举办成人礼活动。除此之外，日常礼仪活动也在恢复，如孔庙时常举行的"演礼"。

其次，孔庙和国子监博物馆是国学教育的重要场所。每逢春季学期，走进国子监博物馆常会遇上中小学生在国子监进行国学教育和参观。国学教学是部分中小学教育的必修课，课程设置内容常包括到孔庙和国子监学习和参观。虽然学校并没有要求家长参加课程，但每次随行的家长都数量众多。

在儒学不断复兴的背景下，北京孔庙和国子监不仅以无言的形式向众人述说着过往的历史故事，也以礼仪的形式宣扬着儒家在新时代的价值，更是北京青少年游览参观、举行成人礼和国学教育的首选场所。而这一切都发生在有限的空间范围内。《周易》有云"观乎人文，以化成天下"，现在的孔庙和国子监正诠释着这样的功能。站在国子监街，回首祖先们留下的遗迹，不免感慨万千，在日益繁纷的世界里，我们民族的文化是否已经渐渐消融在绚烂的繁华之中？如今全国上下推崇国学，尚儒之风日盛，追寻泱泱华夏的精魂，人们循着先贤的足迹来到孔庙和国子监，嗅一嗅古树和石碑的清凉，静静地聆听来自历史的回响，于心灵无疑是一种荡涤。

From the end of the 1970s to the present, all circles of society—official, academic, and folk—have actively engaged in efforts to return Confucianism to Chinese society. They have rediscovered the value of Confucian traditions, reexplored the spirit of Confucian ethics, reattached importance to the Confucian classics, and reestablished the significance of Confucian teachings.

The Confucius Temple and the Imperial College plays a brand-new role in this revival. Once again, the Confucius Temple serves as a ceremonial site, holding an annual Confucius Memorial Ceremony on Confucius' birthday (September 28) to promote traditional Chinese culture. Likewise, the Imperial College Museum has become a site for coming-of-age rites for young people, with many high schools in Beijing holding ceremonies here. The Confucius Temple and the Imperial College also daily reenact Confucian rituals for tourists.

The Confucius Temple and the Imperial College is also an important venue for offering *guoxue* education for elementary and middle-school students in Beijing. Visitors can always find school students studying or sight-seeing here in the early spring. *Guoxue* is an optional course for some elementary and middle school students, with recent textbooks written on this subject. One curriculum activity for the course is a site visit to the Confucius Temple. Although parents are not required to accompany the students, they often do.

The Confucius Temple and Imperial College continues telling stories of the past, revealing Confucianism's renewed values for a new era, maintaining its role in education, and offering a smell of ancient trees and touch of ancient tablets. As visitors listen, look, smell, and touch, they also reflect: How can traditional culture co-exist with modern prosperity? Where shall the old traditions stand today in the lives of the Chinese people, the Chinese nation, and the world?

东四清真寺

马斌

历史

出了北京故宫博物院后门,沿着景山前街一直向东走,第三个十字路口叫"东四",它的全名是"东四牌楼"。明永乐年间中后期,政府在这个十字路口四面各建了一座木制牌楼,又因其位置在皇城之东,故称东四牌楼。四座牌楼早在1954年因拓宽街道而被拆除,但是"东四"这一地名留了下来。

进入东四南大街,行100米就可以看见一座古建筑,青砖砌成的墙面古朴而庄严,中间是一扇朱红色的大门,门的两侧各书两个金色大字,四个字合起来是"清真古教",这便是"东四清真寺",它因地理位置而得名。"清"意为清净无染,"真"意为真实无伪,"古"意为恒古不变,"教"意为教化。"清真"原本是道教的术语,伊斯兰教传入中国之后,中国穆斯林开始使用"清真",之后,这个词成为中国穆斯林的专用词汇。"古教"的意思是"古老的教导",穆斯林认为,伊斯兰教并非始于先知穆罕默德,而是自人类祖先亚当时代真主就启示给人类的教导,因此中国穆斯林用"清真古教"指代伊斯兰教。

东四清真寺始建于1447年,由一位名叫陈友(卒于1460年)的明代穆斯林官员出资建设。1450年明代宗朱祁钰(1449–1457年在位)为东四清真寺题写了匾额"清真寺",这块匾额已经遗失,但是留下一块记载陈友捐建以及皇帝敕字的石碑。寺内还有一个铜制的宣礼塔塔顶也能证明这座清真寺的历史,塔顶上刻的铸造时间是"成化丙午年",即1486年。由于皇帝敕字,这座清真寺被称为京城四大"官寺"之一,其余的三座分别为:牛街礼拜寺、锦什坊街普寿寺、安内二条法明寺。值得一提的是,明代时候穆斯林的寺院可能并没有被固定地称呼为"清真寺","普寿寺"和"法明寺"都可以用来称呼,这些词都是道教和佛教的术语,以此给清真寺命名也体现了伊斯兰教传入中国后对中国传统文化的借鉴。

东四清真寺不仅是一座历史悠久的清真寺,也是北京穆斯林的文化中心。近代中国穆斯林知识分子创办的"成达师范学院"有一段时间就设置在该清真寺内,学院的图书馆至今尚存。20世纪早期中国穆斯林最著名的报纸《月华》的编辑部也曾设置在该寺。新中国成立之后,东四清真寺是新政府开展"政训班"培训少数民族干部的地方。据中国伊斯兰教协会前会长陈广元阿訇回忆,"文化大革命"时期,北京的所有清真寺都被关闭,但是周恩来总理批示,东四清真寺继续开放,周总理说:"我们破除四旧,但外国人不破四旧。"(四旧是指旧思想、旧文化、旧风俗、旧习惯)因此,东四清真寺只对外国穆斯林开放供他们做礼拜。

东四清真寺自明代以来,多次修葺,仅中华人民共和国成立以来,分别于1974年、1987年、2003年修葺三次,并于1984年被认定为北京市文物保护单位。

空间

东四清真寺坐西朝东,是中国古代经典的对称式建筑。大门的正上方有一块黑底

Dongsi Mosque

Ma Bin, with Kameron Tomes, editor

History

From the rear gate of the Forbidden City, the third crossroad to the east along Jingshan Street is Dongsi, meaning "East Four." Dongsi is short for Dongsi Pailou, with *pailou* meaning "ornamental arch." At the beginning of the fourteenth century, the Ming government erected a wooden *pailou* at each corner of the intersection, making four *pailou* altogether. Since these *pailou* were located east of the royal palace, they were called "Dongsi Pailou"—"Four Ornamental Arches on the East." Although the arches were removed in 1954 for road expansion, the name "Dongsi" has remained.

Entering South Dongsi Street and continuing for 100 meters, one can see an old building whose gray brick wall gives it a simple, ancient, and solemn appearance. The grand door in the middle is painted vermilion. On each of its sides, two golden-colored characters are inscribed. Put together, they read 清真古教 (*Qing Zhen Gu Jiao*)—"Pure Genuine Ancient Teaching." The first two characters, *Qing Zhen*, used to be a term for Daoism. When Islam was introduced to China, Chinese Muslims borrowed the name, which has since referred specifically to Chinese Muslims. The second two characters, *Gu Jiao*, suggest the long

33. 坐在清真寺内的信徒 Member of Dongsi Mosque sitting in the prayer hall

东四清真寺

34. 东四清真寺小净室 Ablution (*wudu*) room at Dongsi Mosque

history of Islam. Muslims believe that Islam did not start with Prophet Mohammad; rather, Islam is a religion revealed by Allah to humans at the time of Adam. Islam is therefore referred to as *Qing Zhen Gu Jiao* by Chinese Muslims.

Funded by Chen You (d. 1460), a Ming Dynasty Muslim government official, the construction of Dongsi Mosque began in 1447. The Ming Dynasty emperor Zhu Qiyu (r. 1449–1457) inscribed 清真寺 ("*Qing Zhen* Temple") on a plaque outside the mosque in 1450. Although the plaque has since disappeared, a stone tablet documenting Zhu Qiyu's imperial inscription and Chen You's funding still exists. Another proof of the temple's history is its copper minaret. At its top, the carving indicates the time of casting as 成化丙午—the year 1486. Thanks to the imperial inscription, the temple is known as one of the "Four Major Official Mosques" in Beijing, the other three of which are Niujie Mosque, Jinshifangjie Pushou Temple, and Anneiertiao Faming Temple. In the Ming Dynasty (1368–1644), "Qing Zhen" was not the only term for mosques; there were also names like "Pushou Temple" and "Faming Temple," which were derived from Daoism and Buddhism. The former (*pushou*) means "May all have a long life"; the latter (*faming*), "Shining the truth." These names show that Islam has been immersed in Chinese culture from its earliest days in China.

In addition to its storied history, Dongsi Mosque serves as the cultural center for Muslims in Beijing. For some time, the Chengda Teachers College, which was founded by Chinese Muslim intellectuals, was set up inside the temple. The college library is still there today. The editorial office of *Yue Hua*, the best-known Chinese Muslim newspaper in the early 1900s, was located here too. Since the establishment of the People's Republic of China (1949), Dongsi Mosque has served as the site for the government's Political Quality Cultivating Classes, which develop government leaders from minority ethnic-group regions. According to Imam Chen Guangyuan, the former director of the Chinese Islamic Association, Dongsi Mosque was the only mosque in Beijing not to be closed during the Cultural Revolution. Premier Zhou Enlai (1898–1976) ordered Dongsi Mosque to remain open, saying, "We broke the Four Olds [old thinking, old culture, old tradition, and old habits], but foreigners did not do that." At that time, Dongsi Mosque was open only for foreign Muslims to worship.

Since the Ming Dynasty, Dongsi Mosque has gone through many repairs and reconstructions. Three repairs have been made since the founding of the People's Republic of China: in 1974, 1987, and 2003. In 1984, the mosque was designated as a Cultural Relics Protection Unit in Beijing.

Space

Dongsi Mosque runs from east to west, a symmetrical structure typically found in classical Chinese buildings. On top of the main gateway sits a black wooden plaque inscribed with three golden characters 清真寺 ("*Qing Zhen* Temple"). A vermilion pillar guards the gateway on each side, together with two stone drums ornamented with auspicious walking beasts—a practice rarely seen in Chinese mosques. Islam forbids any animal paintings or carvings. Because Dongsi was an official mosque, however, it was bestowed with this privilege.

The entire temple is a three-enclosed-courtyard structure. The north wing of the front yard is a shower room. Muslims are required to cleanse the body before prayer. This can involve full ablution (the washing of the entire body) or partial ablution (the washing of only the hands, face, and feet). The south wing of the front yard is the bedroom and living room of the imam.

Between the front and middle courtyards, there are five arches, with the center arch functioning as the passageway. On each side of the passageway is a

东四清真寺

金字的木质匾额，写着"清真寺"三个汉字。大门的两侧各有一根朱红色的柱子，以及两个抱鼓石。抱鼓石上雕刻着象征吉祥的走兽，这在中国清真寺中是十分罕见的，因为按照伊斯兰教的教义不可以绘画或者雕刻任何动物的形象，东四清真寺大概因为是"官寺"才会有这种现象。

整座寺院是三进式院落，前院的北厢房是沐浴室。穆斯林在做礼拜前都要先清洗身体，清洗分为两种：一种是沐浴全身，中国穆斯林称之为"大净"，一种只是清洗手、脸和脚，中国穆斯林称之为"小净"。前院的南厢房是阿訇的卧室和起居室。

由前院进入中院本来有五个拱门，只有中间一个是真正的通道，其余四个只是拱形的门廊。通道的两侧是陈列室，放置着见证这座清真寺历史的文物。穿过通道就进入了中院，在进入中院的过道口正上方有一副极具中国特色的阿拉伯文书法砖雕，其内容是"奉普慈特慈的真主之名"，书写采用中国古代自上而下先右后左的书写顺序，被认为是阿拉伯伊斯兰文化中国化的典型产物。中院是古尔邦节宰牲的场所，这可以从两个大的下水道口，以及旁边用来挂肉的铁架子看得出来。

中院和后院之间是"敏纳热"，中国穆斯林称之为"望月楼"或者"宣礼塔"，"望月楼"的意思是用来观看月亮的楼。伊斯兰教历是按照月亮的出现和消失计算一个月时间的，尤其是到了斋月的时候，穆斯林必须看到新月之后才能宣布斋月开始。称之为"宣礼塔"是因为，到了礼拜时间宣礼员要登高疾呼召唤大家来做礼拜。中国传统清真寺的宣礼塔和世界各地的宣礼塔风格不同，在阿拉伯世界宣礼塔是高高的尖塔，中国传统的宣礼塔并不高，只有两层楼，更像观景楼。

穿过望月楼就进入了后院，后院的南北厢房都是中国古典木质门窗，是阿訇的办公室以及接待室和会议室。后院的中心是一块宽敞的广场，用来举行盛大仪式，在我访问清真寺的前两天，中国伊斯兰教协会会长杨发明阿訇被东四清真寺聘请为首席阿訇，就在这里举行了欢迎仪式。

正对望月楼是礼拜大殿，大殿古朴而庄严，能同时容纳500人做礼拜。在大殿的屋脊上蹲坐着许多石刻走兽，有的屋脊上有五只，有的有七只，这在中国古代建筑中被称为"五脊六兽"，只有皇帝和权贵人家才可以使用，是等级社会不同阶层地位的象征。中国清真寺内的走兽雕刻，体现了伊斯兰教传入中国之后的变通，以及对中国传统文化的接受。礼拜殿台阶左侧竖立着一块名为《清真法明百字圣号》的石碑，落款日期为万历七年（1579年）。碑文的内容主要是赞颂先知穆罕默德，中国穆斯林认为这块碑文的作者是明太祖朱元璋。

推开大殿高大古朴的木门，会发出"吱吱呀呀"的声音，仿佛感叹着历史的悠远和变迁的沧桑。殿内有22根柱子，柱子上绘刻着精美的荷花图案，屋顶则是雕梁画栋，这些都是中国文化的体现。有意思的是这些柱子上的荷花有花有叶，却没有根，因为按照伊斯兰教义真主是唯一的创造者，而根象征着花的创造，因此没有绘出根部。横梁上除了装饰图案之外还有很多阿拉伯文书法，这些书法兼具"库法体"的刚硬"纳斯赫体"的圆润，上刚而下柔。大殿的西端有三个室内的穹顶，穹顶具有扩音的作用，穹顶下方是伊玛目站立的位置，这些穹顶属于室内建筑，从外部是看不出来的。穹顶建筑是阿拉伯-伊斯兰建筑的风格，东四清真寺的大殿也因此被认为是综合了阿拉伯和中国的建筑风格。礼拜殿内的右侧有一块区域用一排屏风隔了开来，隔开的空间是妇女做礼拜的地方，以体现伊斯兰教男女有别的观念。

礼拜殿外边的南北两侧分别是两座二层小楼，北侧是储物间和锅炉房，南侧是前面提到的成达师范学院的图书馆。这座图书馆由于20世纪30年代受到当时埃及苏丹

35. 银杏树遮掩的望月楼 Moon-watching tower at Dongsi Mosque

display room that contains artifacts from the mosque. At the end of the passageway, there is an Arabic brick carving near the top that reads "In the name of God, the Most Gracious, the Most Merciful." This calligraphy is written in traditional Chinese order—from top to bottom, and right to left—suggesting Chinese cultural influence on Arabic Islam. The middle courtyard is used to slaughter animals in preparation for *Eid al-Adha,* as evinced by the two big sewers and two iron shelves for hanging meat. Between the middle and back courtyard is the minaret, which Chinese Muslims also call a "moon-watching tower." Muslims use a lunar calendar that goes by the wax and wane of the moon; they must therefore be able to see the crescent moon before announcing the start of Ramadan. The moon-watching tower also serves as a minaret since the muezzin ascends to the height of the tower to call the faithful to prayer. Chinese minarets differ from those of other countries, especially the Arab world, where minarets are tall spires. The Chinese minaret is not conical and is only two tiers tall, resembling a watch tower.

Passing through the moon-watching tower, one enters the back courtyard. Both the south and north wings—currently the imam's office, reception room, and conference room—are fit with ancient Chinese wooden doors and windows. The center of the back courtyard is a spacious plaza to hold grand ceremonies. Two days prior to my visit to the mosque, a welcome ceremony was held here for Yang Faming, the director of the Chinese Islamic Association, who had been newly appointed as the chief imam of the Dongsi Mosque.

Facing the moon-watching tower is the grand and simple prayer hall, which can accommodate 500

福阿德（Fuad I，1868-1936年）的捐助而被命名为"福德图书馆"，当时图书馆的筹备委员会中除了著名阿訇马松亭和著名历史学家白寿彝等穆斯林学者之外，还有不少非穆斯林学者，包括中国著名教育家蔡元培、著名哲学家冯友兰以及著名历史学家顾颉刚和陈垣等人。成达师范学院及福德图书馆不仅开创了中国穆斯林的新式教育，而且在抗日战争中发挥了积极作用。中国清真寺的传统教育局限于宗教学科，成达师范学院则将各种人文社会学科和自然科学也纳入了穆斯林教育，并且向埃及派去留学生。1939年1月朝觐期间，日本企图派人在沙特阿拉伯宣传并美化其侵华行为，马松亭得知消息以后立刻通知在埃及的成达师范学生，学生组成28人团前往沙特阿拉伯，他们痛斥日本在华的罪恶行为，宣传中国人民抗战的英勇行为，揭穿了日本谋划的伪宣传。

人物和实践

笔者来到东四清真寺的时候正好是晌礼（Salat al-Zuhr）时间，院子空无一人，只有银杏树叶在风中沙沙作响。礼拜结束后我们见到了热情友好的何阿訇，何阿訇今年31岁，是一位十分年轻的阿訇，他2012年从中国伊斯兰教经学院毕业之后，就一直在东四清真寺担任阿訇。何阿訇的家乡在距离北京200公里的河北省张家口市，他出生在一个虔诚的穆斯林家庭。何阿訇告诉我，他的外祖父就是一位伊玛目，他从小就跟着外祖父去清真寺，也学习了一些简单的宗教知识。高中毕业后，他在清真寺看到中国伊斯兰教经学院的招生简章，就报考了经学院，经过四年的学习，成为了一名伊玛目。东四清真寺现在有5位伊玛目，除了首席伊玛目外，其余四人实行轮班制。何阿訇告诉我们，星期五聚礼，以及开斋节和古尔邦节的时候，周围有不少穆斯林会来参加礼拜，而平时来这个清真寺做礼拜的人极少，比如当天，尽管是周末，但是只有三个人参加礼拜。其中一位是在某个档案馆工作的宋先生，宋先生十分健谈，他告诉我，工作之余，他最大的兴趣就是去参观清真寺，他对北京各个清真寺的建筑历史和现状都十分熟悉，来清真寺做礼拜，了解清真寺的历史能够让他忘记工作的疲惫和烦恼。有时候家里一些宗教事务需要处理，他还会邀请阿訇去他家。

东四清真寺因为其悠久的历史吸引了不少游客。就在我们交谈时，一位来自斯里拉卡的穆斯林小伙进来做礼拜。他告诉我们，他来中国旅游，在网上查到这座清真寺的信息就想来看看，在这样一座古老而宁静的清真寺做礼拜他感觉自己远离了城市的喧嚣，内心更加平静。何阿訇告诉我们，也有一些高校的师生来参观清真寺，了解穆斯林的宗教生活。在我们谈话快要结束的时候，进来了三位老人，他们直径走到大殿的右侧，许久才出来。经过交谈，我们才知道他们是来寻找童年的学堂。他们说，在新中国刚成立的时候，清真寺大殿的后面是一座回民小学，周围很多穆斯林小孩都在这所小学上学，如今60多年过去了，学校已经换了校址，他们也很早就搬家，不在周围住了，现在想回来看看旧的校址，但是校址早就没有了。这三位老人告诉我们，以前东四清真寺的周围有一个穆斯林社区，来清真寺的人很多，到节日的时候大殿里面无法容纳来做礼拜的人，还要在院子里铺上毯子供人礼拜。但是随着城市化的逐步加深，清真寺的周围发展为商业区，原来的社区也进行了重建，很多穆斯林搬走了，久而久之，穆斯林社区就消失了。面对60年翻天覆地的变化，三位老人唏嘘不已。

何阿訇告诉我们，清真寺的功能不能只限于做礼拜，它同时是穆斯林文化中心。近些年东四清真寺和北京市伊斯兰教协会合作发起了一项名为"福德论坛"的文化论

36. 东四清真寺的礼拜大殿 Prayer hall at Dongsi Mosque

people. Carvings of crouching animals adorn the ridges of the hall. Some ridges have five, while others have seven—a technique of ancient Chinese architecture called "Five Ridges and Six Beasts," which was authorized to be used only by emperors and dignitaries as a symbol of high prestige. The beast carvings reflect Islam's embrace of Chinese culture since its inception.

On the left side of the entrance to the prayer hall stands a stone monument named 清真法明百字圣号 ("The Life of Muhammad in 100 Characters"), which is dated the seventh year of Wanli (1579). The text, which praises the Prophet Muhammad, is widely considered by Chinese Muslims to be the work of Emperor Zhu Yuanzhang (r. 1368–1398).

Pushing open the tall and imposing ancient wooden door, one can hear the squeaky sound it makes, as if the door were languishing about the sorrows and vagaries of its long history. There are twenty-two pillars inside the hall, each ornamented with exquisite lotus-flower patterns, a traditional element of Chinese culture. Only the flowers and leaves of the lotus were painted, not the roots, since roots suggest the creation of life. Islam holds that the only creator is Allah; painting roots would supersede his power. In addition to the decorative patterns on the beams, there is plenty of Arabic calligraphy that combines the rigidness of the *Kufa* font (with hard edges and corners) and the smoothness of the *Naskh* font (with flowing curves), achieving the effect of hard lines on the top, and soft and gentle lines at the bottom.

There are three indoor domes at the west end of the hall, visible only from the interior. The imam stands below them, since the domes amplify sound. Domes are an important part of Arabic and Islamic architecture. Thus the hall combines Arabic and Chinese architectural style. On the right side of the hall,

37. 何阿訇 Imam He

坛。福德论坛是一项大型的学术会议，每年一次，已经召开两届。论坛的主题是倡导温和的伊斯兰教，反对极端主义，推进伊斯兰教中国化，参加论坛的不仅有神职人员，还有大学教授和政府官员。何阿訇还告诉我们，有不少穆斯林来清真寺拍婚纱照，甚至举行结婚仪式。著名男演员王志飞婚礼的宗教仪式就是在这座清真寺举行的，这位男演员是一位穆斯林，但是他的未婚妻不是，因此在婚礼当天先为新娘举行了入教仪式，而后举行了婚礼中的宗教环节。

何阿訇告诉我们，清真寺是宗教场所，但这并不意味着要和世俗社会完全隔绝，东四清真寺门口以前挂了一张牌子写着"宗教场所，谢绝参观"，最后在国家民族工作部门的统一工作下，那块牌子被取掉了。何阿訇风趣地说："宗教神职人员能够正确理解教义，其思想具有包容性，普通信众由于缺乏对教义的深入理解反而思想比较保守。"何阿訇告诉我，东四清真寺很重视和其他宗教的交流和互动，最近他和其他宗教的神职人员一起参加了政府的"宗教界青年骨干"培训，其中有现场培训，就是参观各个宗教的场所，这个活动的第一场就是邀请其他宗教的神职人员来东四清真寺参观。

两个多小时的访谈临近结束，何阿訇说他得收拾一下，各宗教互访活动今天晚上安排的是参观天主教堂。我告别了何阿訇走出他的办公室，午后的清真寺更加安详宁静，两棵巨大的银杏树长出了新叶子，翠绿可爱，望月楼在银杏树后若隐若现，别有一番风趣。

there is a screen that separates the women's prayer area from the main hall, a visible reminder of the distinction between men and women in Islam.

Two-story buildings are connected to the prayer hall on its south and north sides. The north building contains a storage and boiler room; the south, the Chengda Teachers College Library. In the 1930s, the library received a donation from Fuad I, the Egyptian Sultan; thus it is called the Fuad Library. The preparation committee consisted not only of Ma Songting, a prominent imam, and Bai Shouyi, a distinguished historian, but also non-Muslim scholars including the famous educator Cai Yuanpei, philosopher Feng Youlan, and historians Gu Jiegang and Chen Yuan. Chengda Teachers College and Fuad Library were not only innovative in the education of Chinese Muslims but also played an active role during the Second Sino-Japanese War (1937–1945). Traditionally, Chinese Muslim education was limited to religious subjects. Chengda, however, included the humanities and sciences in its curriculum. Some students were even dispatched to Egypt to study. During the month of Hajj in January 1939, Japan conspired to send to Saudi Arabia a delegation to cover up their crimes and embellish their invasion of China. Upon receiving the news, Ma Songting immediately informed the Chengda students who were studying in Egypt at the time. A team of twenty-eight students were dispatched to Saudi Arabia, where they condemned Japan's criminal behavior, praised the Chinese people's heroic rebellion, and revealed the conspiracy of the Japanese.

People and Practice

When we arrived at the Dongsi Mosque, it was time for *Salat al-Zuhr,* the noontime prayer. No one could be seen in the courtyard—only the ginkgo leaves rustling in the wind. When the prayer finished, we met Imam He, a warm and friendly young man of only thirty-one years. Since graduating from the China Islamic Institute in 2012, he has served as the imam of mosque. Imam He was born to a devout Muslim family in Zhangjiakou, a city 200 kilometers from Beijing. His grandfather was an imam. As a child, he always followed his grandpa to the mosque, where he learned some simple things about the religion. After finishing high school, he happened to see the admission guide for the China Islamic Institute and applied. Four years of study prepared him to be an imam.

Dongsi Mosque currently has five imams. With the exception of the chief imam, Imam He, the other four imams are on shifts. Imam He told us that although many people come to worship on Fridays (*Jumu'ah*) and for *Eid al-Fitr* and *Eid al-Adha,* very few people pray at the mosque on other days. The day of our visit was a weekend, but only three people attended the prayer. Among them, one was Mr. Song, a fine conversationalist, who said that his favorite avocation is to visit mosques. He is very familiar with the architecture, history, and context of every mosque in Beijing. He finds a relief from daily exhaustion and life troubles by attending prayers and learning about mosques. Sometimes he invites imams to his home to help him deal with religious issues in his family.

Dongsi Mosque attracts many tourists because of its long history. While we were talking, a young Muslim man from Sri Lanka came to pray. He told us that he was traveling in China and learned about Dongsi online. The antiquity and tranquility of the mosque offered him peace of mind, as if he were far away from the madding crowd. Imam He told us that some teachers and students from the nearby universities and colleges come to visit the mosque to learn about the religious life of Muslims.

Towards the end of our conversation, three elderly people entered. They went straight to the right side of the hall and remained there for a long time. Eventually, we learned that they were looking for their childhood school. They said that when the

38. 伊玛目在敏拜尔作呼图白 Imam He giving a sermon (*khutbah*) in the prayer hall

People's Republic of China was founded, there was a Hui elementary school behind the hall. Many Muslim children attended school here. Sixty years had passed since then. The school had been relocated, and they had moved away. Now they were returning simply to revisit the old site, despite knowing that the building no longer existed. They told us that there used to be a Muslim community around the mosque, many of whom attended the mosque. During festivals, the hall was not big enough to accommodate all the people. Blankets had to be provided so that people could pray in the courtyard. With urbanization, however, the neighborhood became a commercial area. Many Muslims moved out, so there was no longer a Muslim community in the area. While recalling all these significant changes over the past six decades, they couldn't help but sigh.

According to Imam He, the functions of a mosque are not limited to praying and worshipping; it also serves as a Muslim cultural center. In recent years, a forum named "Fuad" (in honor of the benefactor of the library, the Egyptian sultan Fuad I) was jointly launched by Dongsi Mosque and the Beijing Islamic Association. It is an annual event, with two forums held so far. The purpose of the forum is to advocate for moderate Islam, which opposes extremism and promotes the enculturation of Islam. The participants are not only imams but also university professors and government officials.

Imam He also mentioned that many Muslims choose to come to the mosque for wedding photos and ceremonies. Wang Zhifei, a famous Muslim actor, had the religious ritual of his wedding at the mosque. Since his wife was not Muslim, a conversion rite was held before the wedding.

Imam He told us that although mosques are religious sites, they should not be isolated from secular society. Previously, a sign reading "Religious Site, No Visiting" had been hung at the entrance of the mosque. Later, the sign was removed because of some government agencies. Imam He said, "Religious clerics understand correctly the doctrines of the religion and are more embracing; ordinary followers tend to be more conservative because they lack profound understanding of the religion." Dongsi Mosque attaches great importance to exchange and interaction with other religions. Imam He and the other imams recently attended a training called "Youth Backbones of the Religious Profession." The site-visit component of the training involved visiting religious communities. Dongsi Mosque happened to be the first stop for the visits.

My two-hour visit was coming to an end. Imam He said he had to prepare for a cathedral visit in the evening, one of the many religious-exchange events he attends. I bid farewell to him and stepped out of the office. The mosque in the afternoon was even more peaceful and tranquil. Two giant ginkgo trees had just turned out new leaves, fresh, green, and lovely. The moon-watching tower loomed behind the ginkgo trees, creating a scene that was charming and delightful.

东岳庙

田丁丁

北京市朝阳区朝阳门外大街北侧，车流来往不息，火锅店铺门口逸满了辣油的香气，一片喧闹繁华中，一座古朴的寺庙静静伫立着，像一位饱经风霜又满怀慈爱的老人，默默端详着这城市的一角。

亭台楼阁几度秋

这座庙的名字叫东岳庙，里面的主神是泰山的东岳大帝，是掌管人间生死和负责人间帝王任命的神灵。它原是道教正一派在中国华北地区的最大的道场，现亦为北京的一个民俗博物馆，并于2008年5月3日作为道教活动场所正式开放。

东岳庙的创始人是在元朝显赫一时的重要人物张留孙（1248-1322）。现址的对面还有一个大牌楼，上书"永延帝祚"四个大字，显示了这座庙与皇家非同寻常的关系。道观里的一位陈道长介绍，由于受中国古代的东岳文化影响，全国各地都有东岳庙，但只有北京的这座东岳庙有着非比寻常的意义，因为元明清三代北京都是帝都，而古代交通不便，从北京前往泰山路途遥远，只好就在就近的东岳庙中举行祭天仪式，这样一来，这座东岳庙就成了东岳大帝的"驻京办事处"。

东岳庙总共有三道门，不过原先的山门已被拆掉，现址的大门原是东岳庙的二道门，每道门上又有三孔，庙内布局也是东、西、中三路。"三"这个数字对道教而言有很特殊的含义，它代表了"天、地、人"与"天人合一"的观念。正门是"天"，东门是"人"，西门则代表"地"。中间的门一般是不开的，现在为了方便游客观光才打开了。在古代，普通人不能走中门，只有天子才能从这扇门通过。原先的第三道门，也即现在的第二道门叫瞻岱门，依据陈道长的解释，一是指往北正对着主殿岱岳殿，二是指往南遥对泰山，是两个方向的"瞻岱"，隐含着东岳大帝胸怀万里江山的意思。

从庙门进去往主殿岱岳殿，地基不断升高，直到东岳大帝的主殿升到最高。陈道长解释，地基越高，就代表大殿的规格越高，而殿主的身份也相应地越高。他指向大殿两侧七十六司的偏殿，"这两侧的偏殿也是一样的，哪个的规格最高，距离主殿的位置就越近。"尽管是偏殿，但所有的偏殿下都有高高的地基台子，四面相连，没有一处缺口，而这种规格在古代算得上是郡王府的规格了。

庙里还有众多御赐之物：瞻岱门正对着的福路两侧就是御碑亭；东西两个院子里相对的是一对康乾时代御赐的塑像。一个叫铜特，一个叫玉马，这些塑像据说都是文昌帝的坐骑。再往后的碑林中还立着一块有大书法家赵孟頫墨宝的大碑。传闻赵孟頫曾因姓氏在元朝得不到重用，当时的住持举荐好友赵孟頫来撰写碑文后，赵便因此得到了重用，从这一点也可以看出这座庙的宠命优渥。

古今游人去悠悠

不过，它和民间的关系也一直很紧密。

Dongyue Temple

Tian Dingding, with Kelsey Rick, editor

On the north side of Chaoyangmenwai Street in the Chaoyang District of Beijing, the traffic runs endlessly, and the aroma of spicy oil from hotpot restaurants suffuses the air. In the midst of these sounds and smells, a picturesque temple sits quietly, like a weather-beaten and loving old man, silently watching the corner of the city.

Centuries of the Elaborate Temple

This is Dongyue Temple, devoted to the Dongyue Emperor of Mount Tai, who controls the births and deaths of people and appoints emperors in the human world.

Once it was the largest of the prestigious "Ten-Direction Residence System" (*shifang conglin*) Daoist temples in northern China; now it is a folk museum in Beijing. On May 3, 2008, it was officially registered as a site for Daoist activities and reopened to the public.

The founder of Dongyue Temple was Zhang Liusun (1248–1322), a prominent figure in the imperial court in the Yuan Dynasty. The big *pailou*

39. "秩祀岱宗"牌楼 Ornamental gate with the inscription "Worshipping Mount Tai deity according to the royal rites"

40. 通往岱岳殿的福路 Fu Road leading to Daiyue Hall

  据说东岳庙建庙之初，道士不超过二十人，要是办个大型庙会之类的活动，就会缺人手，所以民间就自发组织了许多义工性质的香会，不要报酬，只为留名，于是就立了许多石碑，记录下这些人的名字，直到今天庙里还存留着大量石碑，东西两侧都是碑林。

  到了庙会的时候，香会无疑是最吸引人注意的一部分。《帝京景物略》载："士女瞻礼者，月朔望日晨至，左右门无闲阒，座前拜席为燠，化楮钱炉火相及，无暂熄。"庙会上，各大香会的人身着盛装，鲜艳夺目，腰戴佩环，乐鼓叮咚，手执彩旗，迎风招展——掸尘会、净水会、净炉会、献茶会、献灯会等，名目繁多，应有尽有。同时庙会期间，还夹杂着一些传统习俗，如抢烧头香、打金钱眼等民俗活动。

  直至今日，正月时依旧有人到东岳庙里拜太岁。太岁是道教信仰中太岁神的简称，乃道教值年神灵之一，一年一换，当年轮值的太岁神叫值年太岁(或流年太岁)。我们常说的"命犯太岁"其实指的就是"冲太岁"。"冲"又分为"年冲"和"对冲"，例如龙年，肖龙为年冲，加上六年即肖狗为对冲。还有一种说法是刑太岁，又称"偏冲"，指自己的出生年与六年所属生肖相差三年，龙年的肖牛和肖羊为偏冲。凡遇到这些生肖都要到庙里拜太岁，才不至"流年不利"，而是诸事顺吉。

  拜太岁时，先站在跪垫前，双脚呈"八"字形站好；然后双手于腹前合抱躬身；再左手捂心，表示专心向神致敬，同时俯身，右手按跪垫，两膝下跪；接着，左手离开心口，呈"十"字状按右手背上；然后俯伏叩首，头与脊同时下伏，臀部略低于

(ornamental gateway) facing the temple contains the four-character inscription 永延帝祚 ("Long Live the Imperial Dynasty"), suggesting a special connection between this temple and the emperors. Priest Chen of the temple explained to us that given the popularity of Dongyue culture in ancient times, Dongyue temples were seen everywhere. However, this temple was exceptional because the emperor decided to hold memorial ceremonies for Heaven (*Tian*) at it after the capital moved to Beijing in the Yuan Dynasty (1271–1368), thus making travel to Mount Tai too difficult and long (500 km away). Dongyue Temple thus became the "Beijing Office" of the Dongyue Emperor.

Although Dongyue Temple used to have three gates, the first, main gate—the "Mountain Gate"—was removed. What is now the first, main gate of the temple therefore used to be the second gate. This gate has three passageways, the middle of which stands for Heaven (*Tian*) and therefore could only be used by the emperor; the east, for humans; and the west, for Earth. This gate, therefore, not only exemplifies the special symbolic meaning of the number three in Daoism but also represents the unity of "Heaven, Earth, and humans."

The original third gate (which is now the second one) is called Zhandai Gate ("Watching Mount Tai Gate"). Priest Chen said that the gate faces two directions—to the north it "watches" the main hall of the temple, Daiyue Hall; to the south it "watches" Mount Tai. Watching in both directions implies that the Dongyue Emperor embraces the whole world.

The ground between the main gate and Daiyue Hall gradually rises, reaching its highest point at the main hall of the Dongyue Emperor. As Priest Chen explained, the higher the foundation, the more prestigious the hall and its god. He pointed to the "Seventy-six Divisions" of side halls flanking the main hall (which contain statues of the seventy-six judges of the underworld): "Similar rules apply to the side halls. The closer a side hall is to the main hall, the more important the Division [and therefore the deity in it]." Although these are only side halls, they are laid on deep foundations that are shared by the main hall. This was the standard of princely halls in ancient times.

Many royal gifts can be seen in the temple complex. On both sides of Fu Road, directly in front of Zhandai Gate, lies a "Royal Stelae Pavilion." Two statues, said to be the riding horses of the Wenchang Emperor, were bestowed on the temple during the era of either Kangxi (r. 1661–1722) or Qianlong (r. 1735–1796). Facing each other, the one in the east courtyard is called Tongte; in the west courtyard, Jade Horse. Behind the Stelae Pavilion stands a stela by Zhao Mengfu (1254–1322), a famous calligrapher. As the story goes, he could not get promoted during the Yuan Dynasty because of the family name he carried. His good friend, then abbot of the Dongyue Temple, asked him to write stela inscriptions. Zhao was thus discovered and offered an important position, a sign of the privilege that the temple enjoyed at the time.

Worshippers Now and Then

Dongyue Temple has a long tradition of actively interacting with folk communities. When it was founded, it housed no more than twenty Daoist priests. Consequently, the temple was always shorthanded when activities such as temple fairs were held. People therefore volunteered to help out at the temple, not in return for material rewards, but to have their names documented. Many stela were made to record their names, most of which have remained until today, located on the east and west sides of the temple.

Journeying to the temple in groups was without doubt the most appealing part of temple fairs. According to 帝京景物略 (*A Brief Guide to Tourist Spots in the Imperial Capital City*, published in the seventeenth century), "Groups of visitors arrived on the mornings of the first and fifteenth day of each lunar month. Neither the left nor the right gate of the

背，头磕在双手背上，一俯伏三叩首，叩首时可以祈祷或许愿；最后抬头，左手收回捂心，慢慢起身后收回右手，双手抱拳高拱，如此重复三次，就是三跪九叩。磕完头后，起身，双手合抱于上腹处（即"怀抱太极"）。接着，向神作揖，待双手自上而下收至上腹处并立身站定后，方可离开跪垫。平日朝神也多用此礼，表达的是对"道"的信仰和对神的尊敬。

正月的庙里格外热闹：除了前来拜太岁的人，还有赋闲在家的老人前来游览，也有年轻的情侣在院子里嬉笑打闹，还有几位外国友人在院前与几只猫合照。

道外世人论不休

当天气开始转凉，庙里便显得萧条了几分，只有岱宗殿正门前的大路两旁围栏上系着的祈福用的红丝带在香火气里热情地舞动着。

一天，我在前院七十六司殿外转悠了好久，才有个穿戴时尚的姑娘过来搭话，她说自己闲暇时就会来庙里看看，身边的同龄人也是如此，不过她自己倒并非专门的道教信徒，只是觉得这间庙许愿很灵。当问她是否信徒时，她甚至觉得这问题很奇怪。不过，她有一点倒是和道教所提倡的相近，就是认为多做善事会有福报。这种观念其实在很多中国人身上都能看到，大概也和中国传统儒家伦理道德的熏陶有一定关系。

不过她的态度的确令我深感意外，本来我觉得，从宗教需求上来说，年轻人应该会对寺庙之类不大感冒，而老年人可能会对之更加热衷，然而几天后，一位在庙里扫地的老大爷的话彻底推翻了这一预设。

初见时是在布施的功德箱前面，殿外一片寂静，只有大爷的扫把在刷刷作响，银杏的叶子落了满院，午后的阳光也静悄悄的，洒落在庭院。大爷自称在庙里工作了大概一个月左右，不过他对这庙并无好感，觉得这里比起修炼场所来说更像是骗人布施的噱头，他理想中的道士是类似于武侠小说中的形象，会轻功，懂江湖，衣袂飘飘，风姿卓然。

后来去时碰到和他年纪差不多的老人，他们的回应与之相似，无外乎说这是"封建迷信"之类的。大抵是因为那个年代的人经历了"文革"的淬炼，所以对这种神神鬼鬼的事有些排斥，但青少年时期又受了武侠热的熏陶，还是忍不住对"道士的江湖世界"有所期待。有位老人提及传统文化继承的话题，我猜他们的关注大概和国家近年来推动文化复兴的政策也有些联系。

道内行者亦情仇

不过，庙里的道长并非我想象中那种不食人间烟火的"世外高人"，相反他们有着很"入世"的一面。

有一次我问马道长怎样才能出家。出乎我意料的是他并没有立马就对我表达邀请之意，反而是义正言辞地劝我轻易不要想着出家，"你要是实在喜欢这个的话可以多学习道家经典，把它作为一种人生哲学……出家是要守清规戒律的，有的还会让你修'闭口禅'几个月不让开口说话。你一个小姑娘家，出家了得有多可惜啊。"我说自己想逃避社会责任，他又劝我："你以为出家了就完全脱离世俗了吗？就算出家清修你也依然是要在人世活着的啊，只要你活着，就永远不可能逃离社会的……责任是更不可能逃的了，出家了也有责任，只是责任不同罢了。"他担心我真的动了出家的

temple ever had a free moment. The praying mats in front of the gods were always warm. There were continuous flames in the stoves from the burning of paper money." These groups were dressed in costumes, bright and dazzling, with rings on their waists and flags in their hands. Drums were played and flags waved in the wind. A variety of volunteer activities and rituals were held, some examples of which included dusting the hall, replacing the purified holy water, removing ashes from the fragrance stoves, and offering tea and lamps as tribute. Some traditional folk-activities were also held during temple fairs, such as competing for burning the first stick of incense and hitting the hanging golden coin.

Tai Sui worship is one of the traditional folk-activities that still occurs at Dongyue Temple. There are sixty Tai Sui deities, who take turns guarding the year, one per year. The Chinese often talk about "offending Tai Sui," which happens when there is a *nian*, *dui*, or *pian* clash between the current zodiac year and one's birth year. If the zodiac of the current year and one's birth year are the same (e.g. dragon), this is a *nian* clash. If the zodiac of the current year and one's birth year are six years apart (e.g., dragon and dog), this is a *dui* clash. And if the zodiac of the current year and one's birth year are three years apart (e.g., dragon and ox, or dragon and sheep), this is a *pian* clash. In years when these clashes occur, one should worship the Tai Sui deity of the year in temples to avoid misfortune during that year.

When worshipping a Tai Sui deity, devotees stand in front of the praying mat with their feet in a "V" shape. Then they bow with their hands together in front of their abdomen. Next they put their left hand on their heart, showing dedication to the deity. Then they kneel, first putting their right hand on the mat, then placing their left hand over it in an "X" shape. Then they prostrate, "knocking" their head onto their hands three times, praying while knocking. (In prostration, the head and spine should fall at the same time, with the hips slightly lower than the back so the back is in the shape of an

41. 文昌帝的坐骑 Riding horses of the Wenchang Emperor

arch.) Then they stand up and bring their left hand back to their heart, and kowtow two more times, knocking thrice each time to complete the "Three Kneelings and Nine Knockings" kowtow. After that they stand up and place their hands in front of their upper abdomen with their left hand over their right, to "embrace ultimate oneness" (*taiji*). They raise their hands to the level of their head to greet the deity, then lower their hands, leaving the prayer mat when they come to rest on either side of the body. This procedure is used for ordinary rituals as expressions of belief in the Dao and respect for the god being worshipped.

During the first month of the lunar calendar, the temple is especially busy. Besides Tai Sui worshippers, some elderly retirees also come to visit. Young couples talk, tease, and laugh; foreigners take photos of the many cats.

42. 御碑亭 Royal Stelae Pavilion

念头，又给我们讲了他的一位朋友出家却无奈还俗的故事。

那位朋友原本是在北京白云观挂单的，后来因为和观里的弟子相处不睦，就被方丈介绍至四川青城山，可他去了之后还是受其他小道姑们的欺负，于是他就去找青城山的方丈主持公道，但他又觉得方丈偏心自己的弟子，最后就决定离开青城山，但一时之间他又找不到别的清修团体，索性就还俗了。

马道长说："不要以为出家后就真的能过上不理俗物的生活，你出家后是要和观里别的修行者一起生活的……人际关系这些问题依然是要面对的。其他人也只是些人罢了，不是神仙。退一步来说，你自己就是人，而人就是要和其他人一起生活的。"

"再者，你当真以为修道是那么容易的一件事吗？即使是我们这样不需要出家的在家道士，修行也是不容易的，你要先皈依'道、经、师'三宝，有传统的师承法派。这个师承法派就很不容易有，因为拜师很难，而且拜师之后你最初所做的也不过是些端茶递水的粗活，最短的可能也要先这样生活3到5年——这一方面是为打磨你的品性，另一方面也是师父对你的考验——通过了考验，你才有机会得到师父的衣钵。之后还要经过各个道教协会的多重手续，才能真正成为一个道士。"

他所说的这些倒是与陈道长的感慨不谋而合，陈道长说："不问红尘只一味问道是不能成仙的……要先过好世俗生活才有可能成圣成真。因为修道之人也是人，而成圣成真的前提条件是你要先成为一个人。"

上次我们去参访时，也听马道长说起，他们经常帮助香客解决生活上的困难。有

Earthly Views of Dao

As the weather started to cool, the temple grew quieter. Only the red prayer ribbons tied to the fences on either side of the road in front of Daizhong Hall danced passionately.

I was approached by a young, fashionable girl while I was walking around the corridor of the "Seventy-Six Divisions." She told me that she came to the temple whenever she had time. So did her peers. Although she is not a follower of Daoism, she attended the temple for answers to her prayers. She found it strange that I asked her about this. She said that she shares at least one principle with Daoism—to do good in return for good fortune. This view reflects the minds of many Chinese people, possibly due to the influence of the moral concepts of Confucianism.

Still, what I learned about the young girl came as quite a surprise. One assumes that young people are aloof to places like temples, which are more for seniors. However, the remarks made by an elderly man whom I met at the temple a few days later changed my entire view.

The first time I saw this elderly man was in front of the merit box for alms. It was quiet outside the hall; nothing could be heard except a broom sweeping, collecting the ginkgo leaves that blanketed the ground. The early afternoon sun cast light on the courtyard without disturbing these moments of tranquility. The elderly man claimed that he had been working in the temple for a month, though he had no favorable feelings towards it. In his mind, Daoists should resemble the figures in *wuxia* (martial arts) fiction—skilled with levitation, well-versed in *jianghu* (the community of martial artists or, more recently, outlaw societies), with long, flowing robes that convey an air of heroism and elegance. Therefore he viewed the temple simply as a place to lure people for donations.

In my subsequent encounters with other elderly people, I received similar responses. Most associate temples with feudalism and superstition. Their generation went through the Cultural Revolution (1966–1976) and therefore instinctively oppose gods and ghosts. However, at a later stage of their life, they were exposed to *wuxia* (Chinese martial arts novels) and became fascinated by the *jianghu* world (shadowy gang world) of the Daoists. One older person mentioned the importance of "inheriting our ancient, Chinese, traditional culture," something they probably learned through the current national policy of "resuming ancient glories."

Earthly Views from Daoists

Unlike what I had imagined, the Daoists I met at the temple were not "high-skilled" spirits from another world. They were in fact very "secular" folks, at least in part.

I once asked Priest Ma how to become a Daoist priest. To my surprise, he did not welcome my idea, but tried to talk me out of it. "If you are really interested in Daoism, try to learn more from the classics of Daoism and adopt them as your life philosophy. Being a Daoist means practicing austerity. Some even require 'closed-mouth Chan [Zen],' which means living without talking for months. You are just a little girl. What a shame to become a Daoist priest." I responded by asking if I could avoid the troubles and responsibilities of the secular world by becoming a Daoist priest. But he corrected me, "You assume that you can keep away from the earthly world by being a Daoist priest? You are still living with humans after all. As long as you live, you cannot get away from society and responsibilities. Daoist priests have their own responsibilities, which are just different from those of the rest of the people." Worried that I might really become a Daoist priest, he added a story about a friend.

一位有出轨前科的香客曾来找马道长，向他哭诉自己把妻子挂在车上的中国结弄丢了，害怕妻子怀疑自己又出轨了闹离婚，问马道长该怎么办。马道长建议他去赶紧买一个一模一样的，趁妻子还没发现的时候挂上去，劝他日后一定要改变自己的生活作风，对妻子忠贞。后来这位香客的婚姻得到了改善。我听的时候感觉很不可思议，我原本还幻想着道长们可能会帮忙做一个什么仪式之类的，但完全没想过他们解决问题的方式其实和我们也没什么不同。倒是我们喜欢误解他们，用各种猜想给他们贴上奇奇怪怪的标签，也许是因为不够了解，也许是因为我们根本不愿意深入地了解。

我突然明白，原来修道之人不是只要"修身养性"就够了，在他们的观念里，所谓的"修身养性"固然重要，但首要的应该是先"做好一个人"，并且二者是相辅助相成、互为补充的，几位道长也曾反复强调，"其实生活也是一种修行，只是大家修行的方式有所不同罢了。"

当我无意间说自己有做基督徒的意愿之后，意外地得到了陈道长的理解，他说其实这些信仰都有一定的共性，本质上他也相信，有一个"最高"的东西安排了一切——可能就是天道。他原本在江苏茅山修行，后来突然被调到这里时，很担心自己可能会不适应，但没想到就在他来到东岳庙的同年，庙里迁来了一座三茅真君的神像，这让他顿时有了一种回家的感觉，他说这一定是天道的安排，是"冥冥之中自有天意"。他甚至还鼓励我勇敢探寻自己的信仰之路。这让我触动很深，因为我们总是会很容易觉得自己的宗教是最优越的，于是我们把这些问题进一步极端化、尖锐化，终于有了嫉妒，有了纷争，有了宗教暴力，有了宗教迫害……人们打着神的旗号做那些悖神的事，还要自以为优于他人，但事实上我们谁也无法完全真正认识神，在信仰的道路上，谁也无法体验另外一个人，但至少我们应该怀有一颗包容的心，尊重别人的路；先走好"人道"，才能保守"主道"。

正值初春，院子里的风还是有点大，但阳光晒得人暖融融的，十分惬意，有只怀孕了的狸花猫慵懒地卧在御制碑下面，半眯着眼冷淡地瞧着庙里走来走去的人们。

庙外，成片怒放的玉兰悄然带来早春的气息，如同明亮绚烂的朝霞，映衬着不远处的红墙青瓦，有隐隐约约的檀香在鼻尖萦绕，一切都显得静谧、安详，像一支轻柔的歌谣，又像一首恬静的小令，像邵康节所写的《山村咏怀》："一去二三里，烟村四五家，亭台六七座，八九十枝花。"

This friend originally found accommodations at the Baiyunguan Temple. Since he could not get along with the disciples there, Priest Ma referred him to Qingcheng Mountain in Sichuan Province. There, he was bullied by some female Daoists. When he went to Priest Ma to complain, Priest Ma took the side of his own disciples, the female Daoists. The friend therefore decided to leave Qingcheng Mountain. Failing to find another residence, he returned to the secular world.

Priest Ma concluded, "Do not assume that Daoists live in an isolated world. Daoists live with other practitioners, and they have to deal with human relations. Other practitioners are humans, and you are too—not godly. Humans ought to live with humans."

"Besides, do you think that it is easy to be a Daoist? The practice can be very hard, even for a 'Daoist who lives at home' [*jüshi*, non-monastic Daoist] like me. You have to acquire the three treasures of Dao, *Jing* [the classics], and *Shi* [a master], and follow the rigid '*shi cheng fa pai*' [succession system]. *Shi cheng fa pai* can be as difficult as finding a teacher itself; it is a very challenging task. Once you find your teacher, you will only be assigned simple tasks like preparing tea. This kind of life will last for at least three to five years. The goal is to train your will. It is a way to pass your master's test. Only by passing the test, will you have the opportunity to receive the master's real teachings. After that, you will have to go through multiple procedures of various Daoist associations to truly become a Daoist."

What he said agreed with Priest Chen's remarks. Chen mentioned to me, "Focusing only on Dao cannot make you immortal or a god. Live a good secular life first, then you can possibly become a saint. A man who has acquired Dao is still fundamentally a man. Before you become a saint, you should be a real human being."

During our last visit, Priest Ma mentioned how the Daoists at the temple often help visitors with their troubles in life. One time, a man who had

43. 燃香处 Incense lighter

frequent affairs with women approached him. He said he could not find a decorative knot called *zhongguo jie* in his car. He was afraid that his wife might doubt his fidelity, suspecting him of giving the knot to another woman, and ask him for a divorce. Priest Ma told him to buy another one and replace it before his wife found out. Priest Ma then advised the man to be faithful to his wife. I had assumed that Priest Ma would have instead performed some rituals rather than offering a solution similar to those given by ordinary people. Perhaps most of us never take the time to thoroughly understand Daoists as they really are.

Thus, I came to a sudden realization: Practicing Dao is not just about self-cultivation. First and foremost, learn to be a good person. As Daoists repeatedly say, "Life is self-cultivation, each practices differently."

东岳庙

44. 记录愿望和许愿者名字的祈福红布 Prayer wheels at Dongyue Temple

45. 东岳庙的猫 One of the many cats of Dongyue Temple

When I unintentionally mentioned my plan to become a Christian, Priest Chen immediately resonated with my idea. He said, "All beliefs share one thing in common with which I agree—ultimately the world is decided by a supreme power, possibly the Dao of Heaven [*Tian Dao*], as we call it." Before coming to Dongyue, Chen had been practicing at Maoshan Mountain in Jiangsu Province. When he was dispatched to this temple, he worried that he would not adapt to the conditions here. Coincidentally, however, Dongyue happened to acquire a statue of Sanmao Zhenjun, the deity worshipped at Maoshan, the same year he was relocated. He instantly felt at home, believing it was the work of Tian Dao. Chen encouraged me to pursue my own faith. That encouragement touched my heart. People always want to feel superior for the religion they adopt. Then they go to extremes and start to fight, which leads to religious violence and oppression. People often carry the banner of God, but go against God's will. As a matter of fact, no one knows God completely. We are each on our individual path of our own beliefs; therefore, we each have our own unique experiences. We should embrace each other's beliefs—to try to understand the human Dao first, after which Tian Dao can be embraced.

It was early spring. Although the wind was still strong, the sun offered generous warmth. A pregnant cat found shelter underneath a royal stela, her eyes half open, lazily watching the people passing by. Outside the temple, magnolias were blossoming, as bright and dazzling as the morning light. Not far away stood the gray-walled, red-roofed temple. I enjoyed the peace, as if back in the poem "Praise the Mountain Village":

I see smoke rising from the households
Elegant buildings and pavilions appear here
   and there
Decorated by flowers scattering around
(Shao Kangjie, 1011–1077).

广济寺

李瑶

历史：荣耀与沧桑

在北京故宫博物院往西三公里处有一圣地，其正门石匾上书写着赫赫七个金字——"敕建弘慈广济寺"。此乃康熙皇帝亲笔御书，仅由此便可知晓广济寺的地位曾经非同一般。

广济寺的前身可追溯到金元时期的西刘村寺，据史料考证其建寺时间大抵在1170年，后在王朝更替的战火中被毁坏。明代时，被誉为广济寺开山之祖的普慧法师笃志重建广济寺，期间困难重重。幸得皇室资助，重建之事顺利开展。广济寺在清朝时颇受皇家重视，尊佛重礼的顺治、康熙与乾隆几代帝王都曾亲临此地，或题诗立碑，或赏赐珍宝，使得广济寺在京城中的地位陡升，其历史身份也更显尊贵。

始终位于都城之中的广济寺，也是清代国运转变的见证者之一。八国联军发动侵华战争时，千余名法国士兵攻入内城，气势汹汹地驻扎于广济寺内，直至清政府签订《辛丑条约》后才陆续撤出广济寺。因广济寺在佛教界拥有较大的影响力，故民国时期的社会名流也多与广济寺法缘深厚：1912年9月，孙中山在广济寺与清朝八旗人士谈话，发表了关于民族团结的演讲；1916年8月，美国传教士李佳白曾在广济寺和中国佛教代表们一起讨论世界宗教联合会的议题；作家朱自清的遗体火化超度仪式选择于广济寺进行。此京城中正心弘法的寺宇，也因历经千帆，愈显雄厚有力。

关于广济寺的近代变迁便不得不提民国时不幸发生的毁灭性火灾。1932年正处局部抗战中，现明法师出于爱国之心召集了许多善士，设立和平道场，期望通过诵经为国家祈求太平，因而在广济寺内临时搭建了芦苇所做的佛龛。佛教的法会往往都会点燃香火，以敬神佛，可正值人们潜心拜佛、闭眼念经之时，香火却不幸引燃了芦苇佛龛的垂帐，随后大火蔓延，火光冲天。此场大火损失惨重，寺中佛像、法物、古玩经典等物悉数被毁。面对突如其来的灾害，僧人纷纷表明重建庙宇的决心，使得其在1935年再次修葺落成，重现往日庄严。

广济寺还是律宗重要传承地。律宗，是中国汉传佛教八大宗派之一，以着重传持戒律而得名。佛教的五戒为不杀生、不偷盗、不邪淫、不妄语、不饮酒，这不仅展现了劝人向善，莫行恶业的佛教理念，也是每位僧人日常必须恪守的基本戒条。作为北京律宗传承的重要脉系，太虚大师、能海法师等高僧们都曾在广济寺中讲经说法，得力于他们的奋勉弘法，广济寺日渐戒行精严，佛法昌明。

广济寺作为常驻于皇城之西的寺庙，其近千年曲折的历史与皇室乃至国运的兴衰都联系紧密，也正因如此，广济寺具有了别样的荣耀与沧桑。

空间：传统与非凡

广济寺坐北朝南，周围胡同纵横交错，人流量较大。作为这闹市中一处静谧地，广济寺可谓"大隐隐于市"的典范。

广济寺的山门临街且一分为三，居中的是日常进出的正门，两边驻有威武的铁狮

Guangji Temple

Li Yao, with Madelyn Bjork, editor

History: Glory and Adversities

Three kilometers west of the Forbidden City lies a holy place. On the plaque on top of the main gate seven characters are inscribed 敕建弘慈广济寺 ("According to the Imperial Edict, to Promote Buddha's Mercy, Guangji Temple"). This is an inscription by Emperor Kangxi (r. 1661–1722), a sign of the extraordinary status of the temple.

Guangji Temple can be traced back to an ancient temple in the twelfth century. Although it was repeatedly destroyed in wars, its rebuilding was resolutely championed during the Ming Dynasty (1368–1644) by Master Puhui (early fifteenth century), who thereafter became known as the founding father of Guangji Temple. Although Master Puhui initially confronted tremendous hardship during the process, royal support eventually enabled the temple's reconstruction. Later in the Qing Dynasty (1644–1912), Guangji Temple was highly valued by the royal family. The emperors who esteemed Buddha and prized rituals—Shunzhi (r. 1644–1661), Kangxi, and Qianlong (r. 1735–1796)—all made visits to the temple. They composed poems as stela inscriptions and endowed treasured gifts to it. Guangji Temple thus quickly rose to become one of the most prestigious temples in Beijing.

Located in the capital city of China, Guangji Temple witnessed the rise and fall of the Qing Dynasty. When the Eight-Nation Alliance invaded to put down the Boxer Rebellion (1900), over 1000 French militants fiercely demanded to be stationed at Guangji Temple, refusing to leave until the signing of the Xin chou Treaty (1901). During the Republic of China (1912–1949), many elites and celebrities tried to identify themselves with the temple, given Guangji's reputation around the Buddhist world. On September 17, 1912, Sun Yat-Sen spoke with the nobles of the Manchus at the Guangji Temple, delivering a speech on national unity and peace. On August 17, 1916, an American missionary named Gilbert Reid met with representatives of Chinese Buddhism at the Guangji Temple to discuss the topic of a world association of religions. The soul-releasing ritual of writer Zhu Ziqing (1898–1948) was also held at Guangji Temple.

During the prelude to the Second Sino-Japanese War in 1932, Master Xian Ming patriotically gathered a number of people in Guangji Temple to chant and pray for the peace of the country, erecting a peace ritual site and a reed shrine for the Buddha. However, while people were meditating, praying to the Buddha, and chanting with their eyes closed, their incense ignited the reeds, and fire consumed the temple. With the exception of Chan (Zen) Buddhist Hall, all the Buddhist statues, ceremonial tools, and other classics and antiques were completely destroyed. The catastrophe did not, however, deter the will of the monks, who were determined to rebuild the temple. In 1935 this reconstruction was completed, and the magnificent temple reemerged.

Guangji Temple is an important site for Lü Zong, one of the eight major schools of Chinese Han Buddhism. Lü Zong is known for its advocacy of Buddhist monastic code (*vinaya*) and the Five Precepts for lay Buddhists (not to kill, steal, engage in sexual misconduct, lie, and consume intoxicants). These commandments not only reflect the Buddhist value of promoting goodness and refraining from wickedness, they also constitute the daily discipline for the monks. Given Guangji Temple's importance in Lü Zong succession, senior monks such as Master Taixu

46. 康熙皇帝御笔亲书的石门金字"敕建弘慈广济寺" Emperor Kangxi's inscription on the main gate of Guangji Temple

一对,似正严守着佛寺要道。佛经中将佛祖讲法比喻成狮吼,即能降服邪魔外道并调伏一切众生。步入前院,可见一幅幅随风飘舞的五色佛旗,呈现一派欢喜之相。

广济寺的建筑整体上保持着明代传统佛教寺庙的格局,寺院按中轴线自南向北分布着天王殿、大雄殿、圆通殿三座主建筑,殿内分别供奉着弥勒佛、三世佛和观音菩萨。天王殿的弥勒佛属天冠弥勒,是古印度弥勒佛形象。汉地寺院多为"大肚弥勒",其态笑容可掬,肚大能容天下难容之事,以提醒世人应当学习包容。寺院核心建筑大雄殿内供奉着三世佛像,从东向西依次为"过去佛"迦叶佛、"现在佛"释迦牟尼佛、"未来佛"弥勒佛。供桌两旁竖立着雕刻有善财童子求教佛法故事的明代木质宝幢,实属精巧,而大殿两侧则供奉着形态各异的十八罗汉,使得殿内更显庄严。圆通殿内供有观音像,正中便是木质观音。观音是佛教中慈悲和智慧的象征,众人遇到困难时,只要诚挚地感念观音菩萨,便会得到救护。主线两侧殿则是五观堂和般若堂,日常分别用以施斋与讲经等。

除传统建制外,广济寺尚有一些与众不同之处。广济寺的大雄殿是帝王敕建,故顶部为皇家专用的黄色琉璃瓦,殿身为绛红色,别致雅观。康熙御赐的石碑屹立于殿前,因积年风雨的消磨现已不可看清其碑文,实则成为"空有碑",亦应了佛法真空妙有之巧意,充满了哲学的辩证思维。

广济寺国宝级的佛教艺术珍宝——《胜果妙音图》悬挂于大雄殿后壁上。此画为乾隆皇帝送给母亲的生日贺礼,由画家傅雯用手指绘成。高6米、宽11米,墨色素雅,刻画精细,属国内现存最大的一幅描写佛祖说法情景的壁画。画正中为释迦佛,

47. 大雄宝殿里的罗汉像 Buddhist *arhat* in Daxiong Hall

其侧是骑狮的文殊，骑象的普贤，有菩萨、罗汉及各类神将，甚至有民间人物关羽以及大鹏金翅鸟、善财童子等，画中人物虽姿态各异，但都在虔诚地聆听佛祖说法，似有所悟。此图从清宫转至寺庙中，在八国联军攻占北京城时，几次险被掠去，因寺僧藏护得当才完整保留至今。

广济寺寺内景色四时各异，意境清幽。寺外的现代城市建设与寺内的传统佛教建筑，相得益彰，使得广济寺成为雅俗共赏的宜人之地。

人物：虔诚与友善

时下的人间佛教，主张温和地解决普罗大众社会生活中的种种苦恼，故除虔诚信众外，常可见忧思重重的人们来此上香散心。按照传统，寺庙主殿前都设有一个香炉。信众们在香炉前点燃三炷香后，双手便会把香高举过头顶，或朝东南西北四个方向分别鞠躬，或面向大殿深鞠躬三次，最终将三炷香插入香炉中。信众们磕头一般是在佛像前或殿门口的蒲团上，双腿半跪，掌心相对、双手合十于胸前，在心中默默祈祷完毕后便可叩首三次。

广济寺的管理分工明确，以方丈为中心，又下设监院、知客、库头等职务，僧人各行其是，犹如企业的部门管理制度。德悟法师是广济寺的知客，日常多在客堂当值。作为广济寺面向信众的窗口，德悟法师每日需处理各类问题，工作量较大。德悟法师生于1971年，安徽人。他坦言自己20多年未回家，因每年春节是寺庙最为忙碌的时分，故其渐无中国人传统的春节归家过年的概念了。法师茶余饭后喜爱吹奏的传统乐器尺八，音色空灵，极富禅意。法师的客堂内有福建信众寄来的枇杷，山东居士带来的素煎饼，也有新茶的踪影。整间小屋陈列简单，却满是各方信众供养师父的心意。对于虔诚的信众而言，供养僧人是他们的一大

幸事。德悟法师坦言，这类信众很多，也正是他们使得广济寺充满了暖意。

与此同时，广济寺也常遇到另一类对于佛教认知不深，将之视为"交易"的"信众"。深冬的一天午后，一位面容憔悴的病人在亲友搀扶下来到客堂，她祈求报名参加广济寺的超度法会，希望超度走自己曾经堕胎的婴灵。佛教中堕胎属于严重的杀业，是切不可行的。而超度法会即通过诵经、供灯等仪轨使堕胎婴儿尽早超度解脱，亦可使得在世之人所犯的罪业尽快消除。对于此类法事，因万事万物的因缘难明，故不能保证一次便可超度成功。病人得知后，便质问道"为何不能保证超度成功？"对此，法师与她避谈法会一事，转向开导她应多行善事，多诵读经书，多调节内心。事后，法师说，对于此类将佛教信仰当作商品交易的信众，寺里不会收取他们的功德钱财。企图通过交换得到相应福报的行为有违佛法，此举是对佛教的误解。面对类似的"信众"，法师都尽量对其困扰之事作开解心灵的安慰。佛教讲人生有"八苦"，包含生老病死、爱别离等苦。现代人们也常为此八种苦而伤心难过，而寺庙便为世人打开了一扇疏解苦闷的窗户。

广济寺的常来访客中，值得一提的便是这附近胡同里的大爷大妈们，他们常会到广济寺礼佛上香，往往一待便是一天。笔者常见一位九十岁高龄的老奶奶坐在前院的石阶上，而几乎每一位前来广济寺的老者都会亲切的和她打招呼，并会犹如老友一般闲聊。原来他们都是常来寺庙的信众，原本互不相识，但因广济寺结缘，经年累月大家便逐渐热络起来。寺中老人们的交友有别于年轻人通过手机通讯联结，他们是单纯依靠着对佛教净地的喜欢，并无约定，有缘恰巧在此遇见便相聚谈心，无缘见面时也

48. 天王殿内景之弥勒像与天王像 Statues of Maitreya and the Heavenly King in Tianwang Hall

(1890–1947) and Master Nenghai (1866–1967) have expounded the texts of Buddhism at Guangji Temple. Thanks to their efforts, the temple has sustained its rigor and prosperity over the years.

Due to its close proximity to the Imperial Palace, Guangji Temple's glories and adversities usually corresponded with the rise and fall of the royal families, the dynasties, and the nation.

Space: Tradition and Wonder

Guangji Temple is "situated in the north and faces south," nestled among the crisscrossed hutongs and streams of people, offering a good example of "great seclusion hiding in the bustling city."

Guangji Temple has a Mountain Gate with three arches, the middle one functioning as the passageway. Flanked on each side by mighty lions, the gate evokes the analogy between the Buddha's teachings and roaring lions, both of which have the ability to subdue evil demons and bring creatures to obedience.

Guangji Temple adopted the architectural style and layout of Ming Dynasty Buddhist temples. Its three main buildings lie on a south–north central axis: Tianwang Hall, which is dedicated to Maitreya Buddha; Daxiong Hall, which contains the Trilokya Buddhas; and Yuantong Temple, which is for the bodhisattva of compassion.

The Maitreya Buddha housed at Tianwang Hall is a "Heavenly Crown Maitreya," which is a representation of the ancient Indian Buddha Maitreya. This is different from most Chinese temples, which instead house "Giant Belly Maitreya," whose smiling face and giant belly show that he is able to accommodate any imaginable difficulty on Earth,

49. 过去佛像 **Statue of the Past Buddha (Kaśyapa)**

reminding people to be embracing and tolerant.

Daxiong Hall is dedicated to the Trilokya Buddhas, which from east-to-west are the "Past Buddha" Kaśyapa, the "Present Buddha" Śākyamuni, and the "Buddha of the Future" Maitreya. On either side of the tribute table stand exquisite wooden treasures from the Ming Dynasty, engraved with the stories of fortunate children who sought advice from the Dharma. Eighteen *arhats* of different shapes are enshrined on either side of the solemn-looking hall.

Yuantong Hall is dedicated to statues of the bodhisattva Guanyin, with a wooden Guanyin in the middle. Guanyin is a symbol of compassion and wisdom in Buddhism. When people encounter difficulties, they can always be assisted or rescued by Guanyin, as long as their thoughts for Guanyin are sincere.

Standing outside the central axis are Wuguantang Hall and Prajna Hall. The former is used for serving meals to the needy; the latter, for teaching Dharma.

Guangji Temple has plenty of distinctive characteristics. Daxiong Hall was built by imperial order; thus the building has yellow-glazed roof tiles and crimson walls, majestic and elegant. A stela endowed by Emperor Kangxi stands in front of the hall. Over the years, wind and rain have eroded the inscriptions. Now it is an "empty" tablet, representing the Buddhist ideal that "real existence derives from real emptiness."

Hanging on the rear wall of Daxiong Hall is a rare Buddhist art treasure, the painting "Fruit of Realization and Sound of Emptiness." The work of Fu Wen, it was a birthday gift from Emperor Qianlong to his mother. During the invasion of the Eight-Nation Alliance (1900), the painting was moved from the royal palace to the temple, successfully avoiding falling into the hands of the invaders, thanks to great efforts by the monks. The gray-and-black colored painting with extremely fine lines is exquisitely delicate and elegant even though it is six meters tall and eleven meters wide. It is the largest mural painting in China, depicting the scene of the Buddha expounding the scriptures. In the middle is the Buddha Śākyamuni. On his side are the lion-riding Mañjuśrī and the elephant-riding Samantabhadra, as well as Sudhana, the Luohan (eighteen *arhats* of the Buddha), and a variety of other gods. Even some folk figures such as Guan Yu and the Dapeng Golden-winged Bird appear in the painting. Although each figure assumes a different pose, they all listen with great reverence, gaining inspiration.

Although the view inside Guangji Temple changes with the season, it is forever peaceful and charming. The ancient Buddhist monastery fits well with the modern architecture outside the temple, mutually enhancing each other's beauty. It is no surprise that Guangji Temple is a popular destination for people of various tastes and interests.

People: Devoutness and Kindness

Chinese Buddhism today advocates a moderate solution to people's distress. Alongside devout followers, people with great worries and anxieties can be seen at the temple, coming there to seek relief. All offer incense—three sticks in accordance with tradition. There is an incense burner in front of each main hall. After lighting their incense, worshippers raise it above their heads, offer it in the four cardinal directions, bow three times towards the hall, and place the incense into the burner. Worshippers also kneel on mats in front of the Buddha statues, place their hands in "praying position" with prayers in their hearts, then kowtow three times.

As far as management of the temple is concerned, Guangji Temple has a clear division of labor, with the abbot as the head of the temple, assisted by different staff, including a superintendent and receptionists, just as with many modern corporations today. Master De Wu, the receptionist, is usually on duty in the guest room. As the

50. 胜果妙音图 Qing Dynasty mural "Fruit of Realization and Sound of Emptiness" in Daxiong Hall

不强求，颇有"君子之交"的意味。由此，广济寺俨然成为了信佛老人们共同的乐园。老人们在此礼佛的同时，也可在群体中化解孤独之情从而有利于身心的调节。广济寺正默默发挥着它的社会功能——为老人们提供了一大怡然自在的平台，一方闹中取静、养心养身的天地。

在圆通殿前的绿垫上，一位赵姓的中年男子陷入了沉思。赵与广济寺的渊源颇深。很多年前，他爷爷初到北京，窘迫交加未有安置之地，幸得广济寺提供偏房居住一年有余，而后事业有所起色，才搬出寺庙，逐步在北京城站稳脚跟，生儿育女，颐养天年。故赵先生在爷爷奶奶去世之后，决定将他们的牌位供于他们最初的进京之地，也算作是一圆满。赵先生闲暇时便会来广济寺礼佛上香，以寄对逝者的相思之情。

广济寺僧众的交互关系体现了当代佛教走下神坛，开始逐步转向于贴近人们生活，关怀信众心灵的世俗化趋势。胡同里的广济寺立足于现世社会生活中的人，带着人性的关怀去替信众分忧，在温暖人心的同时也传播了人间佛教的理念。

活动：神圣与慈悲

寺内的僧人勤于做功念佛，每日晨钟暮鼓、早晚功课皆未曾懈怠过。大雄殿佛像前整齐摆放着一排排蒲团，可供僧众叩首跪拜。早晚课的主体内容为众人持诵佛经，随木鱼声进行叩拜，绕大殿三圈并齐声念颂佛号。每一天的诵经礼拜，是寺庙千百年

"window" of the temple to the public, Master De Wu busies himself with different issues every day. Born in 1971 in Anhui Province, he says that he has not returned to his hometown for over twenty years since the Chinese New Year is usually the busiest time for the temple. Thus the tradition of reuniting with one's family during the Chinese New Year has disappeared from his life. Master De Wu enjoys playing *shakuhachi* after meals, an instrument that creates a sound both vast and bleak, celestially hollow, full of the feel of Chan (Zen). In his guest room, there are loquat plants mailed to him by a lay Buddhist from Fujian, plain pancakes brought by a lay Buddhist from Shandong, and some new tea. The room is small and simple, but full of human warmth. For devout believers, they consider it a blessing to give offerings to Buddhists.

There are times when the monks at Guangji have to deal with "believers" who do not understand Buddhism, treating the temple as a place of transaction. One winter afternoon, a pale-looking patient arrived at the guest room, hoping to sign up for a soul-releasing ritual for the baby she had just aborted. Abortion is forbidden in Buddhism; by releasing the soul of the person killed, the living person hopes to be relieved from his or her sins. However, success for those who perform the ritual only once cannot be guaranteed. The woman wondered, "Why can't a guarantee be made?" The master avoided further explanation, instead advising the woman to do more charity, chant scriptures, and maintain a peaceful mind. The master said the temple would not collect merit money from believers who consider Buddhism a platform for transaction. Any attempt to exchange rewards through transactions is against Dharma and a misunderstanding of Dharma. In such cases, the masters try their best to offer spiritual comfort to believers. According to Buddhism, there are "Eight Sufferings" of human beings: birth, aging, illness, death, love, separation, leaving, and waiting. People in the modern world are often distressed by these issues, so temples serve as a means to help them relieve their pains and sorrows.

Among the frequent visitors to Guangji Temple, elderly men and women are especially noteworthy. They often visit the temple, usually staying for the day. A few times I noted a ninety-year-old lady sitting on the stone steps of the front courtyard. She greeted every elderly visitor passing by and chatted with them like old friends. She had not known any of them before meeting at Guangji Temple and developing relationships there. Unlike the younger generation, who are connected mainly through cell phones, the bond for these elderly is their love for the peace and purity of Guangji. They never set a time to meet; they only meet by chance, like a gentlemen's social agreement. Thus Guangji has become a paradise for older people—not only a place to worship but also a way to avoid loneliness. The temple fulfills its social function by offering tranquility and health for seniors.

On the green hassock in front of Yuantong Hall, Mr. Zhao, a middle-aged man, began reminiscing. Zhao's connection with the temple can be traced back years to when his grandfather had just arrived in Beijing. At the time, his grandfather had no financial means to afford a residence, but was lucky enough to get a free room at the temple. His grandfather stayed here for over a year. When his grandfather's job started to progress, he moved out. Later his grandfather established himself in Beijing, got married, and had children. When his grandfather and grandmother later died, Zhao moved their memorial tablets to the Guangji Temple—the place where his grandfather first arrived in Beijing, which is now the place where his grandfather's Beijing story both begins and ends. Whenever he has the chance, Zhao comes to the temple to offer incense in memory of his ancestors.

The interactions between the monastery and the people show that contemporary Buddhism has stepped down from the altar and become more involved in the secular world, caring for the day-to-day lives of ordinary people. In the midst of

51. 跪拜在大雄殿前的信众 Visitor worshipping in front of Daxiong Hall

来严格秉承的佛教传统，是僧人与神圣相连接之所在。

广济寺面向社会信众展开的佛教讲经活动每年分上下两期，每期时长四个月，于周末上午进行。新一期的讲经活动由道宏法师主讲，讲座内容围绕《四圣谛》展开。上午8时，广济寺讲经堂内已坐满了听众，其中以中老年人居多。道宏法师主张向信众通俗地解读佛教文化，当天的讲解主题为"三宝"（佛、法、僧）是什么，以及为何要皈依"三宝"？通俗的比喻是：佛类似于医生，佛法便是药，众生就如同病人。病人找医生（佛）看病，医生开方（法）治病，护理病人的护士便是僧。法师的讲解风格诙谐幽默，常与信众互动。他谈及宗教信仰是自由的，各信众皆可在比较中选择，并举例到基督教中也有博爱思想。广济寺展开的讲经活动，对于信众而言是一研习佛法的平台，受益颇多之人比比皆是。

历史上的广济寺便有兴办平民教育的义举，倡导慈悲为怀、众生平等。抗日战争期间，广济寺也曾挑选青年僧人组成一支战地救护队赴前线救死扶伤，并举行法事为战争死者超度，祈祷和平。广济寺济世利生的高尚情怀延续至今。广济寺方丈演觉法师便是一位佛教慈善的践行者。2008年，广济寺拿出寺院积攒多年的90余万元善款援建汶川地震中受灾严重的弘慈小学，为学生购置电脑，安装暖气，挖凿饮用水渠等，实实在在地为贫苦地区的教育带去了甘霖。

五观堂，系僧众进食的场所。名字来源于戒律规定僧人进食前应观想五方面事宜，即感念食物的来之不易；回想自身德行是否对得起眼前食物；观想应谢绝贪念，适量进食；谨记应将食物视为良药；进食是为了成就道业。每到周末，广济寺便会在

52. 圆通殿前诵读佛经的信众 Visitors reading Buddhist scriptures in front of Yuantong Hall

hutongs, the temple establishes a foundation in modern life and society, helping people steer clear of troubles, spreading the message of the Buddha by offering warmth to people.

Activities: Sacred and Merciful

The monks at the temple are diligent in their daily religious work. At the calling of the bell and drum in both the morning and the evening, they engage in daily worship—chanting scriptures, bowing with the sound of a wooden fish, and making three circles around the interior of Daxiong Hall while praising the Buddha. This daily worship has been a Buddhist tradition for centuries. It is when connections are forged between Buddhists and the holy.

The temple holds open lectures for the public on weekend mornings. Two courses are held each year, one in the first half of the year, another one in the second half, each lasting four months. The new series, conducted by Master Dao Hong, is about the Four Noble Truths. At 8:00 a.m., the lecture room was already full, mostly with middle-aged and elderly attendees. Master Dao Hong has a unique way of vividly delivering his message. The theme of the day was what the "Three Jewels" are and why we should acquire them. He made an analogy: "Buddha is like a doctor, Dharma is the medicine, and the folk people are the patients. Patients seek treatments from the doctor, the Buddha; the doctor prescribes medicines, which is Dharma; and the nurses are the monks [sangha]." The master has a good sense of humor as he interacts with his audience. He talks about freedom of religion and encourages people to make comparisons between different religions.

宽敞的讲经堂内为人们提供免费的素斋，信众们多早早地排好长队，等待义工们将其一一领入堂内进食。男女信众需按性别分坐在两侧。开饭前的仪式大致有十分钟，主导人道宏法师边敲木鱼，边庄严念诵"南无阿弥陀佛"佛号，而信众们则双手合十端坐在桌前，跟随法师一同念诵，而后齐声颂佛经，以此感念诸神诸菩萨，感恩能够生而为人，有饭可食。随后，义工们便会手持铁桶，给众人分食。佛教提倡静声进食，珍惜粮食，因而几十僧众共同进食的过程中只能听见咀嚼声，未见喧哗之音。汉传佛教僧团历来将进食视为一种重要的修行仪轨，而圆融通透的广济寺使得都市人们亦有机会能够亲历佛教素斋，更生动地体悟佛教感恩惜福、慈悲平等的理念。

佛教与中国传统文化交融上千年，相伴相生，早已成为九州大地中不可或缺的文化一隅。佛教庙宇虽小，却承载着文化传承的使命。胡同，本是充盈着市井之气的地方，而胡同里的广济寺在走向世俗、立足人间的过程中澄明依旧。

"Christianity embraces philanthropic love too," he highlights. Ordinary people benefit greatly from this learning platform

Throughout its history, Guangji Temple has always offered education for ordinary people, part of their mission of compassion and ideal of equality. During the Second Sino-Japanese War (1937–1945), some young monks formed a medical-aid team that went to the battlefield to rescue the wounded, hold soul-releasing rituals for the dead, and pray for peace. Traditions of caring for the sick and serving the world have been carried on up to today. Master Yan Jue, the abbot of Guangji Temple, is a Buddhist charity practitioner. In 2008, the temple donated over 900,000 Yuan to Hongci Elementary School, which had suffered severely from the Sichuan earthquake. For the school, the donation came like rain after a drought. They could use it to purchase computers for the students, install heating, and dig drinking-water channels.

Wuguantang ("Five Reflections") Hall is the dining place of the monks. Its name derives from the five things that the monks think about before eating: reviewing one's virtue to see if one is worthy of the food, refraining from greed, eating in moderation, remembering that food is a good medicine, and remembering that good deeds help one achieve great virtues. On the weekends, Guangji Temple offers free vegetarian food for the lecture attendants. The believers line up, waiting for the volunteers to lead them to the hall. Male and female believers sit on different sides of the hall. Ten minutes before the meal, Master Dao Hong knocks a wooden fish and solemnly recites "Namo Amitābha." The believers sit with their hands crossed and recite with the master. They then chant together the Buddhist scriptures, thanking the Buddhas and bodhisattvas and expressing their gratefulness for the food being offered. Thereafter, the volunteer carries an iron bucket with food, offering a meal to each person. Buddhism recommends quiet eating and frugality with food. Only the sound of chewing can be heard while eating. Chinese Buddhism has always regarded dining as an important ritual for cultivation. Guangji Temple offers this experience to people so that they can further understand the Buddhist concepts of gratitude and mercy.

Buddhism and traditional Chinese culture have intertwined for thousands of years. Even today, Buddhism continues to interact and integrate with Chinese culture. Although Guangji Temple is small, its mission is big—reaching out to the surrounding hutongs and beyond, while staying as clear, pure, and bright as always.

海淀基督教堂

谷俊锋 王迎梅

时间与空间

从海淀福音堂宣教之初,信仰的礼赞声响彻在历史及未来的旅程之中,在这片水土润泽的海淀区,伫立于被誉为中国"硅谷"的中关村的基督教堂,中华传统与基督教传统在这里碰撞并融汇,在沟通中理解。海淀教堂已逐渐融入寻常百姓的生活。在时间和空间的坐标系中,信仰者追寻着属于自己的人生价值。

北京市海淀区源于金朝所建制的海淀镇,这里曾是一片浅湖区,在湖边逐渐形成居民聚落,亦以"海淀"命名。1900 年后,基督教公理会开始宣教工作,成为基督教在海淀区最早的思想导源。1928年北平海淀中华基督教会成立,这片水土丰美、优沃润泽的平凡土地,伴随着福音的传播变得不平凡。

随着福音的传播,基督教会在海淀区建成"福音堂",并为后来的海淀教堂发展奠定了根基。1937年后的抗日战争时期,在一年左右的时间里,有300多名妇女在海淀福音堂避难,而免遭日军蹂躏。海淀区蒙受着福音堂的光照,随着教会影响力及信众的增加,这里不仅成为战争的避难所,也是和平时期的育儿院,教会在此兴学兴民,开办学校和慈善事业,提倡革新社会风气,提高教育水平。面对纷繁复杂的国内外环境,这里已成为北京的一片净土。1958 年后,海淀福音堂经历短暂的停歇。

随着中国的改革开放,海淀教堂重新复堂,在尘封27年后(1985年),福音堂又唱起了上帝的赞歌。进入21世纪后,海淀教堂堂址被划入北京市中关村高科技园区建设中,昔日的福音堂成为了历史的记忆,海淀新堂的重建应运而生。

今天的海淀新堂是在2007 年建成使用的。海淀新堂在功能上,着重于现代教堂的设计理念,将聚会场所和办公区融为一体,突出环境与功能的协调。在造型上,由193根洁白的立柱围合而成,寓意"诺亚方舟",又象征教会的合一,纯粹而典雅。同时,也让人联想为一卷打开的《圣经》,日落时分,伫立于教堂之上的十字架,在夜色中荧光泛红,令人心向往之。教堂的钟楼高48米,顶层安置三座铜钟,预备在每一个主内重大节日和每一堂主日礼拜开始时敲响。

这座伫立于中国硅谷的"诺亚方舟"承载着新的福音,继续传承历史的足迹,伴着教会圣所的钟声;伴着车水马龙的喧嚣;伴着阳光弥漫的赞美;他们前往应许之地,信仰之礼赞在这里回荡。

信徒与敬拜

肖恩出生在一个基督徒家庭,从小就阅读《圣经》,偶尔也会随母亲去教堂礼拜,在懵懂的少年时代,他并没有明确的"信"或者"不信",而是在求学阶段才逐渐明确了自己的信仰。大学期间,读书是最美好的时光,知识在其中涌现,他开始对真理有所思考。他觉得,世界如此美妙,真理即运行于之中。他阅读了大量关于宗教学的典籍,包括:佛教、道教、儒教等。一次偶然的机会,肖恩陪同师友(基督徒)前去教堂礼拜,牧师讲到"认罪、悔改"的主题时,触发了内心的情绪。在那一刻,他

Haidian Church

Gu Junfeng and Wang Yingmei, with Kameron Tomes, editor

Time and Space

The praise of faith resounds throughout the journey of Haidian Church. Located in Zhongguancun, the Chinese Silicon Valley in the district of Haidian, the church is where Chinese traditions and Christianity communicate, clash, and eventually converge. The church today is part of the life of many ordinary people who continually seek to position their values in coordinates of time and space.

Haidian District was first founded as Haidian Town during the Jin Dynasty (266–420). At that time, it was no more than a shallow lake along which people started settling, giving rise to the name "Haidian," meaning "shallow lake." In the early 1900s, the Evangelical Church began preaching in Haidian, making it the earliest source of Christianity in the district. In 1928, the Chinese Christian Church of Haidian was formally established. From that time on, the spread of the Gospel transformed this land of richness and beauty into an extraordinary place.

With the successful spread of the Gospel, the Christian Church of Haidian built a "Gospel Church," laying the foundation for the future Haidian Church. When the Japanese invaded Beijing during the Second Sino-Japanese War (1937–1945), women took

53. 现代教堂风格，像一本打开的圣经 Front of Haidian Christian Church

54. 肖恩服侍于教会青年诗班 Sean, who serves in the youth choir *(photo by He Yinglong)*

refuge in the Gospel Church to avoid being sexually assaulted by the Japanese. Blessed by the Gospel, the church's influence continued to grow and its followers increased. After the war ended, the Gospel Church began serving as a childcare center, school, and charity, all aiming to promote the social morale and education of the general public. No matter how chaotic and complex the domestic and international environments, the Gospel Church has always remained "a land of purity."

Although church activities came to a halt in 1958, they later resumed in 1985 in the wake of the Chinese "Reform and Opening" policy. Hymns to the Lord were sung again in the Gospel Church. At the turn of the twenty-first century, the site of the church was included in the construction of the Beijing Zhongguancun High-Tech Park. The former "Gospel Church" was demolished to make way for the new "Haidian Church" to come into being.

Today's Haidian Church was built in 2007. It was designed to be a modern church, integrating spaces for social gathering and office work. Its elegant and simple exterior is made up of 193 white columns that look like Noah's Ark or an open Bible and also symbolize the unity of the church. At dusk, the cross on top of the church emits fluorescent red light, warming the hearts of onlookers. The bell tower stands forty-eight meters high, with three bronze bells that ring out at the beginning of each Sunday service and festival.

The "Noah's Ark" in China's "Silicon Valley" proclaims a new Gospel, embarking on its route towards a new "Promised Land," while continuing the path of its glorious past. Accompanied by the bustling traffic of the busy city and the clear ringing of its bronze bells, the hymns to the faithful echo in the air.

Believers and Worship

Sean (a pseudonym) was born into a Christian family. He read the Bible from an early age. Occasionally he went to church with his mother. During his "unenlightened" youth, he was not sure whether to believe or not. During his time in college, he devoured books on Buddhism, Daoism, and Confucianism, which triggered his curiosity to pursue the truth. One day, he accompanied a Christian schoolmate to church. The pastor's sermon that day on "confession and repentance" awakened emotions within him. He came to realize that Christianity was the only path for his pursuit of truth. He was firm in his decision of faith. After college, he left his homeland and arrived in Beijing, an "alien" city. He became one of the millions of "Beijing Drifters" (Chinese immigrants to Beijing without permanent residence status). In a highly competitive and market-oriented city like Beijing, he was forced to continually stretch his capacity to adapt.

As a "drifter" and a Christian, Sean's primary task upon arrival was to find a church, a harbor in which to anchor his soul. Christianity is such a wonder that it can offer great peace for those solitary minds deeply rooted in family traditions while far away from home. Its magic is the power of faith. For Sean, hometown identity and geography became secondary; his priorities in life were now to discover God and himself through church, family, and work. This new perspective quickly shaped the "new drifter" to be more determined and stronger willed. In his spare time, he often participated in church services and activities, including choir, spirituality, and fellowship.

Sean has been in Beijing for nearly ten years now. At first, he kept changing jobs. Each change enabled him to better understand himself, better position himself, and better improve himself. Currently he is an office administrator, a key member of his department. Whenever he encounters difficulties, he prays or attends worship at Haidian Church, seeking power from within. The guidance he receives from church, along with the support of his family,

55. 海淀教堂的聚会 Worship service at Haidian Christian Church

　　认为只有在基督教内才能获得对真理的解答，并坚定了自己的信仰。大学毕业，肖恩踏上了"北漂"的生活，逃离故乡，拥抱城市，在高度发达的市场分工之中，他的生命张力也在陌生环境中得以激发。

　　作为一名北漂基督徒，肖恩来到北京的首要事情，便是寻找心灵的家园：海淀基督教堂。基督徒的生命体验是独特的，让习惯于生活在中国传统家庭的人们，难以理解如何在陌生的大城市可以安静度日。这种隐含在内心深处的生命体验是信仰的力量，对于肖恩而言，故乡、身份、地理都是不重要的，而重要的是穿越生活的沉重细节，在教会、家庭、工作中认识自己和所要赞美的上帝，海淀教堂成为了心灵寄居的场所。这样一种全新的理解生活的方式，令刚刚来到北京的肖恩，更有目标、更有力量、更有决心在外北漂。在工作之余他经常参与教会的服侍，包括诗班、灵修和团契活动。

　　肖恩来北京打拼已近十年，他的职业在此期间曾不断转换，在这段经历之中，重新认识着自己，在北京的市场分工中实现专业领域的细分，个人的工作能力获得了极大的锤炼，目前在一家公司做文职工作，并成为公司部门内的重要成员。在工作中面临困难时，他常常通过祷告，或前往海淀教堂礼拜，以此来缓解内心的压力，寻求一种由内而外的力量涌现，并通过教会的引领，以及家庭的鼓励，使得自己在工作中继续前行。在谈到自己的家庭时，肖恩会心一笑，坦言"感谢上帝的保守"，回首与妻子相识、相知的历程，他感慨万千。

56. 海淀堂的领祷员 Minister leading prayers at Haidian Christian Church

are the driving forces that keep him working hard and moving forward. When speaking about his family, Sean smiles and thanks God for His protection. Reminiscing about his journey with his wife, he becomes choked with emotion.

As the saying goes, a seemingly casual encounter is actually the result of destiny. Through the church choir, Sean met the most important partner of his lifetime—his wife. The Chinese widely believe that a good marriage should be from a good match, which includes the match of two entire families. Sean was from a Christian family; his girlfriend, however, was not a Christian believer, even though she did respect Sean's faith and attend the church's fellowship activities with him. Because of Sean's influence over an extended period of time, she eventually decided to be baptized. Later, she and Sean got married. There is another Chinese saying, "travelling for thousands of miles to meet is predetermination; remaining strangers even while face to face is also predetermination." The "predetermination" here is the love of God. The two got married at Haidian Church.

The life of "Beijing Drifters" is filled with stress from work and daily life. Sean is no exception. The family sometimes has issues too. When husband and wife fight over differences, it can be exhausting. For Sean, the balance of career, family, and serving the Lord is the biggest challenge in his life. After worrying about these difficulties, he came up with a solution—to admit their individual fragility and become sympathetic about each other's problems. His family relationship is increasingly stable, smooth, and harmonious, thanks to the love and guidance of Christ. Haidian Church has been the holy witness of the couple's relationship journey.

因缘际会，肖恩在青年诗班的服侍中，遇到了一生中最重要的伴侣，在谈到自己的婚姻生活时，一条普遍的观念认为，婚姻讲究门当户对，基于共同信仰的基督徒的彼此结合是婚姻生活的稳固保障和基石。肖恩虽生于一个基督徒的原生家庭，与其谈恋爱的女友却是一位非信徒，女友非常尊重伴侣的信仰事实，并常常陪同他参加海淀教堂的青年团契活动，在长久的恋爱与观念的磨合中，女友受洗并与其结为夫妻。中国一句老话："有缘千里来相会，无缘对面不相逢"。在他看来，这里的"缘"即是上帝的爱，是上帝的引领，在海淀基督教堂缔结成为了夫妻。

北漂族的生活每天都充满压力，肖恩也常常被生活和工作的琐事所困扰，甚至于家庭硝烟时而弥漫，常常出现分歧，有时甚至无力改变，力不从心。如何平衡家庭、事业、服侍，是他所面临的问题，在感慨生活的种种不易时，肖恩对此的理解是"正视软弱、彼此怜悯"。一路走来，正如其所言，"藉着基督的大爱和引领"，肖恩的家庭越来越稳固、越来越和谐，也越来越幸福，海淀教堂便是见证夫妻二人生活的圣所。

节日与活动

中华民族有春节、元宵、清明、端午、重阳、中秋等节日，每一个节日对于中华民族都蕴含着丰富且深刻的故事，基督教的节日亦有着丰富的内容。近年来，海淀教堂在圣诞节、圣周、复活节等教会节日，都会举行盛大的节日庆典。同时，海淀教堂也会在中华传统佳节和社会节日期间，举行相应的庆典活动，力图用中华民族语言和时代语言诠释基督教所信仰的上帝恩典。肖恩参与到节日活动的敬拜中，并在每一个特殊节日向孩子们讲述发生在海淀教堂的故事。

圣诞节是庆祝耶稣基督生命的诞生，也是海淀教堂重要的节日庆典之一。在圣诞月之初，肖恩会在家里布置圣诞树，并向孩子们讲述圣诞节的故事。"她将要生一个儿子，你要给他起名叫耶稣，因他要将自己的百姓从罪恶里救出来"（马太福音1:18）。十二月的第一个周日，海淀教堂进行了一年一度的圣诞树点亮仪式，北京的冬夜十分寒冷，海淀教堂广场外相聚的人心却是暖的。喜庆的音乐和唱诵的赞美诗，在挥舞的荧光棒下响彻星空，广场内人群的脸上洋溢着微笑，已抑制不住心中的感动。在全场倒数声中，圣诞树被点亮，人们的心也被点亮，圣诞的欢喜在人群中弥漫，圣诞月的节庆开始了。

圣诞节当天的海淀教堂，成为了一个开放的欢乐殿堂，这里伴有掌声、歌声、笑声和祝福声。这一天，没有地域、没有国界、没有性别、没有肤色等一切差异，人们欢聚一堂，像是中国的农历新年一样，成为了一个团圆的日子，在赞美声和欢呼声中，迎接着耶稣基督的诞生，盼望着新的一年的到来。这一天是新的起点，海淀教堂的圣诞颂歌响彻中关村，广场中的圣诞树所点缀的荧光格外耀眼，光照着当夜的北京。

在复活节的圣周，海淀教堂举行了泰泽式祈祷会。追溯历史，泰泽是一个法国勃肯地省的小村庄。泰泽修士们追求普世教会合一，希望泰泽修会可以成为普世基督徒在世上可见的合一的标记，以耶稣基督为楷模，活出福音的精神，藉着祈祷为全人类大家庭带来和平的希望。

泰泽祈祷会是海淀堂圣周重要的活动，主要通过简短的歌词，表达出信仰的核心和真谛；简单的旋律，使参与者很快便能加入咏唱；反复咏唱，能用心去歌唱，使歌

57. 圣经与十字架 Bible and cross

Festivals, Events, and Activities

Chinese celebrate important festivals such as the Spring Festival, Lantern Festival, Qingming, Dragon Boat Festival, Chongyang, and Mid-Autumn Festival, each of which has its own significance. In recent years, not only has Haidian Church celebrated Christmas, Holy Week, and Easter by hosting grand ceremonies; it has also held events and activities for Chinese festivals, demonstrating God's grace in the language of the Chinese nation and the modern era. Sean attends these festivals, telling stories to the children about the history of the church.

Christmas Day is one of the important celebrations for Haidian Church. At the beginning of December, Sean will help set up the Christmas tree indoors and tell the children stories about Christmas: "She will have a son, and you will call him Jesus, for he will save his people from their sins" (Matthew 1:21). On the first Sunday of December, Haidian Church holds an annual Christmas-tree lighting ceremony. Winter nights in Beijing can be very chilly, but the hearts of the people inside and outside the church are warm. Celebratory music is played and hymns are sung. People wave fluorescent sticks with smiles on their faces. After a countdown by the entire crowd, the Christmas tree is lit. People's hearts are illuminated, and the air is permeated with great joy. So begins the Christmas celebration.

Haidian Church on Christmas Day is a hall of great happiness, filled with applause, singing, laughter, and blessings. People from all countries and regions, of all colors and genders, gather together. Like the Chinese New Year, Christmas Day has become a day of "reunion." With great

词融入我们的心灵的深处；读经静默，使个人安静自己，沉浸在与上帝相遇的美好中，敞开心灵，迎接上帝、敬拜上帝。短暂静默后，牧师和传道分别带领信众为人类、教会、国家、苦难、家庭及个人献上祷告，每一次祷告的间隙，会众齐唱:《求你俯听我》。

肖恩也是本次赞美诗班的一员，吟颂的诗歌与教堂的环境合二为一，营造了一种神圣、庄严、安静的氛围，令人肃然起敬。教会希望藉着这样的祈祷，在赞美、默想和读经中，使得信众增进与上帝之间的关系，寻求上帝在自己生命中的旨意。使其他参与者(包括非信徒)能有机会感受到基督教会带给人的"温和力量"，在静默的环境中，感受到信仰对人心灵的安抚。

在基督教的传统之中，最重要的节庆是复活节，耶稣复活是基督教信仰的根基。复活节象征着一个人的重生和希望，为的是纪念耶稣基督被钉死在十字架之后第三天复活。"人子必须被交在罪人手里，钉在十字架上，第三日复活"(路加福音24:7)。在这一天，肖恩会带着家人来到海淀教堂纪念这一重要节日。基督徒正是对耶稣基督死而复活的相信，而建立对未来的盼望。

在海淀教堂，复活节庆典从最后的晚餐、受难到复活是一个完整的序列程序。在复活节前一周，海淀教堂要准备两支大蜡烛，放在圣洗地或祭台旁。在这一周中，烛光闪耀在主堂，烛光是喜乐的象征，复活节是喜庆的节日，在信徒看来，蜡烛象征着基督，祂燃烧自己，照亮他人，驱散黑暗迎接光明。每一位参与敬拜的会众都将获得一枚复活蛋，并写有一句经文，这是礼物，也是祝福。

这一天的活动充满了喜乐，礼拜仪式中的音乐、舞蹈、启应经文不再是赞美诗班和神职人员的互动，而是在一种艺术美学的渲染下，最终与信徒们一起的合唱。这极大地提高了信徒们的参与性；极大地调动了教堂内的活跃度；极大地激发了参与者的崇拜感。

藉着感恩与祝福，海淀教堂为人类、为教会、为国家、为家庭和个人献上真挚的祝福，信仰之礼赞将回荡在北京的每一个"今天"。

anticipation and praise, people greet the birth of Jesus and await the coming of the new year.

The day is a new starting point. Christmas carols from Haidian Church resound round Zhongguancun. The fluorescent lights on the Christmas trees dazzle, as if all of Beijing is glowing.

In the Holy Week of Easter, a Taize-style prayer service is held at Haidian Church. Dating back to historic times, Taize was a small village in Burgundy, France. The Taize monks advocated the unity of the Church; thus the Taize symbol became a sign of the unity of Christians throughout the world. They promoted living the spirit of the Gospel by following the example of Jesus Christ. They brought hope of peace for the entire world through prayers.

The Taize-style prayer meeting is an important Holy Week event for Haidian Church. The lyrics are concise but contain the core message of the faith. The melody is simple, easy for everyone to follow, repeat, and remember. Reading and meditating on the scriptures offer people a peaceful mind to embrace and become immersed in moments of beauty with God. After the short meditation, the pastor and evangelist lead prayers for the people of the world, the churches, the country, those who are suffering, families, and individuals. Between each set of prayers, the congregation sings "Please listen to me."

Sean is a member of the choir. The songs they sing are solemn, holy, peaceful, and awe-inspiring, creating harmony with the sanctuary. Through singing and chanting, the followers seek communion with God, feeling the warm power of Christianity, and enjoying the comfort that faith brings to their minds. The bond between God and His followers also becomes strengthened.

Easter is the most important celebration for Christians since the resurrection of Jesus is the foundation of the Christian faith. Easter commemorates the resurrection of Jesus Christ on the third day after crucifixion. It symbolizes the rebirth and hope of a person. "The Son of Man must be handed over to the sinner, crucified, and resurrected on the third day" (Luke 24:7). On this day, Sean will commemorate this important festival at Haidian Church with his family.

The Easter celebrations at Haidian Church are a complete procedure from the "Last Supper" to crucifixion and resurrection. A week before Easter, the church prepares two giant candles, which are placed next to the baptistery and the altar. During the week, the candlelight shines in the sanctuary. Candlelight represents joy, and Easter is a joyful celebration. In the eyes of the believers, candles symbolize Christ, who burns himself but illuminates others, dispelling darkness to bring light. Each member of the congregation will receive a "Resurrection Egg" with a verse from the Bible as a gift and a blessing.

The day is full of delight. Inspired by the atmosphere, the church members join the choir. The music, dance, and responsive reading in the liturgy are no longer mere interactions between the choir and the clergy like on ordinary days, but an activity participated in by all, filled with passion and a feeling of worship.

The praise of the faith reverberates around Beijing every day, as Haidian Church sends its sincere blessings to every person, family, church, and the entire world.

后桑峪天主教堂

张睿

后桑峪坐落于北京市门头沟区斋堂镇，是京西的一个古老的村落。村子三面环山，一条蜿蜒流过的清水河将桑峪村与周围的村落联系在一起，沿河而建的109国道是进村的主要路径之一。

桑峪村大约建立于公元1271年，因为这里的桑树茂密成林而得名"桑峪"。公元1294年，意大利方济各会会士孟高唯诺（1247–1328）以教宗钦使的身份来到北京，并获准在元大都设立教堂传教，这被视为天主教正式传入中国的标志。同年，在桑峪村的村落文化志记载中，村子里来了两位外国的宣教士，他们一边行医一边传教，天主教在后桑峪的传播，自此拉开了序幕。此后40余年的时间里，后桑峪的教友迅速发展至数百人。那时村里还没有教堂，于是众多教友在一间民房中，设立了后桑峪的第一座天主教堂。

桑峪村的行政区划十分特别，早在明清时期，桑峪村就因信仰的不同开始分村而治，即分为前桑峪和后桑峪。新中国成立以后，虽然前后桑峪的行政区划已经合二为一，但在当地仍然保留着原来的叫法。从信仰状况来看，前桑峪以中国民间信仰为主，有个别几户人家是天主教徒；而后桑峪几乎全村信仰天主教，教堂和圣母山也坐落在后桑峪。虽然信仰不同，但这两个村子之间仍然保持着密切的联系。每年的农历三月初三是前后桑峪共同祭祀中华始祖黄帝的日子。这一天村民们会聚在一起吃村宴，虽然后桑峪的人并不会真正参加祭祖这样的祭祀活动，但是教堂的乐队也会受邀在典礼上表演几首通俗的乐曲。

大约七百多年前，第一位传教士在深山之中播下了福音的种子，天主教信仰就在这里生根发芽。历史裹挟着神秘的故事，一辈辈的流淌在村民们的记忆之中。对于村里的老人们来说，从他们的祖辈流传下来的天主教信仰，才是这个村子的传统。

空间构造

后桑峪的教堂首建于1334年，当时仅由两间平房组成，是有文字记载的北京地区建立最早的一批教堂之一。在历史上，后桑峪的教堂几经扩建，也数次遭到损毁。明清时期，后桑峪的教友日益增多，教堂也经历了两次较大的扩建。据《门头沟区志》记载，明朝嘉靖十年（1531年），小教堂被拆除并改建成大教堂，建筑形式采用了中国传统的寺庙风格。清光绪二十一年（1896年），教堂依欧洲哥特式风格再次翻修扩建，当时已有两位外国神父常驻此地传教。

19世纪末，中国发生了一场以"扶清灭洋"为口号的义和团运动。这场运动后来演变为针对天主教徒和基督教徒的集体屠杀事件，直接冲击了天主教在中国的生存和发展。据《门头沟区志》记载，因为都信仰天主教，后桑峪村和附近的张家铺村也受到了义和团的攻击。张家铺村几乎被屠村，百十口村民无一幸免。而后桑峪因为圣母显灵的圣迹，免于一劫。传说义和团围攻后桑峪时，曾在夜里看到村子后山有一道白光出现，随后数百位身着白色盔甲骑着白马的将士将村寨护住。义和团见此异象，只

Housangyu Church

Zhang Rui, with Sara Feldman and Kelsey Rick, editors

Housangyu is an ancient village west of Beijing in the jurisdiction of Zhaitang Town in the Mentougou District. The village is surrounded on three sides by mountains, through which the sparkling Qingshui River winds, connecting it with other nearby villages. National Road 109, which was built along the river, is the main entrance to the village.

Established in 1271, Sangyu literally translates as "Mulberry Valley," with *sang* meaning "mulberry," and *yu* meaning "valley." In the past, the mulberry woods here were densely forested, so the locals made a living by reeling silk.

Commissioned by the Pope, Giovanni da Montecorvino arrived in Beijing in 1294, where he was granted permission to build churches. This marked the beginning of Catholicism in China. The Sangyu village log recorded that in the same year, two foreign missionaries arrived in the village, preaching Christianity and practicing medicine. This was the prelude to the development of Catholicism in the village. In the following forty years, a few-hundred people converted to Catholicism. Since there was no church at the time, the members decided to build the first Catholic church at a residential bungalow.

Although the founding of the People's Republic of China (1949) ended the division of Sangyu village into two parts, the reason for its initial division into *qian* (front) and *hou* (rear) is quite unique. As early

58. 后桑峪村全貌 **Village of Housangyu**

59. 礼敬圣母处 Place of prayer in front of a statue of the Virgin Mary

能撤退。那天刚好是圣母升天日，于是圣母显灵救护后桑峪的传说自此流传了下来。当地村民为了感激圣母的保佑，就依教堂后山修建了圣母山，并请圣母作为村中的主保。后桑峪的圣母山始建于1902年，这也是北京地区唯一的一座圣母山。

  令人遗憾的是，在抗日战争时期（1937-1945），当地的教堂因作为传递情报的秘密据点，被日军发现而被烧毁，圣母山也未能幸免于难。在"文化大革命"期间，教堂再次遭到重创。此后近30年的时间里，村里都没有一个正式的宗教场所。据老教友张大爷回忆，文革结束以后，宗教政策一直不太明朗，因为没有教堂，教友们就聚集在村民家中做弥撒，他家正是其中一户。平日的弥撒没有神父，教友们就聚在一起念念经。每逢大瞻礼，村里就派几个年轻的小伙子，走上几十里的山路，到周围的乡里去请神父来做弥撒。后来政策渐渐宽松，教堂的重建工作也逐步进入正轨。

  现如今的后桑峪天主教堂，建成于1999年。教堂整体采用了中国传统的院落布局。在院子东侧，摆放一座纯白色的圣母塑像，周围常年以鲜花作装饰，到了冬天，就换上艳丽的塑料花。鲜花代表奉献，即信众将他们认为最好的东西奉献在圣母面前。来到堂里的每一位信徒，都要先面向圣母像鞠躬祈祷，再进入圣心堂。耶稣圣心堂延续了清朝的哥特式风格，大门和窗体都呈尖拱形。教堂内东部为举行弥撒典礼的祭台，西部是音乐楼，供教堂的乐队平时排练使用。

  紧依教堂的后山就是圣母山，越过标有"上天之门"的拱门，就进入了这与俗世分隔的秘密之境。教友们依山势修建了一条"苦路"，盘旋隐没在密林之中。苦路的

as the Ming and Qing Dynasties (1368–1644, 1644–1912), the villagers have mostly followed two different kinds of religions. Except for a few households, the people from Qian-sangyu largely follow Chinese folk religions, while villagers in Hou-sangyu are mostly Catholics. The church and Mount Virgin Mary are both located in Housangyu. Their different faiths, however, did not stop the villagers from communicating and interacting with one another. Each year, on the third day of the third month according to the lunar calendar, all villagers gather together to memorialize the Yellow Emperor, the ancestor of the Chinese nation. A big village feast is offered to all. Although Housangyu villagers do not perform the rituals, they accept invitations to play popular songs at the ceremony.

Ever since the seeds of the Gospel were planted by the first missionaries 700 years ago, the Catholic faith has taken root in Housangyu. Over the centuries, numerous stories and myths about the faith have been passed down. For the senior Housangyu villagers, it is the Catholic faith inherited from their ancestors that is the dominant tradition of their village.

Space and Structure

Documents attest that Housangyu Church was first built in 1334; it was therefore one of the first churches in the Beijing area. At that time, it consisted of only two bungalows. Although several expansions have been made since its initial construction, it has also suffered repeated damage.

During the Ming and Qing Dynasties, the church went through two major expansions because of the steady increase of church members. According to the Mentougou District log, the small church was torn down and replaced by a bigger church of traditional Chinese temple style in the tenth year of Emperor Jiajing of the Ming Dynasty (1531). Later, in the twenty-first year of Emperor Guangxu (1896), the church underwent another expansion and renovation, and was also converted to Gothic style. At the time, two foreign missionaries were permanently stationed in the village.

Towards the end of the nineteenth century, a nationwide revolt called the Boxer Rebellion swept across the northern plain of China, with the slogan "Destroying the West and Supporting the Qing." This revolt led to a massive slaughtering of Catholics and Christians, directly impacting the survival and development of Catholicism in China. The Mentougou log records that Housangyu and the neighboring village of Zhangjiapu were attacked by the Boxer Rebellion since they were both Catholic villages. Over 100 villagers from Zhangjiapu were killed. Housangyu, however, miraculously survived the raid, thanks to a manifestation of the Virgin Mary. Legend has it that the Boxers saw a white beam of light emerging from the back of the village after they sieged it. Immediately, hundreds of militants wearing white armor and riding white horses appeared and came to rescue the village. Having never seen anything like this before, the Boxers had no choice but to flee. That day happened to be the Assumption of the Virgin to Heaven. The legend that the Virgin Mary appeared and rescued the villagers therefore became part of the village's history. To express their gratitude, the villagers built a statue called "Mount Virgin Mary" on the hill behind the church, inviting her to be the main guardian of the village. Construction began immediately after the rebellion in 1902. It is the only Mount Virgin Mary in the Beijing area.

During the Second Sino-Japanese War (1937–1945), the church was used as a secret intelligence communications site. This was however discovered by the Japanese, who burned down the church and Mount Virgin Mary. The Cultural Revolution (1966–1976) shattered the church once again. For thirty years, there was no formal religious site in the village. Mr. Zhang, an elderly church member, recalled

后桑峪天主教堂

60. 教堂院子里的圣母像 Statue of the Virgin Mary in the church courtyard

61. 神父祝圣圣餐 Priest serving Eucharist *(photo by He Yinglong)*

that religious policies were ambiguous after the Cultural Revolution. Since there was no church, villagers could only hold the Mass in their homes. His home was one of the sites. There was no priest on ordinary days, so they gathered together and recited the scriptures themselves. However, on major Catholic feasts, the village would send a few young men to walk for several dozen miles to look for a priest in neighboring villages to perform the Mass. When religious policies were loosened up several years later, the reconstruction of the church was back on the agenda.

The Housangyu Church we see today was built in 1999, using the layout of a traditional Chinese courtyard. On the east side of the courtyard, a pure white Virgin Mary statue is on display, decorated with fresh flowers. The villagers only present the most beautiful offerings to the Mother of Christ.

Everyone bows and prays to the Virgin Mary before stepping into the "Sacred Heart of Jesus" hall of the church. This hall inherited the Gothic style of the Qing Dynasty, with pointed-arch doors and windows. Inside the hall, the altar for the Mass lies on the east, with music rooms in which the band regularly practices on the west.

The hill behind the church is Mount Notre Dame. After passing through the arch inscribed 上天之门 ("Gate to Heaven"), one enters a hidden path that is separated from the secular world. This is the *Via Dolorosa* ("Way of Suffering") that the villagers built among the trees on the hill. The beginning of the path is marked by a stela inscribed with the "Peace Prayer" of St. Francis and the Beatitudes of Jesus. Four crosses are placed along the path, in remembrance of Jesus's sufferings. The path ultimately leads to an open altar, with a stone dome

62. 后桑峪乐队 Housangyu church band

起止点分别立有和平祷词和山中圣训碑，沿途的十四个十字架，作为耶稣受难十四处的标识，最后通向一个开阔的祭台，祭台后的石堆形似蒙古族的敖包，有圣母像置于正中。祭台两侧分别立有圣保禄和圣伯多禄的雕像。每到夜里，圣母像上就亮起一明灯，守护着在夜色之中沉睡的山村。

每年都有来自全国各地的信众，来圣母山朝圣。在中华圣母节这天，北京教区的主教也会协同其他堂区的神父、修士、修女等几百余人，一同前来后桑峪朝圣。在村中的广场上举行隆重的弥撒，特别敬礼圣母玛利亚。

文化血脉

若不是教堂的哥特式钟楼使村落带有一丝异域风情，后桑峪和周围的其他村子相比，似乎并没有什么不同。但天主教信仰在这里传承数百年的同时，也深刻浸染了后桑峪的村落文化。

现在教堂的弥撒全程使用中文，但在相当长的一段时间里，后桑峪举行的都是拉丁弥撒。杨树民大爷（1947–）回忆到，村里原来有好几任外国神父，他们懂拉丁文，就将拉丁弥撒的礼仪一句句地教给村里的教友们。那时的人们大多没有接受过正规的教育，但对拉丁弥撒却非常熟稔，能读能背诵弥撒所使用的拉丁文。"文革"结束后，拉丁弥撒一度中断，村里一位姓高的教友是教师，也懂拉丁文，就和村里几位

behind it and the statue of the Virgin Mary in between. The altar is flanked by statues of Saint Paul and Saint Peter. When night sets in, the light on Mount Virgin Mary is illuminated as it guards the sleeping village.

Every year pilgrims from all over the country come to Mount Virgin Mary. On Chinese Holy Mother's Day, the bishop of the Beijing Diocese, accompanied by a few-hundred Catholics, including priests, monks, and nuns from different parishes, makes a pilgrimage here. A grand Mass is held as a special dedication to the Virgin Mary.

Cultural Inheritance

Housangyu Village would look no different from other nearby villages if it were not for the Gothic-style church. The church brings a touch of exoticism, but more importantly, deeply influences the culture of the village.

Today, the Mass at the church is given in Chinese. For a long period of time, however, it was conducted in Latin. Mr. Yang, an elderly church member, recalled that in the past, the church had several foreign priests. Sentence by sentence, they taught the villagers the Mass in Latin. Even though most of the villagers were not formally educated, they did learn to recite the Mass in Latin. Although the Latin Mass stopped during the Cultural Revolution, it was later resumed by a teacher from the village by the family name of Gao, along with the help of several other church members. When talking about Latin, Mr. Yang grew excited, scarcely able to contain his desire to show off his Latin: *Sit Dominus vobiscum et cum animus tuus!* ("May the Lord be with you and your soul!"). After the Second Vatican Council in 1965, the Beijing Diocese started to perform new Mass rituals. Over time, the Latin Mass was replaced by the Chinese Mass. Now, hardly anyone remembers the Latin Mass.

Mr. Yang suffered from a measles outbreak as a child and lost his vision as a result. His home is in a courtyard in front of the church. He makes his living by offering massage services. The walk from his home to the church takes three minutes. In the past, he had to fumble his way along the stone path, but he is now completely familiar with it. Besides attending the Mass each morning, he returns to the church every other day for band rehearsal.

Housangyu has a brass band made up of church members with an average age of sixty-five. About five years ago, the priest at the time, Father Song, started the band. He organized the band members to buy musical instruments and learn music theory together. Without scores, they copied each piece of music by hand and circulated them to one another. Yang recollected that when the purchased musical instruments arrived, no one knew how to play them since there were no teachers. With a little instruction from Father Song, members took their instruments home, experimented with them, and figured out how to play Do-Re-Mi. From the simplest note, they went step by step. Now the band is of a decent scale and sound. Before each rehearsal, they always play the same tune, "The Holy Spirit Runs Here," asking the Holy Spirit to join them. Almost all the tunes they play are holy songs from the Mass, such as the Lord's Prayer and Kyrie. On important occasions, the musicians wear uniforms with the words "The Holy Orchestra—All for the love of God" embroidered on their armbands.

Numerous priests and church members have come to Housangyu, bringing with them knowledge and religious culture. They have witnessed the growth of the religion in this place. If it were not for the love of God, which is silent but powerful, we would not be able to experience this Catholic presence in such a small village in the countryside of Beijing.

老教友一起，把拉丁弥撒又搞了起来。杨大爷一边说着一边高兴的展示他记得的拉丁文，"愿主与你们同在，也与你的心灵同在"，并用拉丁文翻译了一遍。1965年梵蒂冈第二次大公会议后，北京教区全部实行新礼弥撒，后桑峪的拉丁弥撒也逐渐被中文弥撒取代，现在堂里已经鲜有教友记得了。

杨大爷是一位盲人，因为幼时发麻疹导致双目失明。他住在教堂前的院子里，靠按摩为生。从家门口到教堂的一段石板路摸索着走大概需要3分钟，杨大爷早已经轻车熟路。除了参加每天早上的弥撒外，杨大爷每隔一天还要去堂里一次，去参加乐队的排练。

后桑峪的教友们组建了一支铜管乐队，乐手们的平均年龄在65岁左右。大概五年前，当时的本堂神父宋神父将教友们组织在一起，买乐器，学乐理知识。没有谱子，他们就将弥撒套曲中的曲子一首首手抄下来，再互相传阅。杨大爷回忆说，乐器刚刚买回来的时候，队里没有老师，大家就拿着各自的乐器回家摸索着吹出了哆来咪，再从最简单的谱子开始练起。现在的乐队已经颇具规模，每次排练开始前，他们都要先演奏一曲《圣神运行在这里》，将圣神请到乐队里来。乐队排练的乐曲几乎都是弥撒中的圣歌，如《天主经》《垂怜曲》等等。每逢重要的演出，乐手会穿上队服，队服侧面的袖章上写着"圣乐团 一切为了爱天主"。

无数位神父和教友来到后桑峪，将文化和知识也带到了这里，浸润在村民们的身上，印证着他们的信仰：天主的爱悄无声息。这也使我们今天还能在京郊的一个小村落，窥见天主教信仰的身影。

宗教人员

后桑峪是一个相对独立的村落，既保持着他们独特的信仰，也并未完全与周围村子分割开来。这个村落以天主教信仰为主，也保留了中国传统文化的遗存。每逢旧历新年，家家户户也会贴春联、吃饺子，庆祝农历新年。

教友们形成了这样的团体：一位本堂神父、八位辅祭、六位读经员，和其他的平信徒。神父是由北京教区派下来的，大约每三年会更替一任。信徒相信神父是教会内有神权的人，可以代表天主"赦他们的罪"。现任的本堂神父姓庞，除了负责后桑峪教堂的事务外，庞神父也会去斋堂镇的其他祈祷场所主持弥撒。

常来堂里参加弥撒的信徒以后桑峪的村民为主，还有一些来自附近的村子。辅祭全部是后桑峪的村民，他们出生时便受洗，幼年时就开始在堂里做辅祭。有些辅祭长大后要外出求学或者工作，就由村里更小的辅祭来代替。教堂每天早上都会准时举行弥撒，神父会根据弥撒的日子来确定辅祭的人数，如果是庆日或主日，需要有辅祭持香炉、捧福音书，就会多安排几个人。而读经员大多是女性，主要负责在弥撒中领经和读经。不论是辅祭还是读经员，并没有严格的选拔标准，主要依照自愿的原则。堂里所有的人事安排都是根据弥撒的需要而进行的。在教徒们的眼中，辅祭和平信徒只是从事的职位不同，在天主面前，他们并没有其他分别。

张宝成（1958-）就是堂里的一位辅祭，和村中其他老人比起来，还属于年轻的一辈。张宝成一出生便受了洗，二十出头的时候就开始在教堂里当辅祭。不仅要在弥撒中协助神父，也要维护教堂的日常运转。每次弥撒前后，常常能看到他在堂里忙碌的身影，或是准备香炉里要烧的炭火，或是把祭台的物品归置妥当。

张宝成家就住在教堂的后面。据他回忆，他家现在住的这座房子原本是属于教会

The Church Staff

While keeping its unique faith, Housangyu does not isolate itself from the neighboring villages, nor does it cut itself off from Chinese traditions. During the Chinese New Year celebration, villagers partake in traditional Chinese festivals, where they hang Spring Festival couplets on their doors, eat dumplings, and hold celebrations with others who are not of the Catholic faith.

The church staff consists of a priest, eight altar servers, six lectors and commentators, and the laity. The priest is sent by the Beijing Diocese; each priest preaches for a three-year term. The followers believe that the priest is the one whom God has empowered and who can pardon their sins. The current priest is surnamed Pang. Besides managing the church affairs, he also hosts Mass for other preaching sites in Zhaitang Town.

Most of the people who attend the church Mass are villagers from Housangyu, though some come from nearby villages. All of the altar servers are from Housangyu. Baptized at birth, they have fulfilled this role since they were kids. Sometimes servers have to leave the village for schooling or career opportunities elsewhere. When this happens, their positions are filled by other younger altar servers. Every morning, the church starts Mass on time, at 5:30 a.m. in the summer and 6:00 a.m. in the winter. The priest determines the number of altar servers based on the date. On Sundays or holy days, a few more servers will be assigned to raise the incense burner or hold the Gospel. Lectors and commentators, those who proclaim the readings or read the introductions, are mostly female. The selection of lectors, commentators, and altar servers does not follow rigid rules and is mostly on a voluntary basis. All personnel arrangements are made depending on the needs of the Mass. The followers consider that the altar servers and lay believers differ only in their careers; in the eyes of God they are all equal.

Zhang Baocheng is an altar server at the church. Born in 1958, he is considered part of the "younger generation" of the village. Zhang was baptized at birth and has been an altar server since his early twenties. He not only assists the priest in the Mass but also manages the daily operations of the church. He is often busy before and after the Mass, having either to prepare charcoal for the incense burner or to light candles in preparation for Mass.

Zhang's home is behind the church. According to him, the house where his family lives used to be owned by the church. In the early nineteenth century, the church possessed a lot of land and farms. Seeing how poor some farmers were, the priest offered free land to them for their survival. This land, which now contains more than a dozen households, used to belong to the church.

Housangyu Church was also once a welfare home, where many abandoned, disabled, or widowed women were cared for by the church. Zhang

63. 怀抱耶稣的圣若瑟 Statue of St. Joseph with baby Jesus

的。在十九世纪初期，教会在后桑峪村里已经拥有了许多田产和土地，那时中国农村的经济普遍非常落后，神父若见到有的村民家中的日子太困难了，就将教堂所有的一小块地送给他，帮助他们生活。现如今村中有十几户人家的土地，都是原来教会捐赠的。后桑峪教堂曾一度作为村里的福利院，许多被遗弃、残疾的人或丧偶的妇女在这里得到教会的照顾，他们也协助并维持教会的正常运转。张叔家有个亲戚，老家是清水河上游东胡林的，当年她的父母嫌弃生下的是个女婴，就将她遗弃在河边，恰巧被路过的刚刚做完弥撒的神父拣到，便将她带回了教堂，在堂里养了起来。若按常规，她本应会成为堂里的修女，只是那时刚好赶上文革，堂里的神职人员都被遣返了，宗教活动也被迫取消，于是便不了了之。"我家这座房子就是她走之前留下的，她现在也大了，在镇里就结婚了。"张叔回忆到。

按照天主教的礼仪，辅祭只能是男性，且大多数为幼童。后桑峪的情况却并不相同。和中国大多数乡村的现状一样，后桑峪也面临着人口流失的问题。这原本是一个靠煤矿产业致富的村子，2005年，为了实现门头沟区"生态涵养区"的定位，桑峪村将矿产资源型企业全部关闭。没有了传统的煤矿产业的支撑，村里的年轻人大多选择外出务工，孩子们也随父母在镇里读书，留下来的几乎都是老年人。走在村里的石板路上，鲜少看到年轻人的面孔，平日里来堂内参加弥撒的基本都是老年人，只有在大的瞻礼前后或者假期时，小孩子才被家人带来堂里参加活动。每到这时，当天的弥撒大多会让一两个孩子充当读经员或者"奉献"的角色，参与到仪式当中来，并以此作为信仰的传承。

后桑峪坐落在京郊的深山之中，这里的交通并不发达，一条弯弯曲曲的清水河将这个村落与周围联系在一起。伴着圣母山上的那盏灯，后桑峪的村民们每天清晨在弥撒的吟咏声中得到祝福。弥撒的结束，也是一天生活的开始。他们聚在一起，聆听上主的真言，作世人中的光；散居于世，而成为地上的盐。所谓作光作盐，荣神益人，便是如此。

64. 在耶稣圣心堂祈祷的信徒 Parishioner praying at the Church of the Sacred Heart of Jesus

has a relative who was originally from a village upstream on the Qingshui River. When she was born, the parents pitied her for being a girl and abandoned her in the river. The little baby floated downstream, where she happened to be discovered by a priest who had just finished the Mass. The priest took the little baby back to the church and raised her there. She planned to be a nun when she grew up. At that time, however, the Cultural Revolution broke out. All clerics were sent away, and all religious activities were forced to stop. "It's said that she is now married," Zhang proudly noted.

Catholicism stipulates that the role of altar server can only be undertaken by males, usually boys. Housangyu does not follow this practice. Like most rural areas in China, Housangyu has been experiencing population loss. In 2005, this coal-mining village had to shutter all mineral resource businesses in response to the "Ecological Conservation Area" of the Mentougou District. Without the traditional coal mining industry, most young people were forced to find jobs elsewhere. Their children followed them, leaving mostly just elderly in the village. When one walks around the village on its stone paths, a young face is rarely seen. Only on days of feasts or holidays do little children appear at the church with their parents. On these days, one or two children will be asked to join the ceremony by taking the role of lector or another role of "dedication" that shows the commitment of their faith.

Lying in a deep valley in the countryside of Beijing, Housangyu is not conveniently accessible. The Qingshui River is the bond between the village and others nearby. Guided by the light on Mount Virgin Mary, the villagers receive their first blessing of the day from their chanting of the morning Mass. With the end of the Mass, the villagers' day begins. Housangyu villagers gather together to listen to the true words of the Lord, and be the light of the world. When the gathering finishes, they become the salt of the earth. Be it light or salt, they forever honor God and serve the world.

火德真君庙

张筱嘉

火德真君庙的新年从春节里的祈福法事开始。

微信昵称为"实习神仙"的魏道长早早地在微信朋友圈里发布了手机录制的拜年视频和火神庙的法事安排表，以便于信众与香客了解详情与网上预约。

虽然人们庆祝这一最重要的传统节日的方式越来越现代，但古老的习俗仍然沿袭至今。春节期间的火德真君庙人潮涌动：正月初一要"抢头香"，在新年的第一天烧第一柱香的人，能够获得最多的保佑与福祉。古代中国使用天干地支配合成六十甲子作为纪年法，六十甲子对应六十位太岁神，他们分别当值某一年份，于是正月初二要进行拜太岁法事。到了正月初五，则要迎财神，主管世间财源的神明，将为信众保佑一年的财运。

2018年冬天的北京没有下雪，东风解冻，蛰虫始振，太阳直射点逐渐向北回归线移动，什刹海的冰层发出第一声解冻的轻响，火神庙的春天来得比以往更早一些。

重生

北京的地安门外，什刹海沿岸，长久以来被认为是旧京风水最好的地区。火神庙所处的这一地区，靠近湖水与被称之为"龙脉"的北京中轴线。中国人相信风水，认为房屋所处的地理位置和内部构造能够影响住户的运势。这里有诸多王府大院和

65. 火神庙的前院 Front courtyard of Huode Zhenjun

Huode Zhenjun Temple

Zhang Xiaojia, with Ireland Larsen and Rosalind Carey, editors

The Chinese New Year at Huode Zhenjun Temple—otherwise known the "Fire God" Temple—begins with prayer rites during the Spring Festival.

Daoist Priest Wei, nicknamed "Intern Immortal" on WeChat, has traditionally shared not only New Year's video greetings but also the temple's yearly calendar of rituals on his WeChat "moments," so that the temple's attendees can arrange online appointments.

Although the manner in which people celebrate this most important traditional festival is becoming more modern, ancient customs still prevail. On the first day of the New Year, visitors "compete for the first stick of incense" (*qiang tou xiang*), as the person who burns this stick is rewarded with the most blessings and protections. On the second day, attendees worship the Tai Sui deity who is in charge of managing the year. This is in accordance with the ancient "Heavenly-Stems and Earthly-Branches Sexagenarian Cycle," according to which there are sixty different Tai Sui deities who take turns managing the years. On the fifth day, people greet the God of Wealth, who controls the financial resources of the human world, blessing years of fortune.

There was no snow this past winter in Beijing. Wind from the east helped thaw the frozen ice. Insects could not wait to dig out of the earth. The vertical incident solar rays kept moving northward. The icy layers of Shichahai Lake (on the shore of which the temple rests) made the first sound of thawing. Spring this year came earlier than ever.

Rebirth

The area outside Di'anmen and along Shichahai has long been considered to have the best Feng Shui in Beijing. Chinese believe in Feng Shui, according to which both the geographical location and internal structure of a dwelling directly impact the luck of the people living in it. The neighborhood where Huode Zhenjun Temple is located is close to the central axis of Beijing, which is called the Dragon Meridian. It is where many princely mansions and Buddhist and Daoist temples are located. Huode Zhenjun Temple is one of the oldest "tenants" here. It was built in the sixth year of the Zhenguan Era of the Tang Dynasty (631), rebuilt in the Yuan Dynasty (1271–1368), and prospered during the Ming and Qing Dynasties (1368–1644, 1644–1912).

"Fire God" refers to the "Southern Fire Star Law Enforcement God," one of the four-direction deities in ancient China, who controlled fire. For ancient Chinese city dwellers who lived in houses made of wood, worshipping the Fire God was an important way to prevent fire. The special status of Huode Zhenjun Temple is thus evident. In the meantime, belief in the Fire God also reflected people's wishes to reward good and punish evil, acquire a high position as a government official, earn a large sum of fortune, and remain protected and in peace.

When the People's Republic of China was founded, the Daoists at the temple had to leave and return to secular life. In 1956, the temple property was taken by the government. Huode Zhenjun Temple no longer existed, not until the beginning of the twenty-first century.

The first person who proposed repairing the temple was Ma Yi, then a member of the Cultural Committee of Beijing's Xicheng District. On January

66. 王灵官：道教护法神之一，在火神庙中为镇守山门之神 Wang Lingguan, guardian deity at the gate of Huode Zhenjun

67. 祈福法会 Daoist priest leading prayer ritual

　　道观佛寺，火德真君庙是资格最老的"住客"之一。它建于大唐贞观六年（公元631年），距今已近1400年。它重修于元代，兴盛于明清两朝。

　　"火神"指"南方火德荧惑执法星君"。中国古代有四方神，南方之神主火，对于拥有大量木质结构房屋的中国古代城市来说，祭拜火神是预防火灾的重要环节，火神庙在旧北京城的地位可见一斑。与此同时，火德星君的信仰中亦寄托了惩恶扬善，求官求财，庇佑平安的心愿。

　　1949年后，火神庙的道士们离开了寺庙，回到世俗生活。1956年庙产划归公有，火神庙消失在北京人的视野中，直到新世纪来临。

　　腾退修缮火神庙建议最早由彼时在北京西城文委的马毅先生提出。2002年1月1日，这片区域被中国道教协会重新接管，北京市文物局、中国道教协会、北京市西城区人民政府拨划款项，组织起了修缮工作。作为道教协会代表来全权负责火神庙修缮工作的金道长，坐在十多年后焕然一新的后院办公室里，依然能记得自他带着一床被子住进火神庙以来，近八年修缮的日夜。

　　重新将几近荒废的火神庙复原并非易事。因为年久失修和乱搭乱建，火神庙不大的前院里居住了四十三户人家——每户平均只有9平方米的居住范围；临时居住的办公室内没有电暖气与空调，夏热冬寒；火神庙原有的格局与规划亦不甚明晰。马毅先生在2001年底将居住其中与附近的居民迁出安置，将钥匙交付到金道长的手上，道教协

1, 2002, the property of the temple was transferred to the Chinese Daoist Association. Funds for reconstruction were appropriated by the Beijing Cultural Relics Bureau, the Chinese Daoist Association, and Beijing's Xicheng District government. The project was planned, organized, and initiated. While sitting in his brand-new office in the back yard of the temple over ten years later, Daoist Priest Jin, who was delegated to oversee the renovation project at the time, recalled vividly the first night he moved in with a blanket, as well as the eight years to follow.

To restore the nearly abandoned Huode Zhenjun Temple was not an easy task. The buildings had gone decades without maintenance. Makeshift structures had been added here and there, with the front yard of the temple accommodating forty-three households averaging nine square meters each. A temporary reconstruction office was established, though without heating or air conditioning, so it was cold in winter and hot in summer. By the end of 2001, Ma Yi had finally resettled the households inside and around the temple, after which he handed over the keys to Daoist Priest Jin. At that time, the Chinese Daoist Association officially took over Huode Zhenjun Temple. Daoist Priest Jin located the original blueprint of the temple from the State Administration of Cultural Heritage, from which he was able to delineate the exact scope and structure of the temple.

There was no shortage of difficulties and challenges. Nevertheless, on December 12, 2010, after eight years of reconstruction and repair, the new Huode Zhenjun Temple emerged along Shechahai Lake. The Zhengyi Sect of Daoism ("Way of Orthodox Unity") assumed its management. Shaking off the historic dust, the temple started a new era in a brand-new manner.

Huode Zhenjun Temple came back to life.

Joining and Parting

Ms. Li, who is on duty at Sanguan Hall, still recalls a snowy winter day two years ago.

During the freezing cold December of the lunar year, Li came down with a severe toothache. The pain tortured her, preventing her from eating and sleeping. Several days of medication and infusion did not alleviate her condition; the inflammation even worsened. On the second day of the Chinese New Year, she heeded the advice of her friend to make the lengthy journey from Tongzhou District to Huode Zhenjun Temple to offer incense.

On that day, Shichahai Lake was covered with a thick layer of ice. Huode Zhenjun Temple was coated by silver white snow. Tree branches were glued with ice crystals.

The Fire God in the main hall is the first deity everyone worships. A banner on the wooden railing in front of the statue announces: "Answer to all prayers."

"Ok, answer to any prayers." With this thought in mind, Li closed her eyes. When she reopened them, they were fixed on the round and bright eyes of the Fire God. She then stepped out of the hall to see the courtyard fully covered by snow. Li opened her mouth with her hand covering her right cheek, exclaiming, "Ah." It was the first sound she had made since her toothache. She then turned to her right, arriving at Sanguan Hall on the west side of the temple. These "Three Officer Great Deities" (*san guan*) are Daoist deities who are in charge of Heaven, Earth, and the ocean. The Heaven Official blesses, the Earth Official pardons, and the Water Official relieves misfortunes.

Li kneeled down in front of the Heaven Official. When she raised her head, the aching was totally gone.

From that day, retired Li chose to serve at Sanguan Hall of the Huode Zhenjun Temple.

Similar stories occur to visitors, believers, and volunteers. Although urban high-rise buildings of reinforced concrete and steel have replaced the

会正式接管火神庙。金道长从国家文物局找到火神庙原有的布局图纸，得以划定出火神庙准确的范围与结构。

凡此种种，不一而足。直到2010年的12月12日，火德真君庙历经八年的修缮，重新出现在什刹海边，由正一派道士接管。它抖落一身历史的尘埃，以新的方式开始了它与崭新时代的共处。

火神庙开始热闹起来。

聚散

在三官殿值殿的李阿姨，时至今日依然能回想起两年前那个下着雪的北京冬日。

在天寒地冻的腊月，李阿姨患上了严重的牙疾，疼痛使她无法进食甚至夜不成寐，几日的输液和服药并没有让牙疼缓解，甚至加重了炎症。但在正月初二她还是应朋友之约从北京通州区来到什刹海边的火神庙进香。

什刹海结上了厚厚的冰层，火神庙被落雪笼罩在一片银白里，树枝上凝结着冰棱。进庙必然先拜正殿的火神，神像前的木质栏杆上，挂着信徒送来的锦旗——"有求必应"。

"行，不是有求必应吗？"李阿姨这样想着闭上眼睛，跪拜之后再睁开眼，撞上荧惑宝殿正中端坐的火神"又圆又亮"的眼睛。她转身跨出正殿的门槛，大雪已经落满了院子。李阿姨捂着右腮张了张嘴，发出了一声"啊"，这是患牙疾以来她第一次能够张嘴发出声音。向右转是火神庙的西配殿——三官殿，其中供奉的三官大帝指的是道教中掌管天堂、地府、海洋三界的"三官"之神："赐福天官"、"赦罪地官"和"解厄水官"，又称"三元大帝"，是极为崇高的神祇。

李阿姨跪在赐福天官面前，再抬起头的时候，疼痛已经消减了。

退休之后赋闲在家的李阿姨，从这一天开始，就留在了火神庙的三官殿。

类似的故事发生在香客身上、信徒身上、义工身上。尽管钢筋混凝土的城市高楼替代了原有的木质结构房屋，现代社会对于火灾的防范程度亦随着科技发展提高。然而这并非意味着北京城再也不需要火神庙，恰恰相反，在火神庙重新回归北京人视野的八年时间里，越来越多的人聚集到了这一小方天地里，如溪流聚成江河直至海洋。

作为管理人员之一的魏道长见证着这里的往来与聚散。每一年，有信徒从其他宗教团体离开，来到火神庙拜师或者担任义工，又或是定期组织群体的祈福法会；也有人离开火神庙，改信其他宗教，或回到日常的工作中。

"许多人对'道教'的认知来源于艺术作品。影视剧里的修道者们'御剑飞行，无所不能'，于是不少人带着懵懂的冲动和梦想来到这里。不过现实里的道长也不是每日念经喝茶讲道，也要面对琐碎的事务和人际的关系往来。"魏道长对于这样的聚散显得坦然而洒脱："修行并非一定要留在庙里，无论他们最终去向何方，我们为每一个能够找到更适合自己生活方式的人感到高兴"。

体悟

位于西配殿的财神殿，因着"财神"的功能，总是吸引着大量香客。值殿的义工王哥本职是一名广告从业者。对他而言，在世俗繁琐的工作之外，庙里的日子忙碌但宁静。

original wooden-structure houses, and although modern fire-prevention technology has been much improved, Beijing still needs Huode Zhenjun Temple. In the past eight years, more and more people have congregated at the temple, like streams converging to rivers and flowing into the ocean.

One of the managers, Daoist Priest Wei, witnesses the coming and going, joining and leaving. Every year, there are people who leave their religions and join Huode Zhenjun Temple to honor a master, to be volunteers, or to organize periodic prayer rituals. There are also people, however, who leave Huode Zhenjun Temple and convert to other religions or return to routine jobs.

"Many people's knowledge about Daoism originates from artworks. The Daoists in movies or soap operas are incredibly powerful: The priest flies to anywhere he wants while standing on the sword he holds. Quite a few people come to the temple with such images in mind. In reality, however, Daoists do not chant scriptures, drink tea, and preach every day. No one can live without dealing with daily trifles and human relations. Daoist Priest Wei takes the joining and parting that he witnesses in his stride. "Cultivation does not have to happen in the temple. Wherever they go, we are happy for the better and more suitable lifestyle they choose."

Contemplation

The Wealth God Shrine on the west side of the temple has always attracted a lot of visitors because it is dedicated to the God of Wealth. Mr. Wang, the volunteer on duty, works in the advertising industry. For him, days inside the temple are busy but peaceful.

Three gods of wealth are worshipped here: Zhao Gongming (God of Wealth); Bi Gan (Civilian Wealth God); and Guan Yu (Military Wealth God). Wang uses a side table directly in front of the Military Wealth God, Guan Yu. Once a visitor asked, "Guan Yu was not a business man, nor was he rich: Why is he worshipped as a god of wealth?" Through his days in the temple, Wang has learned to "see the gains but think of righteousness." Guan Yu is the embodiment and manifestation of loyalty and righteousness. Business people tend to value material things over justice. They often ignore ethics for the sake of business interests. The fact that Guan Yu is the God of Wealth reminds people of the saying "Gentlemen love money but should obtain it rightly."

Wang sees many visitors trapped in false thinking: always praying but never self-correcting. They pin all their hopes on the blessings and protections of the gods, forgetting to reflect on the righteousness of their own behaviors.

The logic of Chinese religions sounds simple and straightforward: people fulfill their wishes by praying to gods for their blessings and protections. However, Chinese religions actually emphasize introspection and self-correction. Many gods have been given an "ideal personality"; Guan Yu, for example, is the embodiment of loyalty, righteousness, and courage. It is also undeniable that Chinese religions have played a historically important role in enlightening people about morality. They contain a set of ideal ethical standards and their applications in real-life scenarios.

Mr. Zhao is a frequent visitor to the temple. But he never requests the gods to answer his destiny. Instead, he bows, kowtows, and leaves. No wind and rain can stop him from visiting. For a long period of time, he appeared only in the afternoons. When asked by some volunteer acquaintances, he said that he had to take care of his mother in the mornings and finish all his tasks at home before he could come to visit.

Now Zhao's mother has passed away. He still shows up at the temple every day, with steady steps and good spirit. He believes in the gods' protections and in living a good life daily.

火德真君庙

68. 在财神殿担任义工的王居士 Mr. Wang, on duty at the Wealth God Hall *(photo by He Yinglong)*

"Take good care of your family, and then ask for divine help. Carry out your own duties first, then listen to the heavenly instructions"—this is the philosophy of life that Mr. Zhao expresses without saying.

Answers

The Moon Elderly Hall on the east side of the temple is hidden by peach blossoms, hanging red cords, and praying cards. The hall is dedicated to the Moon Elderly Immortal, Fox Immortal, Peach Blossom Immortal, and the Immortals of Harmony and Union. The Moon Elderly Immortal is in charge of marriages between men and women. For those couples that have been predetermined, he uses a red cord to connect them. The rest of the deities control affairs such as the luck of romance, good looks, and appearances. They fulfill people's wishes of "keeping the wrong man or woman out of the way" or "preserving youth and beauty." Nowadays, people offer not only fresh fruit and flowers but also lipstick, lotion, and other cosmetics. The followers believe that using cosmetics that have been enshrined can give them better looks.

People visiting the Moon Elderly Hall arrive in endless streams: worried-looking elders who fret about the marriages of their children, youth who are undecided about their dating candidates, young girls distressed about never being able to find the right man, or couples who are troubled in their relationships.

They kneel down devoutly in front of the statue of the Moon Elderly Immortal, reciting silently their worries and issues, praying to him for luck in romance, asking him to fix their relationships with loved ones, or drawing lots to obtain his guidance.

In China's traditional religions, the concept of Heaven (*Tian*) and the gods associated with it have far-reaching effects. These gods have foreknowledge about all operations in the universe, including social issues and personal life. Using lot-drawing or divination to interpret and forecast one's difficulties and issues can be traced back about 3000 years. This method is still common in Daoist and "folk religion" temples.

At the Huode Zhenjun Temple, interpreting lots is usually the job of the lay volunteer and Daoist priest on duty. The volunteer Yü Lu and Daoist Priestess Li are more like caring sisters. They listen to the bewilderment of a person, then offer comfort or solution. For those who worry about their children's marriages, they suggest "refreshing their values": "Marriage is not a compulsory task of a certain age." For young men and women who are traumatized by break-ups, they offer comfort and encouragement. For husbands and wives who are in relationship crises, they help them identify the root causes and find solutions.

In *Religion in the Chinese Society* (1967), C. K. Yang (1911–1999) explains the multifaceted social function of Chinese traditional religions as including explaining extraordinary social and natural phenomena, dealing with existential tragedies and crises, making humans less selfish and bonding them together, and justifying the moral order. Without a doubt, all of these functions are still very much needed by the Chinese people today.

Huode Zhenjun Temple has become a place to share what is on your mind and to seek answers and solutions.

The main hall of the Huode Zhenjun Temple is dedicated to the southern Huode Zhenjun (Fire God). Its roof is a sunken panel suggesting water; the rear hall of the temple contains the Xuanwu Emperor, the Water God. This arrangement entails the coordination of fire and water. The wisdom of Chinese Daoism is reflected in its balanced approach, which emphasizes combining rigidness and softness, the harmony of yin and yang.

火德真君庙

　　财神殿内供奉三大财神，赵公明、比干、关羽，王哥值殿的一方小桌就位于关羽的正前方。曾有香客询问，关羽并非商人出身，亦非拥有巨额财富，何以位列财神之位。在财神殿的时间给予了他"见利思义"的体悟："关羽是忠义的化身与承载者，而从商者总易滑向'重利轻义'，为了商业利益与金钱纠葛可以置伦理道德于不顾，作为财神的关羽恰恰是在提醒大众——君子爱财，也应取之有道。"

　　关羽的财神身份是在防止人们陷入"只求不改"的误区，即寄生活的希望于神灵的恩赐与庇佑，却遗忘反省自身行事的得当与否。

　　这里信仰的逻辑看似简单明了：人们祈求神灵以期获得庇佑实现心愿。但它实际上也在强调内省与自我纠正，诸多神灵被赋予了一种"理想人格"，譬如关羽即是忠、义、勇的化身。不可否认的是，它们在历史的长河中共同承担起道德教化的作用，承载着一种理想主义式的道德要求和生活图景。

　　赵伯伯是火神庙的常客，不过他从未求签问卦，只是叩拜一圈神灵便离开。无论刮风下雨从不间断，并在很长的一段时间里都只在下午前来。彼时有相熟的义工问起，才得知他需要在每天早晨照顾好自己的母亲，安顿好家里的事务，再前来火神庙。

　　如今赵伯伯的母亲已经离世，但他依然会每天走进火神庙的大门，步履稳健，精神矍铄，他相信神灵的庇佑，也过好日常的生活。

　　"先照顾好亲人，再祈求神灵的保佑，先尽人事，再听天命。"这是赵伯伯不言自明的一套人生哲学。

答案

　　东边的月老殿掩映在桃花、悬挂的红线与祈福牌之中。殿中供奉月下老人、狐仙娘娘、桃花仙子及和合二仙，月下老人是主管世间男女姻缘的神灵，他用"红线"将有缘之人系在一起结成连理。其他配祀的神灵亦掌管着"容貌""桃花运"等"事务"，承载着"挡烂桃花"、"永葆青春美丽"的心愿，面前所呈供品与时俱进，除了常备的水果鲜花之外，更是有口红、润肤露等各种化妆品：信众们相信使用了供奉过的化妆品能够使他们获得更美好的容颜。

　　来往月老殿的人络绎不绝——操心子女婚事，眉眼间尽是担忧神色的老人；在几名追求对象中游移不定的青年；苦恼自己始终未能觅得良缘的少女；婚姻或恋情出现难题的夫妻或情侣。

　　他们虔诚地跪在月下老人的神像前，默念内心的郁结，祈求月老给予自己一段桃花，或是弥合与恋人之间的关系，又或是抽取一根签文以期获得来自神灵的指引。

　　中国的传统宗教思想里，"天"这一概念和附属于"天"的众神体系影响深远，这个体系能够预先知晓包括社会现象、个人生活在内的宇宙万物的运作。运用抽签、占卜等方式解读甚至预示人的生活境况与难题的方式甚至可以追溯至约三千年前。直到如今，这种方式在道观或是民间宗教场所中依然常见。

　　在火神庙里，解读签文的工作通常由当日值殿的义工与道长完成，这里的义工于璐和道长李姐似乎更像是"知心姐姐"。月老殿人来人往，但香客们面临的困境却无外乎几类。她们聆听着情感困境，给予相应的安慰与解答。对于担忧子女婚姻的老人，她们让其理解社会的新价值观——"婚姻并不是要在某一个年龄阶段必须完成的事"；面对被失恋阴影笼罩的青年男女，她们则承担起开解和鼓励的角色；对于情感出现危机的夫妻或是情侣，她们则需要寻找问题的源头和解决方式。

RELIGIONS OF BEIJING

137

69. 在月老殿供奉的化妆品 **Cosmetics left as offerings in Moon Elderly Immortal Hall** *(photo by He Yinglong)*

To the west of Huode Zhenjun Temple now lies the feasting and revelry of the Houhai bar area. To the south is the Forbidden City, the center of the entire ancient empire. To the east of the temple, one can walk to Nanluoguxiang, one of the must-see places for visitors in Beijing to view the International Trade Center with its rows of skyscrapers. To the north of the temple stands the centuries' old and hardship-laden Drum and Bell Tower. Huode Zhenjun Temple connects the realms of modern and ancient, refuses no one regardless of his or her religious origin, and does not reject requests for the nature of secular triviality. In the meantime, the temple never compromises the core of its spirit.

Although times change, people's concerns roughly remain the same: health, money, marriage, career, and education. Guidance can be sought at the temple for all these confusions. Huode Zhenjun Temple is not a mere Daoist temple, but a constantly refreshing box containing the rising and falling of the city and time, the destinies and stories of people coming and going, the joy and suffering of the world.

Rites and activities at Huode Zhenjun Temple last throughout the year: Tangyuan (boiled, sweet white glutinous flour balls) are distributed to every visitor at the Yuanxiao Festival; the soul-releasing ritual is held in drizzling rain on Qingming; red cords are hung in front of Moon Elderly Hall like the rosy dawn on Qixi; the moon and lights are reflected in the ripples of Lake Shichahai at the Mid-Autumn Festival; the elderly are brought to the temple to burn incense for Chongyang Festival. Then one year passes. Countless believers bow and kowtow. All their wishes, requests, worries, and sorrows are carried to Heaven through the rising smoke billowing from their incense sticks, praying candles, and petition cards.

The deities in the halls sit silent without saying a word; their only message seems to be the constant ringing of ceremonial bells (*qing*) at Huode Zhenjun.

火德真君庙

70. 火神像以及信众送来的锦旗 Statue of Fire God and banners

　　杨庆堃在《中国社会中的宗教》一书中指出，中国传统宗教的社会功能在于解释社会和自然的各种非常态现象，处理由包括死亡在内的生活悲剧带来的失望与恐怖。另一方面，中国宗教在于提高人的精神境界，使之脱离低俗的自私与功利，给人以更高的目标，使他与周围的人团结并和睦相处，或者调整道德秩序的正当性以面对单纯道德难以解释的人生成功与失败。毫不意外地，这样的功能在时下依然存在，并为人们所需要着。

　　火神庙成为了一个可以倾诉秘密的地方，同样也为人们寻找答案。

　　火神庙的正殿供奉南方火德真君，殿顶有代表着"水"的藻井，后殿供奉北方玄武大帝，即水神，暗合"水火既济"之意。不偏不倚，刚柔并济，阴阳调和，这是中国道教的处世智慧。如今的火神庙，西边，是灯红酒绿的后海酒吧区；南边，临近曾经是整个古老帝国中心的紫禁城；东边，近能抵达如今已成为旅行者"打卡地"的南锣鼓巷，远能眺望高楼鳞次栉比的国贸；北边，是历经北京城百年沧桑的钟鼓楼。它紧邻着现代与古朴，对到来的无论何种出身何种宗教的人从不拒绝，不抵触世俗的琐碎，却亦有自身坚持的内核。

　　时代辗转，人类所面对的困境大抵依然相同——健康、财富、婚姻、事业、学业，在这里都有了具体的指向。火神庙不仅是一个道教庙宇，更像一个古老但永远在更新的盒子，里头装着时代与城市的历史浮沉与进退；装着来来往往之人的命运与故事；装着人间的欢欣与疾苦。

　　火神庙的种种法事和日常活动，会持续一整年。元宵节的汤圆被分发到每名香客手中，清明节的超度法会在细雨里举行，七夕节的红线朝霞般挂满月老殿的门前，中秋节灯火倒映于什刹海粼粼的波光里，秋高气爽的重阳节最适合带家中长辈上香祈祷。于是一年又这么过去了。无数信众叩拜顿首，所有的祝愿、请求、烦恼、悲喜、疾苦，都在香火、表文、灯烛燃起的袅袅青烟里上达天听。尽管神灵们端坐殿中闭口不言，但听到声声磬音响起，仿佛就听到了他们的回应。

71. 正在烧香的香客 Believer worshipping with incense

潭柘寺

于博洋 刘熠然

空间与历史

潭柘寺最初是名为嘉福寺的一个小庙,建于西晋永嘉元年(公元307年),因山上有龙潭和柘树,民间习惯称之为潭柘寺。后来在唐代武则天时期,以嘉福寺为中心兴建了大型寺院,即为今天我们看到的潭柘寺的格局。潭柘寺享有"京都第一寺"的美誉,距今已有1700多年的历史,比北京建城还早800年,因此民间流传"先有潭柘寺,后有北京城"的说法。

潭柘寺的寺庙园林是典型的中式风格,以对称稳重、南北中轴线布局,构成气势磅礴的建筑群体,与紫禁城的格局十分相似。其中最主要的建筑都集中在中轴线上,有山门、天王殿、大雄宝殿、毗卢阁等。从晋代起,历代帝王就对潭柘寺格外恩宠,各朝代上至皇帝后妃、王公大臣,下至平民百姓都来此进香礼佛;清代康熙皇帝更是把潭柘寺定位为皇家寺院。潭柘寺在北京人心中,不仅仅是一座佛寺,更象征着北京在历史发展黄金时期绽放的灿烂光芒。潭柘寺与禅宗的关系也较久远,五代初期,有一位从湖南来的丛石禅师把潭柘寺作为祖庭,此后,禅宗开始在潭柘寺的历史上兴盛起来。

潭柘寺最负盛名的景观当属伫立在天王殿前的两棵银杏树。相传它们有1400年的树龄,由于富有神奇灵性,被清代乾隆皇帝御封为"帝王树",这是迄今为止皇帝对于树木的最高封号。到了秋天,"帝王树"掉落的金黄叶片会把潭柘寺装点成宛如童话的金色世界。自2009年起,每到金秋时节,寺院都会举办"帝王银杏观赏季"活动,邀请四方游客见证"满寺尽带黄金甲"的美景。

观赏"帝王树"的最佳方位是山门腹地前设置的公共茶座,游人可在此处品茗休憩,在感受古树穿越千年历史气息的同时,品味银杏叶片从萌芽生发到落叶归根的轮回禅境,让饱受俗世物质生活侵染的身心在与古树静谧无言的精神接触中得到抚慰。游客张先生与李先生每年秋天都会相约在此喝茶下棋,感受秋日慵懒的午后时光,"在北京工作压力很大,需要有像潭柘寺这样的地方来放松身心"。

走过茶座,在通往天王殿的石砌甬道中央,矗立着一个带有藏传佛教特色的巨大经轮,上面刻有藏文六字真言(即观音心咒)"唵嘛呢叭咪吽",周围经幡舞动,庄严肃静,前来转经轮的游人络绎不绝。金色的经轮与金秋美景的结合浑然一体,在阳光的照耀下流光溢彩,熠熠生辉。在藏传佛教看来,转经轮、念诵六字真言具有不可思议的功德,是一种简单易行的修行方法。此地汉藏佛教象征的交融,体现了中国文化的多元与包容,同时反映出了中国人信仰边界的模糊与杂糅。

穿过甬道,迎面即是天王殿。殿内正中供奉大肚弥勒佛佛像,天王殿的左右两侧是四大天王,他们各护一方天下,分掌风、调、雨、顺之职,他们各自脚踩面目狰狞的鬼魅,寓意四大天王为使天下风调雨顺,必须镇服人间邪恶。

登上天王殿后的石阶,便来到大雄宝殿。大雄宝殿供奉着佛教创始人释迦牟尼像,是整座寺院的核心建筑,它的建筑形式叫庑殿式,是中国古代最高等级的建筑形式,只能用于皇家和孔庙,这在民间几乎是看不到的,由此可见,潭柘寺与皇家文化

Tanzhe Temple

Yu Boyang and Liu Yiran, with Kelsey Rick and Anna Wondrasek, editors

Space and History

Tanzhe Temple was originally a small temple named Jiafu. It was built in the first year of Yongjia in the Western Jin Dynasty (307). Because of the dragon pond and banyan trees on the mountain where the temple is located, people called the temple *tanzhe*, which means "pond and banyan trees." During the period of Emperor Wu Zetian (624–705) in the Tang Dynasty, a large temple complex was built around Jiafu Temple, forming the layout that we see today. Tanzhe is known for its long history, privileged location, and imposing architecture, enjoying the reputation of being "the first temple in the capital city." With a 1700-year history, it is 800 years older than the city of Beijing. As people commonly say, "Tanzhe Temple came first, followed by the city of Beijing."

Tanzhe Temple "sits in the north and faces the south." Its buildings and gardens adopted a traditional Chinese style, featuring a symmetrical layout, a north–south orientated central-axis, and solemn and majestic building groups, similar to the design of the Forbidden City. The most important buildings are lined up along the central axis, including Mountain Gate, Tianwang Hall, Daxiong

72. 天王殿 Hall of the Heavenly Kings

73. 透过香炉看到的转经筒 Tibetan prayer wheel as seen through incense burner

的联系非常紧密。

潭柘寺内建筑的地势层层拔高，中轴线的终点是一座阁楼式建筑，名曰"毗卢阁"，殿内供奉五方佛。除中轴线上的主建筑外，东、西两路的建筑也别具一格，东路建筑以庭院为主，有行宫院、方丈院、流杯亭、地藏殿、圆通殿、舍利塔等。西路建筑多为自成系统的独立殿堂，有楞严坛、大戒台殿、药师殿、文殊殿、观音殿、龙王殿等。

龙王殿位于观音殿西侧，殿前门廊上悬挂着一条石鱼。传说石鱼是由天上掉下的神石雕刻而成，能解人间干旱，游人去潭柘寺，必做的一件事就是摸石鱼。石鱼作为潭柘寺的古迹，展现了古人面对自然灾害的抗争和对美好生活的向往。龙王殿的存在使历史悠久的佛教庙宇与最贴近百姓生计的农业生产问题在同一时空中紧密地联系在一起。

潭柘寺作为北京的旅游胜地，以其得天独厚的地理位置和人文景观吸引大批游客到访，现已成为北京旅游的一块名片。潭柘寺的文化底蕴不仅仅体现在历史建筑和人文景观上，还体现在以"禅茶一味"为代表的中国佛教文化和丰富的民俗文化中。

禅茶文化

潭柘寺内有两处公共饮茶空间，一为上文提到的露天茶座，二为更具私密性与舒适性的玉兰茶楼，位于寺内西路建筑靠南的千佛殿阁楼外廊。禅茶文化，是中国传统文化史上的一种独特现象，也是中国对世界文明的一大贡献。茶与禅本是两种文化，在其各自漫长的历史发展中，发生接触并逐渐相互渗入、相互影响，最终融合成一种新的文化形式，即"禅茶"文化。

74. 龙王殿前石鱼 Stone fish in front of Dragon King Temple

Treasure Hall, and Pilu Pavilion. Emperors had adored the temple since the Jin Dynasty (266–420). People of all classes—from emperors and empresses, to princes and ministers, to ordinary people—have made pilgrimage to Tanzhe. Emperor Kangxi (r. 1661–1722) of the Qing Dynasty endowed Tanzhe with the title "royal temple." For people from Beijing, Tanzhe is not merely a temple; it signifies the glories of Beijing in the past. During the Five Dynasties Period (907–979), Chan (Zen) Buddhism Master Chongshi from Hunan honored Tanzhe Temple as the "ancestral temple." Since then, Chan Buddhism has flourished in this temple

The two ginkgo trees standing in front of Tianwang Hall, which are said to be over 1400 years old, are for many the highlight of Tanzhe. The trees are believed to contain miraculous spirituality. Emperor Qianlong (r. 1735–1796) even offered an imperial name for them: "The Imperial Trees"—so far the highest title granted to trees by emperors. When autumn arrives, the falling, golden leaves turn the temple into a fairyland. Since 2009, the temple has been holding "Royal Ginkgo Viewing Season" to attract visitors.

The best angle to watch "The Imperial Trees" is from the teahouse in front of the Mountain Gate. The antiquity of the ginkgo trees and the cycle of their leaves fascinate people, providing total relaxation for body and mind. Many people visit the temple in the fall. Mr. Zhang and Mr. Li come together every fall to taste tea, enjoy the warm sunshine, and play chess. "Beijing is full of stress. We need a place like Tanzhe Temple. It is an escape."

From the teahouse, a stone pathway leads to Tianwang Hall. In its middle stands a giant Tibetan Buddhist prayer-wheel. A six-character mantra, the Guanyin Mantra 唵嘛呢叭咪吽 ("*Om Mani Padme Hum*"), is engraved on it in Tibetan. Tibetan prayer flags wave in the wind. People visit in streams. The golden wheel reflects the golden ginkgo leaves close by, shining and glowing in the fall sunshine. According to Tibetan Buddhism, rotating the prayer wheel and chanting the six-character mantra have incredible merit. It is also easy to practice. Tibetan

75. 玉兰茶楼 Yulan Tea House

Buddhism and Han Buddhism intersect here, a manifestation of Chinese culture's embrace of diversity and the Chinese people's unbounded approach towards religions.

The paved pathway leads to Tianwang Hall, which is dedicated to Giant Belly Maitreya. Maitreya sits in the middle of the hall, flanked on each side by the Four Tianwang, (Four Heavenly Kings), each of whom is associated with a different cardinal direction and oversees a different function. By their feet are some vicious-looking devils, implying that in order to relieve the world of disaster, the Heavenly Kings must remove the devils.

Ascending the stone steps, one arrives at Daxiong Hall, which houses Śākyamuni Buddha. This is the central building of the temple complex; therefore it was built with a "hip" roof, the highest grade in ancient Chinese construction, used exclusively for the royal palace and Confucian temples. This draws a clear connection between Tanzhe Temple and the royal family.

Along the central axis, the elevation gradually increases, ending at a loft-style building named Pilu (Vairocana Buddha) Pavilion, which is dedicated to the Five Buddhas. Like the buildings on the central axis, those to the east and west of the axis have their own distinctive characteristics. The eastern area is mainly courtyards, such as Xinggong Courtyard, the Abbot's Court, the Stream Cup Pavilion, the Earthen Temple, Yuantong Hall, and the stupa. The western area mostly contains independent halls, including the Yantan Temple, the Great Ring Temple, the Pharmacist Hall, Wenshu (Mañjuśrī bodhisattva) Hall, Guanyin (Avalokiteśvara bodhisattva) Hall, and the Dragon King Hall.

Hanging from the front porch of Dragon King Hall is a stone fish, said to be made from a stone that fell from Heaven that has the ability to relieve drought. All visitors must touch the stone fish, a symbol of the determination of ancient people to counter natural disasters. Dragon King Hall thus connects holy religion with the livelihood of earthly people.

Aside from its geographic location and architecture, Tanzhe Temple attracts a large number of tourists for its ability to embrace diverse Chinese culture such as "the oneness of Chan and Tea" and the colorful Beijing folk traditions.

Chan–Tea Culture

There is another teahouse besides the one mentioned above—Magnolia Teahouse. It is located in the outer corridor of Thousand-Buddha Hall, which is in the southwestern part of the temple complex. It is more private and comfortable.

Chan (Zen)–Tea is a unique element of Chinese culture and a contribution China made to the world. Tea and Chan which come from two different origins, encountered at some point in history. Through mutual influence, they developed into a new cultural form: Chan–Tea, containing in itself the important Chan messages of letting go of the ego and abandoning all that is unnecessary. The flourishing of both Chan and tea in the Tang Dynasty (618–907) led to the development of Chan–Tea culture.

The tea ceremony, which involves tea brewing and tasting, adopts the same principles as the Noble Eightfold Path. When brewing tea, it is necessary to apply mindfulness. Only by using concentration can one make tea of good color, aroma, and taste. When drinking tea, one should sit upright and still, focusing on inner peace. This is similar to the meditation of Chan Buddhism. "The oneness of Chan and Tea" was therefore coined as a Buddhist term. Chan is an indescribably holy state, focusing on the self-awakening of the mind. Tea is the physical carrier of the Chan spirit. Oneness suggests the unity of both mind and tea and of mind and mind. From a religious perspective, oneness is the unity of a holy state and the secular world.

潭柘寺

76. 帝王树 The Imperial Trees

77. 莲灯 **Lotus candle**

In Chan's view, all living creatures are equal and undifferentiated. In the path of learning and seeking enlightenment, one should be self-based, self-cultivated, and self-awakened, just like tea tasting, in which the taste of the tea can only be understood by applying one's own senses. The tea ceremony also reveals the minimalistic approach of Chan—to eliminate all delusions and distresses from the secular world, turn complexity to simplicity, and seek a state of peace and tranquility.

The Chan tradition of tea tasting exemplifies the approach to embed Buddhist philosophy and cultivation into routine activities such as tea tasting. According to Chan, seeing the purified mind of self is to see the Buddha and to be the Buddha. In "the oneness of Chan and Tea," tea is the core that reveals Chan's spirit; Chan represents the philosophy carried by the tea aroma. Tea's spirit is therefore uplifted. Chan advocates sudden enlightenment, which uses parables and *gong'an* (*koans*) to rid ignorance and find enlightenment. The Buddhist philosophy embedded in "the oneness of Chan and Tea" is one application of sudden enlightenment. It talks about tea without mentioning tea, alluding to Chan with tea without mentioning Chan. This is one form of Chan cultivation, namely cultivation through non-cultivation, which is astonishingly similar to Daoism's advocacy of achieving through non-action (*wu wei*). Chan and tea, two originally unrelated cultural symbols, met and merged to form a simple but important term in Chan Buddhism.

The architecture and scenery of the temple are physical representations of Buddhism's localization in China. The temple has carried forward the spirit of Chinese Buddhism in the form of Chan–Tea. Tanzhe Temple not only displays a profound historic mark but adapts itself to the new modern era.

泡茶、喝茶这一过程，可以说与修行佛陀的教诲"八正道"相一致。因为泡茶时，要以正念、正定的心境，集中精神专注于茶道，才能使泡出的茶汤凝聚好的色、香、味。此外，少语端坐、宁静致远的喝茶状态，也类似于佛家的坐禅修行，因此才有"茶禅一味"——喝茶和修禅是一个味道的佛门禅语。其中，禅是一种不可名状的神圣境界，其精髓在体悟自心；茶是禅的物质灵芽，"一味"代表心与茶、心与心的相通，二者的结合从宗教的意义上来说，可谓神圣与世俗的高度融合。

在禅宗看来，众生是平等无差别的，在修学悟道上所有众生都需立足本我，自我修学，自我悟道。犹如饮茶，茶味如何只能通过自己的品尝，由味觉这一自我感官获得信息。饮茶这一的过程告诉我们，若要修学入禅，必须祛除个体在烦扰尘世中生起的诸种分别妄念，要懂得化繁为简，将生活中的一切烦恼执着归于宁静平实。

饮茶这一禅门风俗，是把佛教哲学日常化、日常生活哲理化，并将佛教修行生活化、佛教义理行为化的禅机秘钥，把禅门不可言说的修行奥秘通过日常生活中最平凡、最不起眼的饮茶行为展现出来。在"禅茶一味"的语法中，茶凸显了禅的本质和核心，揭示了禅的特色和精神；禅则代表了馥郁茶香中凝聚的境界和哲理，升华了茶的气质和灵魂。除此之外，禅宗主张"妙悟"，即借用比喻、公案等方式点拨愚痴、启迪众生，"禅茶一味"中蕴含的佛教哲理正是"直指人心，见性成佛"的妙悟方式之一。禅门以茶言法而不讲法，以茶喻禅而不说禅的文化表达方式代表了禅门"无修而修"的修行形式，与道家倡导的"道常无为而无不为"有异曲同工之妙，最终构成了"禅茶一味"这一蕴藏禅门机要于朴素生活的禅门语法。

民间传统

"帝王银杏观赏季"是潭柘寺最负盛名的观赏活动，每年都会吸引大批游客、信众前来，帝王银杏树的观赏季为10月末到11月初，被金黄色树叶覆盖的潭柘寺是孩子们眼中的童话世界，也是大人们眼中的人间天堂，老舍说"北平之秋便是人间天堂"，那么与北京城有着千丝万缕联系的潭柘寺便是把这天堂的美景悉数呈现在游客眼前。

潭柘寺之秋是京城百姓休闲度假的好去处，到了万物复苏的春日，二乔玉兰的竞相绽放，便用斑斓的色彩宣告古刹春天的正式到来。潭柘寺"二乔玉兰观赏季"的举办时间依花期而定，大致为每年的3月底至4月中旬，广大游客和摄影爱好者届时将纷至沓来，共赏潭柘寺的佛光禅影玉兰香。

每年腊八节，潭柘寺都会延续佛教千年的传统，支起粥锅，为八方游客施粥，纪念佛祖成道日。腊八节，俗称"腊八"，即农历十二月初八，源自中华民族的一个传统节日"腊日"。古人在腊八节有祭祀祖先和神灵、祈求丰收吉祥的传统，一些地区有"喝腊八粥"的习俗。据民俗专家介绍，"腊八"一词起源于南北朝时期，本为佛教节日，后经历代演变，逐渐成为家喻户晓的民间节日。相传释迦牟尼出家修行六年无果，静思太过，饿晕在菩提树下，一个牧牛女经过，施以杂粮、野果、清泉同煮的一碗粥给世尊吃。世尊吃完后气力恢复，继续在菩提树下打坐，七天后，终于在腊月初八悟道成佛。故此，十二月初八也被定为佛教创始人释迦牟尼成道之日，亦称"法宝节"。

这一风俗将佛教的盛大节日与中国传统的民俗结合起来，使两种文化相互交织，在一个共同的节日里以特别的方式面向广大僧俗。寒冬里包裹严实的游客和信众，在

78. 观音菩萨 Statue of Avalokiteśvara

Diverse Folk Traditions

Tanzhe Temple holds major rites, organizes scenic-view events, and offers free congee during the Laba Festival. Its appeal to Chinese folk culture is evident.

The annual Royal Ginkgo Viewing Season, held between the end of October and beginning of November, attracts many tourists and worshippers. The golden-leaf-paved temple is a fairyland in the eyes of children and a paradise in the eyes of adults. The famous writer Lao She (1899–1966) once wrote, "The fall in Beijing is the paradise of the human world." Tanzhe Temple demonstrates Lao She's point.

When creatures awaken in early spring, the dual-colored magnolia trees gradually start to blossom, announcing the arrival of spring. The magnolia viewing season is between the end of March and April, subject to the exact days of the blossom. Many visitors and photographers come for the aura of the Buddha and to appreciate the beauty and fragrance of the magnolia flowers.

Every year, Tanzhe Temple carries on the 1000-year-old Buddhist tradition of offering congee called "Laba" to visitors and worshippers to commemorate the Buddha's day of enlightenment. The Laba Festival is held on the eighth day of the twelfth month of the lunar calendar. According to scholars, this day was originally used to pray for a good harvest and worship the ancestors. In some regions, people would eat "Laba" congee on this day. Later, during the Southern and Northern Dynasties (386–589), Buddhists began practicing the festival of "Laba." Even later, it evolved into a folk festival for all.

品尝手中腊八粥的那一刻，体现了腊八节背后蕴含的民俗、佛教文化的双重价值，腊八粥表面袅娜升腾的热气仿佛使整个腊月里的严寒荡然无存了。由此可见，异质文化对中国传统文化的影响之深远，亦可见中国文化兼容并包、有容乃大的宽广胸怀。

个人实践

潭柘寺作为北方地区的一处佛教中心，以皇家青睐和灵验在信众中享有崇高地位，吸引广大游客和信众前来求姻缘、保平安，使内心获得一份暂离俗世的平静。T小姐与潭柘寺的因缘是在获得佛祖保佑的基础上建立的，北漂的她作为一个初入职场的新人，遭遇了工作和精神的双重压力：职场上激烈的竞争和居住在外地的亲人忽得急病住进ICU（重症监护室）昏迷不醒。T小姐来此在潭柘寺供奉的每一尊佛像前鞠躬跪拜，祈祷自己和家人摆脱厄运，在得知亲人从ICU转入普通病房后，T小姐放声大哭，从此成为潭柘寺的常客。"我并不是一个虔诚的信徒，可能只勉强算得上一个信众，我再次来到潭柘寺是为感谢佛救了我的亲人，仅仅这一番机缘就已经足够我到这里来还愿一生了。"

Z先生曾经在潭柘寺山下门头沟城镇里面教书，退休之后因为个人兴趣和朋友介绍开始学起佛法，时常来潭柘寺进香参拜，Z先生认为潭柘寺所见没有让他体悟到佛法真谛，很多信众试图用施舍钱财的方式减轻自身业力，使佛教清净地沾染了俗世的污浊之气。"钱财一物，对世俗中的人固然是可以追求的，让人可以活得顺遂舒适，确实是个好事物。但生财之缘也是在因缘际会当中降临到某个人身上，企图用一段因缘结束另一段因缘，一方面劳民伤财，另一方面更是增添了自己身上要还的因果，反而阻碍了求觉悟的路。"Z先生认为这些人或许可以称得上信众，但绝对算不上信徒，用金钱作为救赎自己的工具，未必能求得解脱。

很多信众，尤其是深度研习佛法的居士认同Z先生的看法，但也有不同的声音出现：认为不管用什么方式，能够得到内心的平静也是与佛教的善缘。"佛教讲求缘分，我学佛，我与佛便有佛法上的缘分；旁人求佛，他们与佛便有他们之间的缘分。众生与佛教机缘不同，但总是殊途同归的。"手捻佛珠的一位信众如是说。

总的来看，潭柘寺在当下快节奏的都市生活中，形成了以佛教为中心，辐射儒道、民俗、旅游等与百姓生活息息相关的多元文化圈。寺庙的宣传更加注重民俗、文化、观赏这三方面，对寺院自身的宗教功能略显忽视，这是潭柘寺现代转型的特点。多元文化的统摄为潭柘寺增添了多样性，但与此同时，也反映出了中国人信仰的混杂性与功利性。这种多元文化的共存模式，是中国佛教的一个缩影。

The Buddhist legend is that Śākyamuni practiced for six years fruitlessly. While meditating, he lost consciousness, suffering from starvation. Then a cow-maiden passed by, offering him congee made of grain, wild fruit, and spring water. This enabled Śākyamuni to recover his energy and continue his meditation. Seven days later, on the eighth day of the twelfth lunar month, he attained enlightenment. Therefore, the eighth day of December is designated as the day when the founder of Buddhism, Śākyamuni, became enlightened. It is also known as the "Fabao Festival" (in commemoration of the Buddha's teaching).

Tanzhe's Laba tradition exemplifies the integration of a Buddhist festival with Chinese tradition, the interweaving of the two cultures. It is a celebration for both monks and laity. The warmth of the congee dispels the chill of winter. Foreign culture has a deep effect on Chinese culture, and vice versa. Chinese culture warmly embraces other cultures.

Practice

Tanzhe Temple's reputation is also a product of its efficacy. Many people visit the temple to seek safety, good marriage, and peace. Ms. T feels deeply connected with the temple, for this is where she receives Buddha's protection. When she began her career as a "Beijing Drifter," the stress and loneliness was unbearable. At the same time, a member of her family was sent to intensive care unconscious. Ms. T came to the temple, bowed, kneeled, and kowtowed to every god. When the family member was later transferred to an inpatient unit, she exclaimed, "I am not a devout believer and hardly can be considered a believer. I merely wish to thank Buddha for saving my loved one. This one-time favor deserves my lifetime devotion."

Mr. Z used to be a teacher in Mentougou, which is a town down the hill from Tanzhe Temple. He started to practice Buddhism after retirement, often coming to Tanzhe Temple to worship. But he is not convinced that what he sees at the temple conveys the true message of Buddhism. Many visitors try to use money in lieu of practice or cultivation. That seems to contaminate Buddhist values. "Money is a good thing for secular people. But money is also a connection, a result of another cause. Trying to use one connection to end another connection aggregates one's debt and hinders the road to enlightenment." For Mr. Z, these people are, at best, followers, not believers. Using money as a tool for redemption is not effective.

Many agree with Mr. Z, including those who are proficient in Dharma. According to one, "The goal is to have a peaceful mind and to make connections with Buddha. How to reach that goal is everyone's choice." While fingering a rosary, another said, "Buddhism believes in connection. I adopted Buddhism; therefore, I have a connection with Dharma. Others pray to Buddha, and they have their connections. The connections are different, but all paths lead to one end."

Although Tanzhe Temple is rooted in Buddhist religion, it also serves as a cultural center and tourist destination. The temple's advertisement emphasizes the latter more than the former, a sign of its transition to the modern era. In taking an integrating and utilitarian approach towards religion, it serves as a microcosm of Chinese Buddhism more broadly.

天宁寺

钟秋思

历史

女性在中国佛教历史上一直占据了独特的位置。据《比丘尼传》记载，净检法师是我国第一位比丘尼。她于西晋建兴年间（313--317）受十戒，并在洛阳宫城西门建立了中国第一座尼众寺庙：竹林寺。这便是中国比丘尼制度之始——证明了女性不只能在家奉佛，还可以深入佛门学法修行。在中国传统的社会里，女性的社会地位和经济能力很低，比丘尼教团的存在为女性开辟了一条"传统家族"以外的出路。在给予出家女性一个心灵抚慰的同时，佛教还赋予了她们新的社会角色，使其能以独立的姿态重新进入了社会，并实现对自我存在价值乃至宗教理想的权利的追求。因此，历经发展、鼎盛、衰落，比丘尼制度对中国社会的影响仍源源不绝。

历史上，作为中国主要政治中心的北京存在过诸多尼寺，也有过为皇家私用的"内寺"。而今，仍保留宗教活动的尼寺仅两所。其中，天宁寺是北京创建年代最早的庙宇之一，位于现在北京西城二环广安门外北护城河西侧的胡同之间。据历史记载，天宁寺于唐代始建，辽天庆九年（公元1119年）建造寺内舍利塔。经多番损毁、重建、修缮，原有建筑现仅余山门殿、东西配殿、接引殿及舍利塔。中华人民共和国成立后，寺院曾一度被工厂陆续占用。直至2000年，政府决定恢复天宁寺为宗教活动场所，在原有建筑基础上重建。2007年前后，天宁寺作为宗教场所恢复使用，成为一座弘扬净土宗的尼众道场，免费向公众开放。

天宁寺第一重的山门殿内，立有一尊面向寺外的铜制弥勒菩萨像，以笑脸接引众生，让有缘接触佛法之人能心生欢喜。其背面站立一尊韦陀菩萨像，面向寺内，以示保护寺庙。前院正北方便是天宁寺主殿"接引殿"，殿内以阿弥陀佛接引立像为主尊，手结接引印。东西两面的墙壁上分别绘有佛陀在世时给众弟子说法及西方极乐世界的场景。围绕着阿弥陀佛像，大殿的东西两侧、排着整整齐齐的拜垫，供香客跪拜礼佛。拜垫是中国佛教用来礼佛、拜忏的一种工具。呈四方形，上边两个角较高，下边两个角较低，这样的倾斜坡度有利于礼佛时不费力气。我本身是不信仰任何宗教的，但是被这阿弥陀佛的庄严所震慑，也被旁边信徒的虔诚所感染，不由自主地也拜了三拜。

接引殿后的"天宁寺塔"，总高度为57.8米，塔的莲座之上建有十三层密檐，每层系缀风铃，每逢风起，铃声铿锵。塔身浮雕金刚力士、菩萨、云龙等纹饰，已有不少破损。由于寺塔供奉佛舍利，在信众心中颇具神圣地位。常有信众按照顺时针的顺序环绕寺塔行走祈福，更有虔诚的居士跪拜绕塔，来表示自己的信仰之心。

天宁寺塔东、西两侧分别为药师殿、弥陀殿。药师殿供奉东方三圣，立的是生者的吉祥牌位。信众将在世的亲友名字填写在红色的吉祥牌位上，僧众念经祈福，祈求生者祝寿康宁，吉祥平安。弥陀殿供着的西方三圣，立的是亡者的往生牌位。信众将往生的眷属名字填写在黄色的超度牌位上，僧众念经超度，消除逝者的业障，助其早日到达西方极乐净土。两个殿内都密密麻麻摆满了居士们书写的牌位，生与死通过这样的方式在天宁寺都得到了安置。

Tianning Temple

Zhong Qiusi, with Sara Feldman, editor

History

Nuns have played a unique role in the history of Chinese Buddhism. According to *The Biography of Bhikkhunī*, which was written by Bao Chang in 516, Master Jingjian (291–361) was the first fully ordained Buddhist nun (*bhikkhunī*) in China. She took the Ten Precepts during the Jianxing Period (313–316) in the Western Jin Dynasty and established Bamboo Forest Temple, the first female monastery in China, at the West Gate of the royal palace of Luoyang. This marked the beginning of the Chinese *bhikkhunī* system. Not only could women worship Buddha at home; they could also further their devotion at a monastery. Women had a very low socio-economic status in traditional Chinese society; therefore, the *bhikkhunī* system offered an alternative to familial life. The monasteries provided women with new social roles, where they were seen as individuals able to pursue their own religious values and aspirations.

As a major political center in China, Beijing has had a number of female monasteries over time, including "inner temples" exclusively for royal families. However, only two are currently active, one of which is Tianning (which was also one of the earliest

79. 山门殿拱门下的天宁寺和佛塔 Main temple and stupa of Tianning Temple

实践

天宁寺作为一个女众寺庙，规模较小。少了大寺的喧嚣，一个人坐在前院的银杏树下，听着风吹过天宁寺塔风铃发出的铿锵之声，仿佛置身于另一个世界中。

霜降那日北京气温骤降，在天宁寺我遇到一位露天打坐的男居士。他席地坐在药师殿的拐角，闭着双眼，忽略了来来往往的行人。受他感染，我也坐在石阶上静默不语。过了好一会，这位男居士与我聊起皈依的原因，突然哭了起来。他说"文革"时候，家附近的寺庙的佛像都被砸坏了。他的父亲当时也参与其中。过了这么多年，他一直觉得内心有所亏欠，因此便皈依了佛门。天宁寺离他工作的地方很近，所以闲暇时便会过来，在寺院里面打坐能让他的内心得到平静。

初冬时，天宁寺举行了一次放生法会，前院里摆满了信众买来的鱼、虾、龟、蛙等。放生法事是佛教中比较重要的一项活动，因为佛教认为一切生命都是平等的。经由法师念经、撒净、祈福之后，把这些生物放回山河湖海，恢复其自由的生命，对信众来说是极有功德之事。因此整个法会过程中都是庄严肃穆的，虔诚的信徒穿着海青服站在前排双手合十与女尼们一起念诵，却仍有些游客在不时拍照或是大声喧哗。义工们就需要走到他们面前不停的劝阻，以维护秩序。这些义工属于天宁寺的义工团队，由一位较年轻的男居士负责管理。主要负责协助寺庙的世俗事务，如打扫、餐饮、日常维护、安全保障等。成员以女性为主，年龄多在四十岁以上。有些义工固定每天都来，更多的义工逢周末和举办法会时才来。

80. 天宁寺里的佛塔底座 Base of stupa at Tianning Temple

temples in Beijing). Tianning Temple is located amid the hutongs on the west side of the North Moat outside Guang'anmen, on the second ring of Beijing's Xicheng District. According to historic record, the building of Tianning Temple started during the Tang Dynasty (618–907). Later, during the ninth year of Tianqing (1119) in the Liao Period, the construction of a stupa inside the temple began. From then on, Tianning Temple went through repeated damage, reconstruction, and repair, leaving only Mountain Gate Hall, East and West Side Halls, Ambassador Hall, and the pagoda stupa. After the founding of the People's Republic of China (1949), the temple was occupied by different factories. It was not until 2000 that the government decided to permit religious activities again at Tianning Temple. Reconstruction was conducted on the basis of the original structures. In 2007, Tianning Temple resumed its function as a Buddhist site, a space for female monastics to promote Pure Land Buddhism. The temple is free and open to the public.

Inside Mountain Gate Hall stands a bronze statue of a smiling Maitreya Buddha. Facing visitors, he greets all with great happiness. Just behind Maitreya is a statue of the bodhisattva Skanda, who guards the temple. The next hall to the north is Welcoming Hall, which houses a standing statue of Amitābha Buddha, whose "reception finger" gestures towards his Pure Land in the West, welcoming visitors not only to the hall but also to the Pure Land. Painted on the east and west walls of the hall are scenes of the Buddha preaching to his followers and of the Western Pure Land (Sukhāvatī).

Surrounding Amitābha are rows of mats for people to kneel on and worship. These mats are sloped for the ease of kneeling. I stood in awe of the Buddha, admiring the piety of the followers. I bowed and kowtowed three times.

Behind Ambassador Hall is the Tianning Temple pagoda. Standing 57.8 meters high, the pagoda has thirteen tiers, each with wind chimes hanging on it. When they blow in the wind, they make a mighty sound. At the base of the pagoda, two guardian Buddhist deities (*dharmapāla*) protect the Buddha. Inside the pagoda there are Buddhist relics. The pagoda is therefore a very sacred place for believers. Many people walk clockwise around the pagoda, praying while walking. Some devout Buddhists "walk" around the pagoda on their knees to show their great determination.

On the east side of Tianning Temple is Pharmacist Hall, which is dedicated to the Three Sages of the East. In this hall are red wishing tablets, on which believers write the names of the living. The nuns will chant scriptures and pray for the health, peace, and prosperity of these family members and friends. On the west side of the temple is Amitābha Hall, which is dedicated to the Three Sages of the West. In this hall are yellow, soul-releasing memorial tablets, on which believers write the names of the deceased. The nuns will chant scriptures to release the souls of these deceased family members and friends, eliminating their karma, helping them arrive at the Western Pure Land. Both halls are filled with tablets for the names of lay Buddhists. Life and death are reconciled in this way.

Practice

As a female monastery, Tianning Temple is relatively small. Absent the noises of a larger temple, I was able to sit down under the ginkgo tree in the front yard and listen to the wind blowing through the pagoda and rustling the wind chimes as if I were in a different world.

On the day of "Frost's Descent" (late October or early November), the temperature in Beijing plummeted. I met a lay Buddhist who was meditating in the open air at Tianning Temple. He sat on the corner of Pharmacist's Hall with his eyes closed, unbothered by all the pedestrians passing by. I

机缘巧合，我认识了一位身穿绿军装的义工，他是一个退役的副师长，在新疆兵团工作过很长时间。他告诉我，义工们把为天宁寺提供服务当作一种念佛之外的修行。其中，前院负责香炉的女居士，自天宁寺重新开放便在此帮忙了，至今已有十余年。聊起皈依的原因，他说道："我的父母就住这附近，去年父亲病重搬回来照顾。闲暇会来天宁寺听师父讲课。我年轻时候脾气很暴躁，并且作为军人，习惯用粗暴的方式解决问题。在天宁寺我找到了一种内心的宁静，对自己以往的人生有了很多反思。父亲去世后，我便皈依了佛教。来天宁寺做义工，一是感念佛祖的恩德，想尽自己的一份力；二也是在积累福报。"

这位男义工的心态，代表了现在大部分信众皈依佛教的原因：寄托心灵的安心之所。居士们因为各自的原因，在佛陀的世界里寻到精神的寄托。又因着天宁寺的魅力聚合在这里。不论信众的性别、年龄、职业、过往，天宁寺仍一如既往地以最大的包容之心容纳世人，并给予他们信念的支持。现在的天宁寺，规模比以往小了。但与此同时，信徒更为多元，寺庙的开放度更高，也更加具有活力。社会功能也得到延展——它不仅在信徒的世界发挥着自己的作用，甚至成为了周围居民日常生活的一部分。寺庙山门的东边是一座大型的菜市场，很多老年人买完菜之后会山门前院的槐树下歇凉休息。我几次拜访天宁寺，都见到几位老人坐在山门两侧的台阶上聊天。山门的南面是一所小学，经常有些接孩子的父母聚在这里，也总看到孩子们在山门前院玩耍。人们说话的声音、车辆交错的喇叭声，和寺院内隐隐约约的梵音同一时间都出现在这一方空间内，世俗与神圣就如此奇妙的融合到这方小小庙宇中了。

信念

在天宁寺一众比丘尼当中，心慧法师显得格外出众。初次与心慧接触，就很容易信服于她，做事麻利，说话简洁，考虑周全又不失亲和，不仅颇具出家人的风范，也有传统"礼"教的痕迹。单看心慧的相貌，就如同才二十出头一般，很难判断出她实际上生于1988年，正逢中国巨大变革的年代。

当然，在发心出家前，她还不是心慧，她是刘福慧，一位普通的高中女生。

一次奇妙的机缘，福慧决心"出家"。这个过程起初并不顺利，作为家里的独生女，她承担了家人太多的期望。而福慧从小到大就是一个有主见且倔强的孩子，毅然退学后，前往五台山，成为普寿寺里一名最最普通的女弟子。个子很高的福慧往往让大家忽略她的年纪，她也不以为意，经常主动承担起比较繁重和麻烦的活计。无论多苦多累的杂事，福慧都坚持下来了。在局外人眼里，一个大都市衣食无忧的女孩未遭遇什么重大变故，就坚定地选择出家，这是很难以理解的。在福慧本人看来，这仅仅是属于自己的缘分。二零零五年农历九月十九日，观世音出家的日子，刘福慧正式剃度，成为心慧。

后来因为生病，心慧回到了北京的天宁寺。凭借自己的努力，考入闽南佛学院学习。同所有的有志青年一样，刚毕业的心慧怀着满腔抱负想大展拳脚，却遭遇了现实的冲突。那个时候的心慧将一切问题都归咎于天宁寺。认为这方小小寺庙限制了她的天地，打着心思想离开这里。天宁寺的方丈法恩法师是一个很睿智的人，将一切都看在眼里。她并不直接训斥或说教心慧，而是在日常的细节中指引心慧自己思考如何自处。两人的相处就如母女一般，有冲突有埋怨，但总会给予最大的理解与包容。在法恩法师的引导之下，心慧慢慢地明白了之前自己的意气用事，日益稳重。而天宁寺，

81. 药师殿内的墙壁上挂满了写着生者姓名的小牌子 **Plaques for the living on the walls of Pharmacist Buddha Temple**

followed suit and sat quietly on the stone steps. After some time, he started to explain to me why he converted to Buddhism. He said that during the Cultural Revolution (1966–1976), all the Buddhist statues at the temple near his home were smashed, and that his father was one of the perpetrators. He burst into tears while talking about this. Although many years have passed since then, his mind is still deep in guilt; thus he chose to convert to Buddhism. Tianning Temple is near his workplace, and whenever possible, he comes to the temple to meditate, seeking inner peace.

In the early winter, Tianning Temple held a captive-animal releasing rite. The front yard was full of fish, shrimp, turtles, and frogs purchased by the believers. It is an important rite, since Buddhism believes that all lives are equal. A Buddhist master chants scriptures, cleans the site, blesses the animals, then releases them into mountains, rivers, lakes, or the sea. The believers consider it an act that accumulates a lot of merit. The entire ceremony that day was solemn. Reverent believers in ceremonial robes stood in the front row, chanting scriptures with the nuns. Some visitors, however, shouted and snapped photos, disrespecting the occasion. The volunteers had to go keep them quiet and orderly. These volunteers are part of the volunteer team-members of Tianning Temple, made up mostly of women above forty led by a young layman. They assist with the secular affairs of the temple such as cleaning, preparing meals, and performing daily maintenance. Some members come to the temple every day, but most can only help on weekends or for special ceremonies.

The laywoman who takes care of the incense burner in the front yard was the earliest volunteer. She started her work when the temple reopened ten years ago. The volunteer whom I met was dressed in

天宁寺

82. 弥陀殿里的亡灵牌位 Statue of Amitābha with plaques for the deceased

a green, military uniform. He told me that volunteering at the temple was part of his religious cultivation, like reciting Buddhist sutras. In telling me about his conversion to Buddhism, he said, "My parents live nearby. I moved to live with them last year to take care of my father who was seriously ill at the time. I took some time off to come here to listen to the preaching at the temple. When I was young, I had a bad temper. Being a military man, I was also always rough. Here at Tianning Temple, I have found inner serenity. I started to review and reflect on my past. I converted to Buddhism after my father passed away. Being a volunteer is a way to show my gratitude to Buddha. I want to do my part. I am also accumulating my merits."

This volunteer offers a good example of those who convert to Buddhism to find a space in which to nestle their hearts and souls. For a variety of reasons, they find spiritual support in the Buddhist world, gathering here for the appeal of Tianning Temple. The temple embraces all and offers religious support for all, regardless of gender, age, profession, or past.

Although the size of the temple is smaller than before, Tianning attracts a more diverse group of people today, and is also more open and lively. The temple not only exerts influence among its followers but is also part of the daily life of the nearby residents. To the east of the temple's Mountain Gate is a big farmer's market. Many elderly people like to take a break at the temple after food shopping, sitting and resting in the shade of the banyan tree in front of the Mountain Gate. Every time I have visited the temple, I have seen older people sitting on the stone steps on either side of the Mountain Gate. To the south of the gate is an elementary school. Parents often wait for their children and children often play in the open area in front of the Mountain Gate. The voices of people on the street, honking of car horns, and chanting of Sanskrit phrases intermingle in the air. Thus this small temple miraculously connects the secular world with the sacred one.

Faith

Master Xinhui stands out among the many *bhikkhunī*. The first time I met her, she appeared forceful—acting quickly and speaking concisely, thoughtful but approachable. She had the air of a Buddhist and was well versed in rites and etiquettes. From her appearance, you would assume her to be a little over twenty. In fact, she was born in 1988, during an era of significant change in China.

Before her ordination, she was of course not Xinhui. She was Liu Fuhui, an ordinary high-school girl. But an inexplicable encounter and mysterious connection changed her, determining her to become a nun. It was not a smooth path. As an only child, she carried the hope of her entire family. Ever since she was a little child, she was decisive and strong minded. She quit school, embarking on a journey to Wutai Mountain, where she ended up the most undistinguished member at Pushou Temple—an ordinary nun. Although young, she was tall and was therefore treated like an adult, required to do hard work. But she did not care, often shouldering heavy and difficult jobs. People failed to understand why a carefree girl like her, who lived in a big city and suffered no major tragic events, decided to enter into nunhood. Fuhui knew that it was her connection with Buddhism. On the nineteenth day of the ninth lunar month in 2005, the day the bodhisattva Guanyin became a Buddhist, Liu Fuhui officially took the tonsure and became Xinhui.

Due to the severity of her labor, however, Xinhui became ill and was required to return to Beijing, where she joined Tianning Temple to continue her practice. With much self-effort, she was later admitted by the Buddhist College of Minnan, which is located in Xiamen in Fujian Province. Upon graduating and returning to Tianning, she was primed to

因为有法恩法师的存在，已被她当成了自己的家。

在天宁寺的信众的心中，心慧是具有神圣地位的法师。但因为比大多信徒都年轻，起初心慧也经历了如何端正自己身份的困扰。即使端坐严肃，也未能得到所有居士的尊重，甚至发生过被亲近的居士背弃的事情。心慧自己用了很长时间找到了自己的位置与定位——即使身份是法师，其本质也只是一个凡夫俗子。以何种面貌展现在众人面前并不是最重要，而在于自己所要去践行与传达的内容。心慧说："过于看重自己身份的结果是被困在伪装里，困在对身份的执着里，以自我的本真的面目去传法、授课，反而更加拉近我与其他信众的关系。这也才是修行之人的本来状态。"

现在的佛教与世俗生活的关系结合得更紧密，心慧在选择了一种宗教的生活方式的同时，与父母亲的联系并未改变。多年来也一直相安无事，直至去年父亲生病了，作为女儿的心慧遇到了出家之后的第一个困境：她没有私产可以回馈父母。反哺父母是中国传统的要求，同时也是法律的规定，而佛家却不允许出家人蓄私产。心慧能接受居士们的供养，但只能使用于自己的生活，其他的都被她捐出用于一些寺庙的重建或其他慈善。作为一个自小就接受传统道德教育成长的孩子，这种养育父母的困局在心慧选择出家之时，就已注定了两难。不过惆怅的情绪并未在乐观的心慧身上停留太久，她反过来宽慰我说："总会有办法的"。这种平静的笃定，仿佛心中有光。心慧养了两只加菲猫，并为其中一只取名为"福慧"。照她的解释，这仅仅是一个与她过去有关的"名字"而已。我俩的聊天话题开始越来越远，猫粮、包裹、暖气、学业……正在中国人民大学修读研究生的心慧法师也会因为作业、考试而抓狂。不觉间，我感到"神圣"并未那么遥远，这样"烟火气"的法师更让我心生钦佩。

刘福慧到心慧的身份转换，是由世俗身份向宗教身份的转换——宗教身份赋予她一个独立的社会地位、追求自我存在价值及宗教理想的权利，也展现了现代的北京对于一个女性选择宗教生活方式的包容与尊重。与此同时，新时代神圣世界中的女性无法像历史上那样偏安一隅，并会面临更多的来自世俗的困境。这同样也是现代的天宁寺在现代社会中寻找自己恰当位置的缩影：不断变化的城市环境、多元并存的文化、世俗与宗教冲突带来的必然。在保持着严苛的修行的同时，天宁寺也以一种严谨而不失活泼的姿态向外界展现自己：在微信上，天宁寺拥有自己的公众号，从中可以查询到寺庙的历史、佛教仪规、近期活动，及佛教知识。除了固定的法会，天宁寺还会开设学习班、讲座，带领信众共修。每年它还会举办慈善活动，帮扶"瓷娃娃"协会、残联等机构。改变正在悄然发生，最终会是什么样的我们不得而知，而不会改变的，可能是天宁寺的钟鼓声，始终会在既定的时刻响起，余音缭绕，不偏不倚；可能还有天宁寺的清香，承载着信众厚重的虔诚，轻烟袅袅，缓缓上腾；还有历经千年仍伫立在那里天宁寺塔，信仰不变，只与时间对话。

83. 天宁寺里的香火 **Burning incense at Tianning Temple**

achieve great things, like every ambitious young person. Her aspirations were however thwarted by harsh realities. At the time, she ascribed her problems to the temple's small scale and wanted to leave. But when Master Fa'en, the very wise abbot of the temple, learned of Xinhui's situation, she guided her through every daily detail and helped her think about how to get along with herself, rather than blaming her. Their relationship was like that of a mother and a daughter. Although conflicts and complaints between them surfaced at times, they retained a lot of understanding and tolerance for each other. Through Master Fa'en's mentorship, Xinhui corrected her previous tendency to act on her impulses and became a more thoughtful person. Because of Master Fa'en, Tianning Temple is still home for Xinhui.

Believers now regard Xinhui as a sacred Dharma master. But for some time, she was not sure how to position herself, as she looked much younger than the majority of the believers. Even though she sat calm and still, she could not earn their respect. Even worse, some of her lay Buddhist followers (who were helping to support Xinhui at the temple) stopped associating themselves with her. It took Xinhui a long time to find herself again. She came to realize that, although a Dharma master, she is still an ordinary person. How she presents herself to the public is of secondary importance. The most important thing is the message she delivers to the believers through her words and actions. Xinhui said, "I was puzzled since I was trapped in the 'disguised me' that I had created for myself. I was stuck with the issue of seeking identity. Actually, I just needed to be myself, focusing on preaching and lecturing. The distance between the followers and me is narrowing. A practitioner is meant to be in this state."

84. 药师佛像下方摆放着举行仪式时候尼姑使用的颂词 Statue of Śākyamuni Buddha with eulogy used by nuns during ceremony

No longer does Buddhism isolate itself from secular life. Though Xinhui chose to devote her life to religion, she did not cut off contact with her parents, with whom she still gets along. Last year, Xinhui's father fell ill. For the first time since she became a Buddhist, she faced a tough situation as a daughter since she had no money or material goods to give to her parents. Reciprocating the favor of parents is an expectation in traditional Chinese society; it was even written into law. However, Buddhism forbids amassing private wealth. Xinhui can accept offerings from lay Buddhists, but these offerings can only be used for her living expenses. The rest has to be donated for renovation of the temple or acts of charity. This dilemma is one she has faced since the day she became a nun. But she was not sad for long. She comforted herself, saying: "I will find a way." She showed great calmness and determination as if the holy light were shining upon her.

Xinhui is raising two exotic shorthair cats. One she named Fuhui, her former name. We started to chat about cat food, packages, heating, and study. Xinhui also spoke about how she is now pursuing her master's degree at the People's University of China, and how the homework and exams are causing her great stress. At this moment, Xinhui, master of the sacred world of Buddhism, was just an ordinary person. Her "secular side" only made me admire her more.

The transition from Liu Fuhui to Xinhui is the transition of identity from a secular individual to a religious person. Religion provides her with an independent social status and the right to pursue self-accomplishments and religious ideals. Xinhui's story reflects Beijing's embrace of and respect for religious practice by women, even if female Buddhists in the modern world can no longer be like their ancient predecessors, nestled quietly in a holy space. On the contrary, they are constantly facing challenges from the secular world.

Today's Tianning Temple is situated in a modern environment—a bustling, changing city of diverse cultures and constant clashes between religious and secular beliefs. Internally, they stick to their rigid practices; however, when presenting to the public, they adopt a flexible and relatable manner. The temple has a public account on WeChat, where one can learn the temple's history, regulations, and events, as well as basic knowledge about Buddhism. The temple also holds classes and lectures for the public and organizes charitable activities, including assisting with the Porcelain Doll Association (which helps children with osteomalacia) and the China Disabled Persons Federation (which helps people with disabilities).

The world is changing. What is going to become of Tianning Temple is unknown. But the sound of ringing chimes, the aroma of burning incense, and the thousand-year-old pagoda will always be the same. Time never stops moving, but faith is eternal.

通州清真大寺

黄婧怡

城市

走在通州新华大街上的时候，我产生了一丝抽离感：这里没有共享单车，没有行道树，没有摩天大楼的玻璃幕墙，一切都被浸在薄薄的灰尘里——尽管这种雾霾景观在北京并不罕见。

作为曾经京杭运河与北京长安大道延伸线的交汇处，和八国联军、日本关东军侵入北京的第一个关卡，中仓社区在一定程度上以一个城市边缘区的空间形态保留，散发着北京这个城市已经褪了色的古城气味。历史上中仓社区是一个传统的移民街区。除蒙古族和满族人外，回族人口也占了大多数。明清时（1368-1912）通县因为漕运恢复人气，越来越多的回族人来到这里"淘金"。他们中的大多数人从事与商船运输有关的苦力工作，其他一些人则靠开饭馆为生。如今中仓社区是整个通州地区最大的回民社区，清真餐饮业也成了通州城市的一道名片。

这里是我们曾经称之为"睡城"的地方，北漂们乘坐着6号线，在公寓和办公室之间来回穿梭。这里也是在《北京市总体规划（2016-2035）》发布后，作为"北京副市中心"而为我们所知的地方。通州清真大寺则位于莲花胡同，回民胡同和马家胡同之间的莲花寺街区西北侧，正对面是民族小学。在寺里的一处院子里挂着这样一幅横幅："立足南街，示范全区，影响全市，面向全国，走向世界"。

据说这是不久前，上级领导来寺里视察时的题词。可见为了响应通州市未来的城市规划，处理清真寺的日常工作也得有迎接四方宾客的国际化视野。我的向导王先生知道每一位来做礼拜的人，有时他会随便和他们聊聊。"清真寺向所有人开放，应该欢迎大家来这里，感受真主的慈悯"，他说。

王先生是这里的"土著"和通州清真大寺新一班"寺管会"的成员，负责寺管会的办公室工作。他是当地社区的回族居民，原先是一位普通的铁道工人，后被委派到寺管会。他有一个正在读大学的女儿，在北京西城区的回民学校接受了高中教育。我第一次见到他时是在大寺的北门附近，他正好骑着自行车到达这里，身着一件黑夹克，自行车的前篮筐里塞着几张报纸。白衬衫和黑夹克是老北京回民最常穿的衣服。"可以说，住在中仓社区的回族人是世代相传的穷人"，王先生这么跟我介绍中仓社区的情况，"据我所知，老一代呢，以卖烧饼，水果为生，还有北京回民最经常做的工作：宰牛。80岁以上的人基本上都是文盲，70岁以上的人只接受过小学教育。一直到80年代后出生的一些人，才开始接受大学教育。"在此之前，我对当地生活条件的窘困有所耳闻，大多数的人一直居住在老旧的杂院里，直到2017年之前，他们仍然要靠烧煤供暖。

胡同

胡同里的景观是均匀的，在整个网络中，每个家庭几乎是相同大小的方块格。胡同里的生活是公共和私人空间的交互穿插，因为我可以看到人们自然地把晾晒地

Tongzhou Mosque

Huang Jingyi, with Kameron Tomes, editor

The City

Hallmarks of Beijing such as shared bikes, sidewalk trees, and the glass walls of skyscrapers do not seem to exist on Xinhua Street in the Tongzhou District of Beijing. Their absence led me to wonder whether I was in the capital city at all. However, everything was covered in thin smog, a common sight in Beijing.

The Zhongcang community used to be at the intersection of the Beijing–Hangzhou Great Canal and the extension of Chang'an Avenue in Beijing. It was the first entry point to Beijing by the invaders of the Eight-Power Allied Forces (in 1900) as well as by the Japanese Kwantung Army (in 1937). Historically, this was a neighborhood of immigrants. Besides Mongolians and Manchurians, the Hui people lived here. The opening of the Great Canal created "gold rush" opportunities for Tong County, and many Hui people arrived here during the Ming and Qing Dynasties (1368–1644, 1644–1912), most of whom engaged in the hard labor of boat transportation. Some Hui people ran restaurants. Nowadays, the Zhongcang community contains the largest concentration of Hui in Tongzhou. The *halal* catering industry is prominent in the area.

At one time this area was nicknamed "Sleep City." "Beijing Drifters" rode Line 6 of the metro, traveling back and forth between offices downtown and apartments in Tongzhou, a distance of over twenty kilometers. When the Beijing Blueprint for 2016–2035 was revealed, Tongzhou began to be known as the second city-center of Beijing since the Beijing city government was to be relocated there.

Tongzhou Mosque is located in Lotus Hutong, on the northwest side of the Lotus Temple Community, between Hui People Hutong and Majia Hutong, across from Ethnic Group Elementary School. However, a banner that hangs in the yard of the mosque, carrying the inscription of a high-level government official, proclaims the influence of Tongzhou Mosque on all of Beijing:

> Well established on South Street as an exemplary temple in the district;
> Extending its influence to all of Beijing;
> Embracing the country and orienting itself towards the world.

85. 清真寺正门 **Main gate of Tongzhou Mosque**

86. 重修清真寺的碑文 Stone tablet commemorating the reconstruction of Tongzhou Mosque

衣服挂在墙上，人们在路上也都会互相聊天。这种社会关系就是我们所说的"左邻右舍"，即一种涉及邻里生活状态的习语。胡同的居民是"土著"，每一个小家庭都是大姓氏的分支。具体看来，清真寺周围至少有五种姓氏家族：马姓、金姓、李姓、张姓和杨姓，他们都是穆斯林家庭。还有一些非穆斯林家庭如鲍姓和谭姓，但他们只是小家族。

居住在胡同里的人们也分享着一种共同的文化价值，并以这种共识来保持邻里和谐。每个穆斯林家庭的门口都有一块小铜牌，铜牌上写的是《古兰经》中的某一段经文，大部分的内部都是关于"认主独一"、"愿主祝福"和"驱逐邪魔"等。回民称这种铜牌加"杜瓦牌"或"嘟啊牌"，装饰"杜瓦牌"是他们的习俗。根据莲花寺街区张贴的广告牌中可见，铜牌的内容是"杜哇宜"。"杜哇宜"在阿拉伯语中本意是"祈祷"，是回族语言中比较常用的词汇，比如"请你给我做个好'杜哇宜'"。在"杜瓦牌"的语境中，"杜哇宜"不仅仅是回民家庭的象征，它还有两个功能：提示住在这里的回族居民必须保持回民的操守，遵主命，习"五功"（念，礼，斋，课，朝），待人要诚恳热情，做生意要讲究诚信，在饮食方面要恪守清真；二是提示外人到回族人家里来的时候，千万别带回族人忌讳的东西，说话要谨慎，切不可信口开河。三是告知那些"要乜帖的"（乜帖是阿拉伯语的音译，意味着'需要'，指的是穆斯林向其他穆斯林分散金钱和物质。回民不愿直接说"乞丐"），这是回民的家，不要走错门。总而言之，这是一个信号，提醒人们要讲胡同里的"规矩"。

Tongzhou Mosque is now equipped with a global vision in response to the latest city planning.

Mr. Wang, my guide, knows everyone who comes to the temple to pray. Sometimes he chats with them: "Everyone is welcome here at the mosque. We want everyone to experience the mercy of Allah." Wang is one of the members of the mosque's management committee, the person in charge of the administrative office. A former railway worker, Wang is a Hui native. His daughter studied at the Hui High School of Xicheng District, and now she is in college.

The first time I met Wang, he was wearing a black jacket and white shirt, standard attire for older generations of Hui in Beijing. He arrived at the temple by bike, with a few newspapers in the front basket. "The Hui people of Zhongcang have been in poverty for a number of generations," Wang said to me. "As far as I know, the older generations lived on selling *shaobing* [baked, layered flatbread] and fruit or slaughtering cows, the job for which the Hui are best known. All the Hui above eighty years of age are illiterate, and those between seventy and eighty have only received a basic elementary-level education. Not until the 1980s did some Hui begin going to university." Most of the residents were also living in poverty, a condition of which I had heard rumor before visiting. Prior to 2017, their houses were heated by burning coal.

Hutong

Many members of the mosque live in the surrounding hutong, the layout of which is uniform, all the houses consisting of similar-sized squares. Here, the border between public and private space is not clear, as every household hangs their laundry on their exterior walls, and everybody is always chatting on the street. This is what Chinese call "left and right neighbors." The hutong residents are all natives of Beijing. Here you will find Muslims with the five most common Muslim surnames—Ma, Jin, Li, Zhang, and Yang—whereas the non-Muslims with less popular surnames such as Bao and Tan have small-sized families.

The hutong has its own culture, serving as the bond to keep the neighborhood together. Hanging on doors are bronze plates with inscriptions of verses from the Qur'an like "Oneness of God," "May Allah Bless," or "Dispel the Demons." Hui people call these *dua* plates, making it a tradition to decorate their doors with them. The inscriptions are called *duwayi*, a common word in Hui languages, which is the equivalent of "pray" in Arabic. One example of *duwayi* is simply "Please make a good *duwayi* for me." Each *duwayi* reminds Hui people of the principles of Islam: the revelations of Allah, the Five Pillars, sincerity and honesty, and a strict *halal* diet. A *duwayi* alerts non-Hui people not to bring offensive objects into a Hui house and not to speak carelessly. It is also a signal to beggars that this is a Hui house that should not be entered. In general, a *duwayi* is a reminder of the rules and regulations.

A temple neighborhood, alternatively called a *zhemati*, is a traditional Hui residential community centered around a mosque. People who live in the same temple neighborhood or *zhemati* share a common set of rules and responsibilities and lead a similar lifestyle. A *zhemati* does not have a clear border. Muslim and non-Muslim residents usually co-exist. Lotus Temple Community is one such *zhemati*.

Space

There are nine mosques in Tongzhou District, the largest of which is Tongzhou Mosque. It is one of the most renowned mosques in Beijing. The construction of the Tongzhou Mosque started during the

87. 穆斯林小帽与念珠 Table with Muslim hat and prayer beads *(photo by He Yinglong)*

莲花寺社区与寺坊共存，寺坊或"哲马提"是回族人社区的传统组织形式，指的是在一定地域内以清真寺为核心的生活共同体。居住在寺坊或"哲马提"的人们有着共同的规范和生活方式，也承担共同的社会责任。寺坊或"哲马提"没有明确的地理区划，大多数时候，穆斯林居民和非穆斯林居民住在和寺坊相重叠的同一个社区里。

空间

通州区有九座清真寺。通州清真大寺始建于元朝，是北京最著名的四座清真寺之一。1959年清真大寺被认定为文物保护单位，但在60年代时经历了一系列的破坏。80年代当地的回族居民重新掌握了清真寺的日常事务，并在1989年增加了女寺，重建了建筑群。1995年10月20日，通州清真寺被正式定为北京市第五批市级文物保护单位的成员。最近的一次全面修缮是在2006年，当地政府为清真寺董事会购买家具和修缮建筑物提供了大量的资金支持。在通州市政工程的一些改造计划中，出于文化遗产保护的提议，政府选择对这块街区进行了保护性维修，而不是直接拆迁。

大寺的门楼看起来像蛮子门（一种中国北方的传统建筑风格），有着红色的飞檐和绿蓝相间的斗拱，挂着一块竖匾"礼拜寺"。清真寺内的建筑群被一面方墙所包围，在前门往左右延伸的墙上，用书法写着四个大字：清真古教。门楼的左侧立柱挂着一个竖形的白色招牌，上书黑字"通州区穆光民族双语幼儿园"。清真寺里的建筑群位于主路的左侧，幼儿园则位于右侧。主建筑群在一个院子里。这个院子里分布着

Yuan Dynasty (1271–1368). In the 1960s it was "pulled down" when all its buildings were destroyed except the prayer hall (which Hui residents took turns guarding). The prayer hall was later requisitioned as an electrical factory. Not until the 1980s did local Hui residents regain control of the day-to-day affairs of the mosque. In 1989, a women's mosque was added, and the entire mosque complex was reconstructed. On October 20, 1995, Tongzhou Mosque was officially designated as a member of the fifth batch of municipal-level Cultural Relics Protection Units of Beijing. The most recent comprehensive repair was in 2006, when the local government provided substantial financial support to repair the buildings and purchase furniture. A conservative approach was taken to the repairs to avoid damaging cultural relics and relocating residents.

The gate of the mosque resembles a Manzi Gate, which features red flying eaves and interlocking wooden brackets painted green and blue. A plaque with the characters 礼拜寺 ("A Place of Worship") sits on top. On either side of the gate is a wall that obscures the interior of the compound. The characters 清真 ("Pure and Genuine") are written on the wall to the left of the gate; 古教 ("An Ancient Teaching") on the wall to the right of the gate. A vertical white board reading "Muguang Ethnic Group Bilingual Kindergarten of Tongzhou District" hangs on the left column of the gate, indicating the presence of the kindergarten across the road. Most of the buildings of the mosque are contained in one courtyard. This includes the main prayer hall, a minaret, a screen wall, an office, and a few other rooms. On either side of the prayer hall are characters, the same number on each side. The left side reads 清真有本千秋远 ("The Roots of Islam Are Thousands of Years Old"); the right side, 正教无变万古传 ("The True Teaching Is Unchanged for Hundreds of Generations").

I asked Wang, "How do you know how many people pray here every day?" "I count the shoes at the doorsteps," he replied. "Every day, about 120 people pray here. Some are as old as ninety. Some are Nigerian, Zambian, and South African students studying at the Beijing Conservatory of Music. Four or five Muslim boys from Qinghai and Gansu Provinces also join us."

Next to the prayer hall is a reading room, where religious books are available for the public. The back door of the reading room leads to the ablution room (*wudu*), the corridor of which connects it to a backyard where people park their bikes or chat.

Wang led me to see some tablet calligraphy, the text of which revealed the history of this mosque. In 2011, Zhu Xiangru, a resident of South Street, donated a tablet, summarizing the series of historical events of the mosque. According to the tablet, Muguang Elementary School was founded in 1938, an achievement that involved the collaboration of the renowned Muslim intellectual Jin Jitang and the committee of the mosque. The goal was to provide free education for the children of local Hui people. "Muguang" was invented as the name of the school, with "Mu" serving as an abbreviation for "Muslim" and "Guang" meaning "light." Prior to the establishment of the school, children learned from the imams at the mosque. It was more like a day-care center, however, and the only subjects taught were religion and basic Arabic. Now Muguang Elementary School offers a diverse curriculum including Chinese, mathematics, history, geography, science, art, and physical education.

Life

Routine life at the mosque is peaceful. Hui people arrive at the eastern gate of the mosque by bike. Senior residents gather together, chatting while enjoying the sunshine. "They mostly talk about family issues, mosque affairs, and political events. That is about native Beijing People," says Mr. Wang.

一座礼拜堂，一座邦克楼，一扇照壁，一间办公室和其他的一些房间。礼拜堂左右挂着一副对联：清真有本千秋远，正教无变万古传。

我问王先生："你怎么能知道每天有多少人礼拜呢？""我就数门口的鞋子有多少双"，他回答说，"每天，我们这里能有120人做礼拜，年纪最大的有九十多岁。现在呢我们这里还有来自尼日利亚，赞比亚和南非的北京音乐学院的穆斯林留学生。有时这里有来自青海和甘肃省的回族男孩，大概有四五个。"礼拜堂旁边的一个房间是一个阅览室，它一个公共活动场所，可以阅读一些关于宗教基本知识的书籍。这个阅览室还有一扇通往水室的后门。沿着水室的走廊走出去是一个后院。这个后院是当地人停放自行车，坐着聊聊天的场所。

王先生带我参观清真寺里不同的碑刻。通过这些碑刻的内容，我得以瞥见这座清真寺的变迁。2011年，南大街的一位乡老朱向如撰写了一块新碑，该碑总结了清真寺在历史上发生的一系列事件。正如这座碑所记述的那样，穆光小学最初成立于1938年，是当时非常有名的穆斯林知识分子金吉堂联合清真大寺委员会通力合作的结果，目的是为当地回民的子女们提供义务教育。穆光小学取名为阿拉伯语，意译为"穆斯林之光"。在这所小学出现之前，当地的穆斯林儿童只能在清真寺里跟着阿訇学习，阿訇对他们的照顾类似于一种托管，他们只给孩子们教授一般的宗教知识和基本的阿拉伯，而这种新型小学的教育要教孩子们语文、数学、历史、地理、科学、艺术和体育等课程。如今这是一所公立学校。

历史上，这座清真大寺同样经历过多次重建和修缮。文化大革命期间，清真寺和小学一并瘫痪了。清真寺原本的建筑只剩下了礼拜殿，而为了保护清真寺，当地的回民晚上轮班驻守在礼拜殿内。清真寺一度被征用为通州区的电器厂，主体建筑也得以保留。好在自20世纪90年代以来，当地政府为清真寺董事会购买家具和修缮建筑物提供了大量的资金支持。

生活

清真寺里的精神生活安静而家常。在清早的阳光下，回民们骑着自行车穿过东门来到清真寺，这时候就已经有一些老邻居们沐浴在阳光之下，悠闲地坐在后院里聊天了。"主要谈的呢就是家里事，寺里事和国家事，这就是北京老人们的特点。"有一块黑板靠在后院的墙上，清晰地写着寺里的捐款名录和其他所有支出的细节，还插播了一条有趣的通知："请值班的志愿者，明日上午九点半，在大寺集中开会，布置安全值班事宜。2019年3月4日。"这座清真寺的日常事务都是由志愿者组织的，大多数志愿者55岁或65岁左右的退休人士，他们也是最常来清真寺里礼拜的人。王先生的解释是，比起在家里待着，退休的老人们更有可能在清真寺找到他们的熟人，这样他们就可以消磨消磨时间。一位带着头巾的大姐刚刚来到后院。她下了自行车，迈步走向通往女寺的水房。"哟！你来了呀，你吃过了吗？"，一位坐在后院里的老邻居向她招呼了一声，这是北京人日常打招呼的方式。"吃过了"，她回过头笑了笑，脚步却没停下来。

中国穆斯林要践行五项基本的宗教功课，分别是念功，拜功，斋功，课功和朝功。念功就是念诵"清真言"，拜功要求一个虔诚的穆斯林每日要礼拜五次，分别在晨、晌、晡、昏、宵五个时间段举行，包括叩拜、立正、鞠躬、面朝麦加的方向祈祷，口中念诵信仰告白和《古兰经》选段。斋功既是课税，每年需要交纳一定额度

88. 女寺里的信徒 Women in women's prayer hall

A blackboard in the back yard lists the donations and expenses of the mosque. There is also a notice: "All on-duty volunteers will meet at the mosque at 9:30 tomorrow for shift arrangements during the 'Two Sessions.' March 4, 2019."

The daily work of the mosque is undertaken by volunteers who are mostly retired people between fifty-five and sixty-five years of age. They are also more common at the prayers. Wang explained that these volunteers prefer the mosque to their home since they can chat and spend time with their acquaintances. A woman in a headscarf got off her bike and headed to the *wudu* room of the women's mosque. She was immediately greeted in the most common Beijing way by an old neighbor sitting in the backyard, "Oh, you are here. Have you eaten?" "Yes, I have." She answered with a smile while walking.

Chinese Muslims must practice the Five Pillars: *shahada, salat, zakat, sawm,* and *hajj. Shahada* is to sincerely recite the Muslim profession of faith. *Salat* is to perform ritual prayers five times a day facing the direction of Mecca: *fajr, dhuhr, asr, maghrib,* and *isha*. The prayer is done in the positions of kneeling, standing, and bowing, all while reciting verses of the Qur'an. *Zakat* is to pay an alms tax: 2.5 percent of one's wealth each year to benefit the poor. *Sawm* is to fast during the month of Ramadan. And *hajj* is to make pilgrimage to Mecca. Some Chinese Muslim scholars give unique theological interpretations of the Five Pillars.

All of the traditional, religious, and life rituals of the Hui are held at a mosque so that every stage of a person's life—from birth, to growth, marriage, and death—will be on God's path. Every detail of every ritual therefore needs to be carried out the way God wishes. The most important ceremonies at a mosque are funerals and Jumu'ah services. A yard inside the mosque is specifically dedicated for funerals. The small restaurants near the mosque are also important sites for life ceremonies. People rent out rooms at

89. 礼拜殿大全景 Exterior of the prayer hall

的财产济贫税，作为给社会的奉献。斋功就是在每年在莱麦丹月的斋戒行为，朝功则指的是去麦加的朝觐行为。在中国穆斯林学者的作品中，他们也有着对"五功"独特的神学解释。传统上，回族人的宗教仪式和生命礼仪都是在清真寺里举行的。这意味着一个人的生命，从出生，成长，婚姻和死亡，所有这些阶段都是在真主的道路上。因此，在每一种仪式中，即使是细节的准备也都是按照真主所希望的标准来进行的。现在在清真寺里，最主要的仪式就是葬礼和主麻拜，清真寺里有一块专门的院子，只负责主持葬礼。清真大寺旁边的小楼饭店也经常成为回民度过生命礼仪的重要场所。除了婚宴请酒外，有时也会在酒店包一个包厢为逝者圆经。圆经是在葬礼办完三年左右后对逝者的纪念活动，一般是逝者的亲友在一起追忆逝者，并一起为逝者诵读全本《古兰经》，为其祈祷。

　　今天是星期五，刚好到了昏祷的时候。这时候我正在王先生的办公室里和他聊天，而当门外呼唤祈祷的声音响起时，他立马直直地站了起来，把身子转向西方，小臂屈伸，嘴里默念。透过窗户，我看着他们静静地祈祷，并悄悄听着讲道的声音。"我们共同来学习一下，关于我们的圣人的一些知识，光阴过得很快，使我们，对很多的事情，无暇顾及，就在匆匆的光阴当中，忽然间，我们自己感觉自己已经老了，于是，很多的忽然间随时而出现，教门上始终嘱咐我们的，就是不要拖延功修，有圣训告诉我们，看待后世，就像今天就像死亡一样，所以呢，今天的事情一定要今天完成，因为大能的真主在《古兰经》当中第十七章，第一节中讲到，……那么既然我们归信真主，就要坚定地走在真主的路上，虔诚地做好各项的功修，那么在经典当

90. 礼拜殿内部 **Interior of the prayer hall**

these restaurants not only for wedding receptions but also for Yuanjing, a memorial ceremony on the third anniversary of the deceased, at which family and friends chant Qur'an verses and pray for the deceased.

It was Friday (Jumu'ah). When time for the *maghrib* prayer came, I was still chatting with Wang in his office. Upon hearing the call for prayer, he stood up immediately, turned to the west, and recited silently with arms bent. I accompanied him to the prayer hall, where I listened to the imam's sermon (*khutbah*) from outside: "Let's learn something about our saints. Time passes so quickly that we haven't had a moment for many things before we realize that we are old. Then many issues came up all of a sudden. Islam repeatedly instructs us not to procrastinate. Hadith tell us to treat the next life the same way we treat death. Therefore, we have to finish our tasks today, for the all-powerful God says this in Qur'anic verse 17:1: 'Then, since we believe in God, we must firmly walk on the path of God and devoutly practice.'" The imam who preached was a young person from Cangzhou in Hebei Province. He quoted the Prophet Muhammad's story of ascension (*isra*) and night-journey (*mi'raj*): "Since we believe in Allah, we should firmly follow the path of Allah and be fully devoted to prayer and worship." The young imam spoke slowly and clearly. I guess his topic and explanation were perfectly suitable for his audience, which was mostly composed of elderly people who had experienced difficult lives of tremendous change.

After the prayer and sermon, Wang showed me the kindergarten. He pointed at a small, deteriorated brick building, "I used to study there. The building is the same as before." I asked, "What happens at the kindergarten during a normal school day?" "Oh, they are mostly Han students now. But, you know, they eat Hui meals." The word "meal" in Chinese implies receiving benefits from some benefactor.

中记载，……"在寺里主持"卧尔兹"是一位来自河北省沧州市的年轻阿訇，他引用了先知穆罕默德"登霄"的故事。"既然我们相信真主，那么我们就应该坚定地走真主的道路，并全身心地投入各种各样的敬拜行为"，年轻的阿訇说话缓慢而清晰。我想这个主题太适合他的听众们了。他们是历经生活变迁的老人，喜欢那种温柔的劝诫。

　　王先生陪我一起去看了穆光幼儿园，"就是这栋楼"，他指着一座低矮破旧的砖房："我以前在这里上小学，这栋楼还和以前一样。""现在民族小学的学生怎么样呢？"我问道。"嗯，他们大多数都是当地的汉族学生。但是……你知道嘛……都是吃回民饭的。"他这样回答。一般来说，"饭"这个词在这里不仅意味着用餐，还表示着某种好处。言外之意是，一来既然都受了对方的好处，那么就不应该再挑对方的毛病。二来既然都吃的是"一碗饭"，因此在生活中虽然规矩不同，但都能接受对方的习惯，也要在相处中学会变通，避免起不必要的冲突。中国人的日常交际总是少不了在饭桌上的事，对穆斯林和非穆斯林而言，为了加深彼此间的联系，维持和谐的邻里关系，尊重彼此的饮食习惯也尤为重要。

　　这时候还有一些老人进到寺里来。"说实话，比起和这些老人家打交道，我宁愿让更多的年轻人来寺里看看"，王先生跟老人们寒暄几句后，面露一丝苦笑地跟我说："清真寺没有年轻人，这是现在面临的一个问题。这里的老人们呢，还是比较保守的。不要说对非穆斯林了，他们老是在给年轻人挑错……他们念经的方式啊，他们礼拜的姿势啊……也不管自己是不是对的，就得按照他们的规矩来，这也难怪年轻人不喜欢来这里。……清真寺应该向所有年轻人开放，不是说来这里就一定要让他们做礼拜，就心胸宽阔一点，欢迎他们开看一看。如果有必要的话，在寺里给孩子们留出一块地，让他们放学后有地方可以补补习，做做数学啊，这样他们就会对清真寺，对我们的传统文化呢，比较亲切。"

　　王先生是诚恳而谨慎的。他的烦恼不只属于通州清真寺，新老之间的矛盾几乎无处不在。当年轻人要选择灵性生活时，他们会再次拥抱他们的宗教吗？我对此较为乐观。然而，处理邻里间的那些事，可能要比处理与真主间的关系麻烦得多。城市中的生活变化迅速，要真正接受彼此间的差异，也并非易事。阳光仍然照进院子，在薄雾下伸展。这里的房子是旧的，但一些新事物也正在建设中。那些朴素的穆斯林居民们感受着这些变化，并等待着，像一场无声的功修。

91. 净室外晾晒的手巾 Ablution (*wudu*) towels hanging to dry in the sun

Wang was hinting that if the Han people living in this area are receiving benefits by working in the Hui *halal* food industry, they should be more tolerant. Moreover, since everyone shares the same meal, people should be more embracing, even though different groups have different lifestyles and traditions. People should learn to be more flexible in order to avoid unnecessary conflict. The Chinese emphasize food and dining a lot. For the health of Muslim/non-Muslim relationships, it is important to respect each other's dietary traditions.

As we talked, more senior residents arrived. "To be honest, I would like to see more young people come to the mosque to interact with the elderly," Wang said to me with a smile and a hint of bitterness. "But young people do not come to the mosque. That is an issue we face. The elderly people are conservative. Let's not mention how they treat non-Muslims. They constantly find fault with the young people: the way the young people chant and pray. They never reflect on their own actions. No wonder young people do not like this place. Mosques should be open to the younger generation. They do not have to come and pray. We should be more broad-minded. Simply invite them to come and take a look. If necessary, we will create a space for children to continue their studies after school or do mathematics. If they have more interaction with the mosque, they will feel more comfortable with our traditions."

This is an issue not only for Tongzhou Mosque. There are tensions between young and old generations everywhere. Will young people return to religion and tradition as they mature? I am optimistic. But dealing with interpersonal relationships within a religious community is challenging. Urban life changes so quickly that it is hard to accept those who change with it. The modest Hui inhabitants of the Zhongcang community and Tongzhou Mosque suffer these changes, waiting peacefully, like a silent spiritual discipline.

西什库教堂

丁柏予

几经修建的教堂

北京西什库教堂，也称北堂，位于西什库大街33号，建于清初，时称"救世主堂"。北堂历史悠久，最初建立于清康熙四十二年。因康熙久病，宫中太医束手无策，法国传教士洪若翰、刘应贡献西药金鸡纳霜(奎宁)治愈了康熙帝的疟疾。康熙帝大悦，把在西安门内蚕池口的空地赐给法国神父，作为修建教堂的地基，便建成了最早的"北堂"，名为"救世主堂"，即为西什库教堂的前身。这也是中国第一座皇家承认的天主教堂。

第二次鸦片战争后，中法签订《北京条约》，教堂产业得以收回。1866年元旦，由法国人布里耶设计，新教堂落成。由于教堂所在地蚕池口临近皇家禁地，在北堂建筑顶层能够看见皇家新建的西苑宫苑，据说，高大的教堂钟楼引起慈禧太后的不悦，于是她命总理衙门与法国教士交涉迁移，教堂才最终迁往西什库。1887年，西什库教堂告成祝圣，建成后即作为天主教在北京的总堂。但在1900年爆发的义和团运动中，西什库教堂成为团民进攻的焦点，在当时的义和团营中曾经有顺口溜道："吃面不搁酱，炮打交民巷；吃面不搁醋，炮打西什库"。1901年，庚子事变后，清政府被迫与西方列强签订了《辛丑条约》，根据条约内容，清政府再次出资修缮了西什库教堂。建国后北堂久被学校等单位占用直到1985年春，北堂返还教会。1987年，北堂被列为国家级重点文物保护单位。2004年7月，天主教华北地区主教府正式移交天主教爱国会。

现今的北堂从1985年政府拨款重修之后，已经30年没有进行过大的修缮，这些年在使用中，北堂慢慢地出现了很多问题：地基沉降，屋顶漏水等。现任北堂本堂神父甄雪斌，组织了新一次的翻修：于2016年开始，2018年竣工。他讲到梵蒂冈第二次大公会议为教会提出的新挑战和机遇——如何在保证历史文物独特的魅力价值和符合教会新时代的牧灵需求方面做到平衡，对于北堂此次的修缮工程来说是个艰难的抉择。比如堂内墙面的翻修，在勘察时发现墙面底下绘有大面积的精美粉色爱情花彩绘壁画，北堂考虑到工程量和资金预算，选择了用可逆的方式覆盖保护墙面的方案，但在堂内二楼唱经台处的管风琴右边，仍可见一块粉色彩绘壁画，上面坑坑洼洼的露出斑驳的痕迹。甄雪斌神父解释说这块墙壁是故意留出来的，因为它见证着北堂的历史和原本的样貌，"虽然重新修缮，但我们也不能忘记历史。"

此次北堂的修缮工程，极大改变了堂内整个礼仪空间。堂内廊柱配色将原先的红配绿改成了金配蓝，因经过历史的考察和谨慎地考量，堂务组最终确定最初北堂内部束柱的配色就是蓝色与金色，如今的配色正恢复了老北堂本来的面貌。此外，北京教区主教府移驾北堂，北堂成为天主教北京教区的中心。昔日已成为北京一处景点的北堂迎来了更多的参观游客。对于甄雪斌神父和郭文武神父而言，如何使一座拥有悠久历史的文物面向现在和未来，在满足现今教会礼仪需求的同时焕发出新的生机，为天主教在中国的传播添砖加瓦，是他们所肩负的更重的责任。

Xishiku Church

Ding Baiyu, with Nicole Margheim, editor

A Church through Several Constructions

Xishiku is one of three names for the church located at No. 33 Xishiku Street. Another name is North Church, denoting it as one of the first four Roman Catholic churches in Beijing, each designated by a different cardinal direction. At the time of its construction in the early Qing Dynasty (1703), however, it was known as the Church of the Saviour. When Emperor Kangxi (r. 1661–1722) came down with an illness that the imperial doctors did not know how to treat, two French missionaries, Jean de Fontaney (1643–1710) and Claude de Visdelou (1656–1737), administered the Western medicine quinine, which cured the emperor's malaria. With great joy, Emperor Kangxi rewarded the two French missionaries with a piece of unused land at Canchikou to be used as the site for the church's construction. Church of the Saviour was the first Catholic church recognized by the royal family, the predecessor of the Xishiku Church that we see today.

92. 哥特式的教堂和堂外的中式黄亭 Gothic Cathedral and Chinese yellow pavilion

沟通中西的精神桥梁

西什库教堂融合了中西建筑风格，是北京最大的天主教堂，也曾是北京内城最高的单体建筑。西什库教堂整体布局和环境建造无不体现教堂的悠久历史和与清朝皇家的密切关联。教堂布局具有典型的官署建筑特征，前有朱红色大门，门扉上横竖有九颗门钉，因为在中国古代，九乃数字之极，最能体现帝王的尊贵，寓意九五至尊，朱红色则表示高贵与权威。

圣堂正门月台建有两座十二红柱双顶黄亭，两亭亭顶坐落着龙，亭内石碑以赑屃为底座，赑屃是古代汉族神话传说中龙之九子之首，形似龟，好负重，长年累月地驮载着石碑。相传上古时它常背起三山五岳来兴风作浪，后被夏禹收服，并立下不少功劳。治水成功后，夏禹就把它立下的功绩刻在碑上，由它自己背着，故中国的石碑多由它背起，尤其多见于庙院祠堂里，为镇宅镇物保平安之意，又因其是龙和龟的结合体，被人们认为具有灵瑞之气，能助人升官发财、辟邪祈福，触摸它能给人带来福气，因此龙头龟的某些部位被摸得很光滑。除此之外，亭前石阶前还有两座石狮，象征王者威严、驱凶纳吉，柱头上雕刻石榴，象征教会多结果子，丰收信众。

圣堂呈十字架形，堂门与圣堂尽头分别为十字架竖直方向的两端，祭台在这次修缮中被放在堂内中心位置，其改变有其神学意义：祭台是天主的子女围绕的中心，将祭台放在中心，以便于全体天主子民围绕在周围。左、右两侧和正前方则为教友座席。祭台后方还有游廊，连接着在圣所周围的几个小堂，堂内由金蓝相间的廊柱支撑，与哥特式尖顶相连接在视觉上呈现出百合花绽放的形状，寓意堂内的信友们是结出的果实。堂内尽头悬挂康熙皇帝于1703年北堂建成时亲笔撰书的"万有真原"匾额（仿品），其上为描绘耶稣再临的彩绘玻璃。在这次北堂的修缮中，彩绘玻璃是一大亮点，修缮保留了八扇1985年修缮时安装的彩绘玻璃用以见证北堂的历史，其余的彩

93. 西什库堂内景 Interior of Xishiku Catholic Church

With the signing of the Beijing Treaty between China and France at the end of the Second Opium War (1856–1860), the damaged church property was ceded from the French to the Qing government. According to official church pamphlets, construction of a new church was finally completed on New Year's Day in 1866. However, the church's proximity to the Forbidden City as well as its height—the top of the church could be seen from the newly built Xiyuan Palace of the Forbidden City—provoked the Empress Dowager Cixi (1835–1908) to anger. She ordered the Ministry of Foreign Affairs to negotiate with the French priests to relocate the church to Xishiku, its current site. When the new church at Xishiku was completed and consecrated in 1887, it was designated "the Cathedral of Beijing," meaning it was the headquarters of the Catholic Church in Beijing. Not much later, Xishiku was targeted during the Boxer Rebellion (1899–1901) by Boxer troops, who developed a rallying cry about the church: "Eating noodles without sauce, our cannons will be aiming at the Lane of Jiaomin; Eating noodles without vinegar, our cannons will be aiming at Xishiku." After the rebellion was finally put down by the Eight-Allied Army, the Boxer Protocol (1901) required the Qing government to fund the repair of Xishiku Church. Later, during the People's Republic of China, the church was occupied by schools and other organizations. In the spring of 1985, Xishiku Church was finally reopened for religious use. On June 25, 2006, it was listed as a Major Historical and Cultural Site Protected at the National Level.

No major repairs were made to the church for thirty years after its government-financed reconstruction in 1985. During this time, problems and issues slowly emerged, such as foundation settlement and roof leakage. In 2016, Zhen Xuebin, the priest of the North Church, finally spearheaded a two-year series of repairs and maintenance to the church. The biggest challenge of this process was to preserve the church's historical and cultural heritage while addressing the functional needs of a church in the modern era. When refurbishing the interior walls, elaborate pink-colored, love-themed murals were found hidden beneath the surface of the wall. Due to budget and workload, however, they had to be covered over. A damaged piece of pink mural can still be seen to the right of the pipe organ and choir loft. Priest Zhen explained that, in this one case, they intentionally left the wall as it once was to show the original construction of the church: "Renovating the church does not mean we should forget about history."

During the renovation, the church interior underwent one especially important change: the colonnades that were once red and green were painted gold and blue, reflecting the original appearance of the North Church. The Beijing Diocese Bishop's Office was also moved to Xishiku, making North Church the center of the diocese. The church now attracts more tourists than ever before. Priests Zhen Xuebin and Guo Wenwu take upon their shoulders the responsibility of preserving the church's heritage while meeting the liturgical needs of modern society.

A Bridge to Connect China and the West

Xishiku Church combines both Chinese and Western architecture. It is the biggest Catholic church in Beijing and was, at one time, the tallest building inside the inner circle of Beijing. Both its interior and exterior designs suggest its long history and close connection with the Qing royal family. One clear sign is the vermilion front gate with nine nails on the door. In ancient China, the color vermilion symbolized nobility and authority, while the number nine was the noblest number, corresponding to the extreme prestige of emperors.

On each side of the church's main entrance is a pavilion with red columns and double-layered yellow roofs, each with a dragon on top. Inside the

94. 堂内举行主日弥撒 Procession at end of Mass

pavilions are stone stelae built on top of the legendary figure Bi Xi, one of the nine sons of the Dragon King. With a dragon head and a turtle-shell body, Bi Xi frequently supports heavy stelae. Legend has it that in very ancient times, the mountains rested on Bi Xi's back; when he moved, it caused natural disasters such as a great flood. Eventually he was conquered by Yu the Great of the mythical Xia Dynasty (c. 2070–1600 BCE), after which he made many contributions to the reign of Yu, which are recorded on the stela that Yu asked Bi Xi to carry. Temples therefore often build stelae on top of Bi Xi, in hopes of winning his protection. Since Bi Xi is one-part dragon and one-part turtle, people believe that he contains the auspicious primordial energy *qi*, which helps others gain promotion, earn fortune, and exorcise evil spirits. Touching the head of Bi Xi brings good luck; this is why his head is always smooth. A stone lion stands in front of each pavilion, indicating the majesty and auspiciousness of the church. Pomegranates are carved on the pavilions' columns, demonstrating the wish to be fruitful and gather more followers.

The church is in the shape of a cross, with the main gate standing at the bottom of the vertical axis. The altar is placed at the juncture of the two axes, with a short stone wall behind it. This is a feature of the recent renovation, motivated by the idea that the altar should be surrounded by the children of God. On three of the four sides of the altar, there are seats for church members. Behind the altar, there is a walkway that connects several chapels, hidden from the crowd by a stone wall. The vaulted ceiling is supported by gold and blue pillars, which together create the pattern of blossoming lilies. On the wall behind the altar hangs a plaque with the characters 万有真原 ("The True Source of the Ten-thousand Things"), a replica of an inscription by Emperor Kangxi when the church was first built in 1703, the forty-second year of Kangxi's reign during the Qing Dynasty.

Above the plaque is a stained-glass window of Jesus's Second Coming. Stained glass is one of the prominent features of the recent renovation. Although eight stained-glass windows that predate the 1985 reconstruction were retained as evidence of the history of North Church, the rest were newly created by artists who are highly accomplished in religious art. These stained-glass windows recreate scenes from the Bible, the early Christian Church, the history of the Chinese Church, and Heaven. From the main gate to the far end of the sanctuary, there are more than 100 stained-glass windows. Together with the altar, lectern, and mosaics on the wall behind the altar, they tell the complete history of salvation, creating a holy space for humans to meet God, performing the sacred liturgy as if moving from Earth to Heaven.

Rituals, Space, and Art

Since the Church of the Saviour is the predecessor of Xishiku Church, the recent renovation drew on the theme of "salvation" to decorate and furnish the church, emphasizing continuity through time.

The new altar artfully prefigures God's eternal kingdom, connecting the Eucharist and Christ's sacrifice on the cross. The colored stone painting on the altar is of an innocent lamb, with a golden glowing cross behind it, symbolizing Jesus's victory over death through resurrection. He sacrifices himself in every Mass to reconcile His followers to the Heavenly Father.

The church's stained-glass windows collectively cover three themes: the history of the Church, the life of Christ, and the Second Coming. The stained-glass windows on either side of the pews in the nave concern the journey of the Church, depicting the events of the Apostles and the salvation history of the Chinese Church.

绘玻璃，均由在宗教美学方面有很深造诣的艺术家根据神学思想进行再创作，将圣经故事、教会、中国的教会史、天堂等景象再现其中。从大门直到圣所尽头，共有一百多扇彩绘玻璃窗，讲述了一系列的故事，并与祭台、读经台和圣所屏风的马赛克装饰画构成完整的救恩史，营造出一个天人共祭的神圣空间，象征在人间的礼仪中，信友预尝并参与那在天上圣城耶路撒冷所举行的礼仪。

礼仪空间与艺术

西什库教堂的前身是"救世主堂"，2016年西什库北堂的维修有意识地将"救世主"的精神表现于艺术装潢和礼仪家具中：除了把基督的救赎奥迹作为主题，也展示出初期教会的建立和基督信仰在中国的延续。

维修后，祭台作为永恒国度的预像，使教堂更能完整地诉说天主的造化和救恩计划，让进堂之人犹如迈进天国——祭台上的彩石画有无玷羔羊，其身后有十字架发出金色光芒，象征他曾被宰杀却又战胜了死亡而复活，在每一台弥撒中为信友向天父献上一次而永久的祭献。

北堂的彩绘玻璃主题以三个部分来布局：旅途教会、基督的救世奥迹、天上教会。"旅途教会"以圣堂教友席两旁的彩窗描述宗徒大事录及中国教会的救恩史。西侧玻璃窗讲述了宗徒大事录的事迹、初期教会的诞生以及福音传至罗马，包含了天主选玛弟亚补宗徒缺、圣神降临、扫禄归化、耶路撒冷宗徒会议、圣伯多禄圣保禄殉道等内容。东侧玻璃窗则讲述了中国天主教会的发展史。

天主教在中国就像一颗远跨大陆的树种，时而无声无息，时而嫩芽微露。约公元635年(唐贞观九年)，一批以阿罗本主教为首的教士从中亚来到中国长安(现今西安)传教，来华后称为景教，基督宗教开始传入中国。但直至十三世纪中叶，中国的土地上才出现第一位天主教传教士——孟高维诺主教。孟高维诺被教宗委任为东方全境总主教，并于1299年在元大都（今北京）建立了首座天主教教堂，但随着元朝没落，基督的福音又陷入两个世纪的沉寂。

1583年9月10日，耶稣会士利玛窦与罗明坚进入中国，开启了天主教在中国的新篇章。中国天主教会有"圣教三柱石"之说，明朝历史上的三位大成就者——徐光启、李之藻、杨廷筠——都深受利玛窦的影响并对教会在中国的发展起到了重大作用。这些重要人物和其他里程碑式的历史事件被形象地刻画在北堂的东侧彩窗上，无论是身穿中式官袍却有着西洋长相的教士，还是熟悉的中国土地上耸立着的教堂，每一副彩窗绘画都无声地表达着教会与中国这片土地的密切交融，正如右侧最后一扇窗最终寓意的那样：北京的东、南、西、北堂形成北京四大殿，基督的福音传扬神州大地。

圣所上的第二部分彩窗"基督降生救世的奥迹"，描绘了玫瑰经二十端所述说基督的救恩故事：从天使向玛利亚报喜，直到天主光荣圣母；天主子透过玛利亚降生成人、显示圣荣、救赎世人，玛利亚蒙召升天。从教堂大门进入，经过教友席感悟旅途教会的福传，到接受基督降生救世的奥迹，最后，迎接基督的再来，迈向"天上的教会"。

教堂尽头祭台后上方的彩窗则是"基督再来"：彩窗上部绘有上帝之手，象征天父派遣子；基督两旁围绕着众圣人，互相对列，以圣母玛利亚为首，与向她报喜的总领天使加俾额尔相对，西面紧随普世教会圣人，东面紧随中国圣人。彩窗之下，祭台屏风以三幅彩石画表达天国快要来临。中央绘有中式太师椅样式的基督宝座和鸽子——与彩窗之手、圣子共同表达天主圣三。

95. 讲述了中国教会史的玻璃彩窗 Stained-glass history of the Chinese Church

The stained-glass windows on the west side of the nave show apostolic events, the birth of the early Church, and the spread of the Gospel to Rome. Included here are God's selection of Matthias to replace Judas Iscariot, the descent of the Holy Spirit on the apostles, the conversion of St. Paul, the Jerusalem Conference, and the martyrdom of Saints Peter and Paul.

The stained-glass windows on the east side of the nave instead tell the story of the Chinese Church. Catholicism in China is like a seed that crosses the continent, sometimes growing, sometimes, not. During the ninth year of the reign of Zhenguan in the Tang Dynasty (about 633), a group of missionaries, headed by Bishop Alopen, came to preach in Chang'an (now Xi'an). With them, Christianity—then called *Jing Jiao* ("Bright Sun Religion")—was first introduced to China. However, it was not until the mid-thirteenth century that the first Catholic missionary, Bishop John of Montecorvino O.F.M., appeared on Chinese soil. Montecorvino was appointed by the Pope as the general bishop of the entire East. In 1299, he established the first Catholic Church in Yuan Dadu (now Beijing). However, after the decline of the Yuan Dynasty, the Gospel of Christ fell silent for another two centuries. On September 10, 1583, the Jesuit missionaries Matteo Ricci and Michele Ruggieri entered China, beginning a new chapter of Catholicism in China. Deeply influenced by Matteo Ricci, the "Three Pillars of Holy Religion" for the Chinese Catholic Church—Xu Guangqi, Li Zhizao, and Yang Tingyun—played important roles in the development of the Catholic Church in China. These three figures and other important historical events are depicted on the stained-glass windows on the east side of the nave. Here we see the

西什库教堂

96. 在西什库教堂祈祷的女信徒 Woman praying at Xishiku Catholic Church

blending of Roman Catholicism and Chinese culture—European priests with Chinese gowns, Catholic churches on Chinese land.

The second theme for the stained-glass windows is the life of Christ. These windows cover the east and west transepts. They follow the path of Jesus's life from nativity to public ministry, passion, resurrection, and ascension. One who enters the church through the main gate can therefore experience the entire life of Jesus while walking along the pews of the church.

The third theme in the stained-glass windows, the Second Coming of Jesus, is illustrated on the three walls of windows behind the altar. The central window facing the nave contains the Hand of God, symbolizing the Holy Father sending His Son to the world. On the other two walls (east and west), there are lines of saints, one headed by the Virgin Mary (east); the other by the Archangel Gabriel (west). On the west wall are saints from the Western Catholic church; on the east, Chinese saints. Below the central window of the Hand of God, there is a stone wall with three colored paintings with the theme "The Kingdom of Heaven Is Coming." The middle painting contains a dove above an empty old-fashioned Chinese chair, which awaits Christ's return. Together with the window of the Hand of God, the chair and dove represent the Holy Trinity.

A Peaceful Mind

The North Church attracts many immigrant working-class people due to its visual appeal, complete set of rituals, colorful group activities, and church culture. One sign of this is the increasing number of people signing up for each "Rite of Initiation for Christian Adults."

Yanzi is twenty-seven this year. She was born and raised in a village in Hebei Province with a long history of Catholicism. Her entire village is like a big "family"—people bless each other in happy events, and pray for the souls of the deceased among them. Yanzi used to go to church in her village with her friends. When she moved to Beijing several years ago, she was overwhelmed at first by difficulties and challenges. The pace of big city life was much faster than that of her village, her familiar circle of friends was replaced by unfamiliar people, and she no longer had friends with whom to attend church. Yanzi attended several different churches in Beijing, but was occasionally tempted to skip church services due to her heavy workload. However, her difficulties and challenges, combined with her loneliness, propelled her to quickly establish a relationship with Xishiku so that she would have a place to rest her soul. For Yanzi, church is like a mother with open arms—always ready for the return of a wandering child.

Yanzi has been to all four of the large Catholic churches in Beijing. She prefers the North Church to the other three for its solemn atmosphere and complete liturgy. When she steps in the door every Sunday, then later hears the entrance hymn begin, she is instantly drawn close to God. Everyone is solemn. Along with everyone else, she concentrates on her love and respect for God. When she listens carefully to the sermon, her mind is in total peace. All the worries and stresses of life are instantly gone. When singing "Gloria" and greeting the others, she feels an increased bond with the people around her, even though many are strangers. She no longer feels like an isolated individual in the big city but a member of a Catholic community. Her doubt and suspicion of strangers are removed during Holy Communion. There is no longer any distinction between Beijing people and Hebei people. All are one under God.

When the Mass finishes, Yanzi goes to "greet" the Virgin Mary, remaining there for a few moments. For Yanzi, Jesus and the Virgin Mary are her family, even more so than her own family. She prays to them, confesses her sins to them, and shares stories from her life with them. The North Church provides such a peaceful environment for

灵魂的安详

由于重视礼仪、各方面条件都比较完善，北堂对越来越多外来进京的人群有着极强的吸引力。北堂以自身优越的条件展现出在信仰上吸引大家的优势：壮美的礼仪空间，完整的礼仪安排，华丽的教堂艺术，丰富的团体生活，与时俱进的文化建设。每期逐渐增长的慕道班人数便是有力的证明。

燕子是一名来自河北的平信众，27岁。她从小就是一名天主教徒，出生在一个有多年天主教历史的河北村庄。村庄的信仰氛围浓厚，整个村子如同一家人，谁家有喜事，邻里都会祝福，谁家有丧事，大家都会为亡者炼灵祈祷，平日也相伴一起去教堂。几年前她来到北京，为了解决工作的问题，起初有些折腾。大城市的节奏远比她曾生长的那个小村庄要快，周围也多了许多形形色色的人，这给她带来了一些挑战和难题：脱离了周围都是相同信仰背景的熟人的环境，再也没有当初能和她一起相伴着去教堂做弥撒的亲密伙伴，她只能独自寻找，一个人去教堂；此外，有时工作紧张，甚至需要加班，便会产生不去了的念头，但城市生活带来的紧张和独自为生存奋斗的孤独促使着她寻找信仰的落脚，教堂就像母亲，她像流浪在外的婴孩渴望回到母亲的怀抱。

北京有四座大的天主教堂，燕子都去过，相比其他三座天主堂，燕子觉得北堂的氛围最好。北堂的礼仪最完整，也最能让她沉浸其中，使她回归宁静。每个周日当她走进北堂，进堂咏在金碧辉煌的堂内庄严地响起，所有人静穆，她便仿佛站在天主面前，和周围的人一起向天主致敬。当神父开始读经，她用心聆听时，内心便获得一种安宁，生活中的烦恼和忧愁便都消散了。而当她与大家一起歌唱圣咏，并微笑着互祝平安时，她感到她与每个人都联结在一起而不是在北京这座城市漂浮的的一叶浮萍，即使身旁的面孔陌生，可心灵却因此而更加欢喜，如同从陌生人那儿得到了一个礼物，彼此便亲近起来。她对这个城市所有的陌生感和身处其中的小心翼翼、紧张恐惧在最后领圣体时彻底消失，她不再是一个惴惴不安的外地人，而作为天主教信徒被整个群体所认同、接受，没有河北和北京之分，只有共同的天主和肢体。弥撒结束后，燕子都会去跟堂外的玛利亚"打声招呼"，静静地站在她的雕像面前祈祷，对于她而言，耶稣基督和玛利亚就像心灵的港湾，如同家人，更甚家人，她向他们祈祷、忏悔，也向他们倾诉。而北堂的礼仪最为完整和有序，礼仪氛围也最静穆，人们可以专心祈祷——在别的教堂有可能会因小孩儿多而受到干扰。

真正的难题出现在她争取一个心仪工作机会的时候。为了获得工作机会，燕子在笔试时违心地选择了不相信"世界上有神、神仙、活佛等"。想到《圣经》中"凡在人面前不认我的,我在我天上的父面前也必不认他"那句话，心里却为此愧疚不安了一个周。一个周日她去做弥撒，向天主诉说了苦恼并祈祷，"如果您认为我需要这份工作，那就请您让我顺利通过吧。"便又恢复了往日的乐观积极。事实上，燕子的性格十分平和，心态非常乐观——这是她最大的特点。在大城市里生存打拼的人身上能够看出的那份焦虑和压力，在燕子身上不见一丝踪迹。对于自己的生活和工作，她的母亲比她更担忧——但她一边工作一边读夜校，并没有哀叹抱怨；对于未来的爱情，她期待但也顺其自然，因为她对当下所拥有的十分知足。即使是对于亲人和自己的生死，她也十分坦然。这份心灵的淡定和从容，正是她的信仰和家庭给予她的最大财富和力量。它使一个人能在这片土地上自由地呼吸，使一个人不惧未来、不怕死亡，使看似娇弱的人强大，使平凡之人透露出天上的光。这份信仰滋养着一群人的心灵，使他们赞美天主，歌颂奉献，充满喜乐，燃烧着永不熄灭的爱。

her to focus on her prayers. At other churches it is noisier since there are more children.

Yanzi once faced a dilemma. In the written test for a job application, she answered "no" to the question, "Do you believe that God exists in the world?" Although it was not what she believed, it was the answer that she thought was expected. Later, she felt guilty for an entire week since the Bible says, "Whoever denies me before men, I shall also deny him in front of Father of me in Heaven" (Matthew 10:33). When she went to Mass the next Sunday, she spoke to God about her guilt. She prayed, "If you think I need this job, please help me pass the test." Her sadness was gone, and her spirit of optimism resumed.

It is this calm and optimistic character that sets Yanzi apart from the majority of immigrant workers who are under constant anxiety and stress. Yanzi's mom, however, worries about Yanzi, especially since Yanzi is constantly busy, working in the daytime and going to school at night. Yanzi, however, never complains. She looks forward to finding a boyfriend, but takes it easy. She is very content with what she has now, never anxious about the lives of herself or her family. This state of ease and calm is the greatest wealth and power that her faith and family give her. It enables her to breathe freely, without fearing death and worrying about the future. Faith makes a seemingly fragile person strong and powerful. Faith can make an ordinary person shine from within. Faith enriches people's minds, filling them with everlasting joy and love—like a burning candle that can never be extinguished.

西直门天主堂

李琳

空间

北京教区四大堂中，西直门天主堂最小（占地约550平方米，圣堂仅能容纳270至300人），像一位小公主，藏在老城内一处不起眼的地方，因位于城西，又称为西堂。高耸的哥特式单尖塔钟楼和白色十架让人从远处便能识别它。常有古老的额我略圣咏萦绕在教堂前小广场上空，而雕刻在院墙上的十二宗徒像在日夜守护这座圣堂。推开圣堂的门：一对带半圆门楣的双掩樟木门，门上雕刻精美，一张圆桌中半张在门楣上，半张在木门上。上面是耶稣和十二宗徒共进最后的晚餐，下面是加纳的婚宴，酒缺了，圣母玛利亚请求耶稣帮助，耶稣于是行了第一个奇迹：他让仆役把六口石缸装满水，那水变成了上好的美酒。餐桌后分垂两旁的婚宴帐幕象征天主亲临的所在。

西堂设计以此神圣婚礼为主题，入口大门象征着饼和酒都备好了，耶稣和圣母遂邀请世人们进入此门，参加天国的婚筵。"我们每个教友的信仰生活就是一个大的宴会，耶稣说：你们到我这里来，到我这里来的，永不会饥饿，信从我的永不会渴。所以就是说，我们的信仰生活就当作吸收耶稣营养的一个过程。我们不断地被耶稣所滋养，他滋养我们的灵魂。"西堂辅祭员方水齐（化名）在向我介绍西堂建筑时说道。

除了门，钟楼正面和两侧的彩窗还描绘着耶稣治愈病人、显增饼奇迹、复活拉匝禄、治好附魔的儿童、山中圣训、平静风浪、复活后在海边显现、向多默显现的事迹。

穿过门和钟楼，进入圣堂，一股神圣的静谧顿时抓住了我，层层叠叠的尖拱顶被柔和地照亮，光线顺着十二根石柱上升到顶部，仿佛能上达天堂、与神沟通，同时往前看又形成笔直透视感，一直通往祭台、至圣所即放置耶稣圣体的地方，而穿过彩窗玻璃射进来的自然光影，红、黄、绿、蓝四色交错，让宁静、祥和、舒适的氛围中又带些许神秘感。跪凳上几个人在跪着祈祷。

历史

圣堂的两侧彩窗除了描绘了中国教会史、主保圣母的显现奇迹、耶稣生平外，还承载着它"三毁四建"的沧桑历史。

西堂最早是由意大利遣使会传教士德格理（1671-1746）神父于1723年兴建，初名"圣母七苦堂"，其建立之初直属罗马传信部管辖。他是康熙（1654-1722）皇帝向罗马教宗申请而委派的乐理老师，教授皇子西洋音乐、乐理、西方科学知识，其中包含将来登基的雍正（1678-1735）。作为曾为意大利皇宫作曲的音乐家，他将西洋音乐引入中国，至今在国家图书馆里仍存有他的十首作品手稿。为纪念他，如今的西堂圣咏团仍以其名字命名。

在清政府禁教的大背景下，1811年，西堂着火，嘉庆皇帝不愿修复，遂荒弃。后西堂四名传教士因违反传教禁令而被驱逐出京，圣堂被拆除，其后五、六十年间，堂址逐渐被民居占用。

Xizhimen Church

Li Lin, with Ireland Larsen, editor

Space

Among the four major Catholic churches in the Beijing Diocese, Xizhimen Catholic Church is the smallest, covering an area of 550 square meters and accommodating only 270 to 300 people. Like a little princess, it is hidden in an inconspicuous place in the old city. Since the church is located on the west side of the city, it is also known as the West Church. The lofty single-spire Gothic clock tower, topped with a white cross, catches people's attention from far away. Gregorian chant is often heard hovering over the courtyard in front of the church. The twelve apostles carved on the fence seem to be guarding the church day and night. The semicircular lintel of the church door is carved from a piece of elm. The carvings on the lintel and door are exquisite: one half of a round table is on the lintel, while the other half is on the door. The carving on top portrays the last supper of Jesus with the twelve apostles; the one on the bottom, the wedding feast at Cana at which the party ran out of wine and Jesus's mother asked him to help. Jesus ordered six jars to be filled with water, then performed his first miracle—turning the jars of water into fine wine. The wedding tabernacle behind the banquet table symbolizes the presence of God in the Hebrew Bible.

The sacred wedding is the artistic theme for the church. The door suggests that bread and wine are ready, with Jesus and the Virgin Mary inviting everyone to join the wedding feast in the kingdom of

97. 教友们聆听张神父讲道 Father Zhang preaching at Xizhimen Catholic Church

西直门天主堂

98. 教堂八角形洗礼池 Baptism font at Xizhimen Catholic Church

God. "The religious life of each church member is like a feast. Jesus said, 'I am the bread of life. Whoever comes to me will never go hungry, and whoever believes in me will never be thirsty' (John 6:35). Our religious journey is a process of absorbing nutrients from Jesus. He nourishes us and our souls," said the acolyte Fang Shuiqi (pseudonym), while he showed me around the building.

Aside from the door, the colorful windows on the front and sides of the bell tower depict Jesus's miracles and deeds: healing the sick, feeding the crowds, resurrecting Lazarus from the dead, healing a demon-possessed boy, preaching the Beatitudes, calming the storm, appearing at the seaside as well as to the Apostle Thomas after resurrection.

After entering the door and passing through the clock tower, I arrived at the nave. I was amazed by its holy stillness. Soft sunshine brightened the vaulted ceiling, with rays of light illuminating the twelve stone pillars that rose upward to Heaven. My line of sight then led to the altar and sanctuary where the Eucharist was placed. The colored sunlight shining through the stained glass added mystery to tranquility. Several people were kneeling and praying.

History

The stained-glass windows on the sides of the nave depict stories of the development of the Chinese Church, the annunciation of Mary, and the life of Jesus. Also pictured are Xizhimen's history of "three destructions and four constructions."

The West Church was first built in 1723 by the Italian Lazarist missionary Teodorico Pedrini (1671–1746). Initially called the "Seven Sorrows of the Blessed Virgin Mary Church," it was under the direct jurisdiction of Rome. Pedrini was a music teacher sent by the Pope at the request of Emperor Kangxi (r. 1661–1722). He taught the princes Western music, music theory, and science. One of the princes later became Emperor Yongzheng (r. 1722–1735). As a musician who composed music for the Italian royal palace, Pedrini brought Western music to China. Ten of his manuscripts are today kept in the National Library. To commemorate Pedrini, the choir of the West Church was named after him.

The Qing Dynasty (1644–1912) later banned the spread of Christianity in China. After the West Church was damaged by a fire in 1811, Emperor Jiaqing (r. 1796–1820) refused to repair it. In the same year, four priests violated the ban and were deported from Beijing. The West Church was then torn down. Over the next fifty to sixty years, the site was occupied by residential buildings.

In 1867, priests requested the church be rebuilt. Inhabitants returned the land without asking for compensation. That started the second construction of the church.

In 1900, the Boxer Rebellion closed in on Beijing under the slogan "Destroying the West and Supporting the Qing." Fang told me, "The French Priest Jin Baoguang was ordered to guard the church. But he locked his two guns in the cabinet and discarded the keys. He thought if the mob desecrated the church, he would lose control and shoot them and thereby violate his vows." As expected, the Boxer mobs chased him all the way up the clock tower. They cut off his arms and legs, after which he fell into the fire that consumed the church. His church members also were not spared. The eight family members of Maria Wu were met by the Boxer mobs as they tried to escape. The whole family was killed. The church was burned down in the riot. Nothing remained.

Not until 1912 did Sister Branssier of Carmelites Benemerita fund the third construction, which was named Carmelo Santa Maria Church. A commemorating monument was erected. An elementary school and a kindergarten were built next to the church.

The third destruction occurred during the Cultural Revolution when the front clock tower was torn down. The West Church was subsequently used

1867年，传教士再次提请恢复圣堂，当民众得知，皆无偿归还该地，于是第二次建造得以成功。

1900年，以"扶清灭洋"为旗号的义和团运动直逼京城，"西堂金葆光神父（法国）受命守护圣堂。但他把自己所持两把快枪锁进柜子，丢弃钥匙。因为他害怕若到时暴民侮辱圣堂，他会开枪反抗而犯诫"，方老师说。后果不其然，义和团和乱民追杀金神父，直到钟楼顶，后砍断其胳膊和腿，使其坠入火海。教友亦未能幸免于难。吴马利亚一家八口本欲逃难，途中遇义和团，满门被诛杀。而堂区亦在这次教难中烧毁殆尽，片瓦无存。

直到1912年，加尔默罗修会的仁爱会修女博朗西耶氏捐资在原址第三次建堂，西堂遂更名为"加尔默罗圣母圣衣堂"，并刻碑纪念。时亦建小学于其侧。

而第三次大毁坏是在文化大革命期间，教堂正面钟楼被拆毁。此后西堂先后被用作过纽扣厂、电扇厂和同仁堂的药材仓库。

1994年，西堂简单装修后恢复正常的宗教活动。2007年进行第四次系统修复，历时两年，成为今天看到的样子。

方老师讲述完西堂教难史后，我难掩心中的震惊与愤怒。"历史上真教会都是在逆境中前进，没有经历苦难的教会是有问题的"。从小就跟随母亲来西堂参与弥撒、亲眼见证了这六十几年西堂的起起伏伏的他如是说。

教堂仅存的其中一块百年旧玻璃重修时被安在了告解室，这寓意宽恕，因为圣经记载耶稣在被犹太同胞钉十字架陷入极大痛苦中时仍说："父啊，饶恕他们，因为他们所做的他们不晓得。"由此他亲自建立告解圣事：天主饶恕了世人的罪过，所以基督徒也要同样饶恕他人的罪过。

更新转化

承载加纳婚宴变水为酒神迹的六口石缸的模型，需人们进门之后，方可看见。它们分别位于教堂最重要的三处：洗礼池、读经台和祭台。

第一口是一个昼夜不停涌着活水的石缸，在一进门的洗礼池前，象征耶稣是生命的活水源头，进堂的每一位教友会在此处用手沾圣水顺着额头、心口和左右肩划十字，再双手合十，接着对红毯尽头的圣体柜深鞠一躬（年轻教友）或单膝下跪（老教友）后再进入。

石缸下面是一方底部镶有金十字架的蓝色马赛克砖洗礼池，呈八角形。每年复活节，都有一批参加完慕道班的预备教友在此接受水和圣神的洗礼。从此，人所有的罪恶由基督在十字架上从肋旁里倾流出来的血和水所洗净，人的生命如同水变为酒的转化那般被更新，成就发生在人身上的神迹，即生命的转变，与基督同浸入水死，同出水活。

冯红（化名）便是其中一员。她和大多数中国人一样，受无神论教育长大，但始终觉得在无神论角度下了解到的宗教不具权威性。她年轻时在附近上班，天天经过西堂，一直想进入了解，却因过于忙碌未能如愿。直到十几年后的2015年，她人到中年，儿女成年、工作轻松下来，再次经过时见"慕道班招生"，遂报名，每周上课直到次年3月。随后在3月26日复活节前夕领了洗，因为她相信只有进入这个宗教才能真正了解它。领洗后的她加入读经班，每周来与教友一起读经，并作为读经员服务弥撒，偶尔探访其他教友，在这个团体中渐渐有了归属感。

99. 弥撒圣祭中张神父 诵念感恩经文 **Father Zhang saying the Eucharistic prayer**

as a button factory, an electric-fan factory, and the warehouse of Tongrentang, the leading manufacturer of traditional Chinese medicine.

After restoration in 1994, religious activities resumed at West Church. In 2007, a thorough reconstruction was initiated. The project lasted for two years, making the church into what we see today.

After his overview of the church's history, I was shocked and angry. Fang explained, "Historically, the church has progressed in adversity. Churches without suffering are problematic." As a child, Fang followed his mom to the Mass at the West Church. In his sixty some years of life, he has witnessed the repeated rising and falling of the church.

The only stained glass from 100 years ago is kept in the confession room. It represents forgiveness. When Jesus endured great suffering while being crucified, he said, "Father, forgive them, for they do not know what they are doing" (Luke 23:34), instituting the Sacrament of Penance. The faithful obtain absolution from God for the sins they have committed. Christians should therefore forgive the sins of others.

Transformation

Replicas of the six stone jars in which the water was transformed to wine at the Cana wedding feast can be seen inside the hall. They are placed at the three most important places of the church: the baptistery, the lectern, and the altar.

The first jar is located in front of the baptistery near the entrance. Water runs from it day and night, suggesting that Jesus is the source of life. Before taking their seats, church members dip their hands into this holy water and make a cross from their forehead to their heart, from their left to right shoulder, and finally put their palms together devoutly. Afterwards they make a profound bow (in the case of young members) or get down on one knee

100. 祝圣圣体的神父 Priest holding sacraments *(photo by He Yinglong)*

(in the case of old members), facing towards the pyx at the end of the red carpet where the consecrated bread of the Eucharist is kept.

Below the first stone jar is an octagonal, blue, mosaic baptistery with a gold-framed cross at the base. Every Easter, a group of catechumens who have just finished the catechism classes are baptized by water and the Holy Spirit here. All their sins are washed away by water and the blood of Jesus. Like water transformed to wine, a person lives a new life from that moment on. He lives with Jesus and dies with him too.

Feng Hong (pseudonym) is one of them. Like most Chinese, she received an education in atheism. But she always doubted that an atheist would ever understand what religion truly is. She used to live nearby, passing the West Church every day on her way to work. She was always curious about the church, though she could never afford the time to get to know it. In 2015, when her life had settled down and her children had grown up, she decided to sign up for the catechism classes. She finished her classes in March 2016. On March 26, right before Easter, she was baptized. She believed that the only way to understand Christianity was to become part of it. After baptism, she joined the Bible reading class that offers the Mass for Bible readers. Occasionally, she went to visit other members. Gradually, she felt that she was becoming part of a big family.

Talking about these changes over the past three years, Feng said that she "is less conceited now." "I used to have a very big ego, and I felt I was immensely capable. I read about the Exodus and how God helped Moses part the Red Sea, but I thought it was a myth and never took it seriously. When I learned the story again at the catechism class, I felt it was very reasonable and realistic." Now Feng reveres and trusts God. Whenever she has difficulties, she prays. As the Bible says, "Cast all your anxiety on him because he cares for you" (1 Peter 5:7), and "Ask and it will be given to you" (Matthew 7:7). Feng finds these verses so true: "Real Catholics will never commit suicide. The Bible talked about the many miracles of God, so there is always hope." Some time ago Feng came down with breast cancer. She went through surgery and chemotherapy, but she never lost her faith in God, nor did she ever complain to God. She is convinced that God's will is above the will of humans. God must have plans for her. When talking about this, Feng shed a few tears. There is sadness, but there is also gratitude.

Communion

After baptism, one becomes a Christian. Then one walks towards the altar and attends "the wedding feast of the lamb," the Mass. There is a lamp behind the altar indicating Jesus' presence in the pyx. The Mass contains two important parts: the Liturgy of the Word, and the Eucharist, which are performed at the lectern and the altar, respectively. The second stone jar is on the lectern. It calls for church members to listen to the Holy Word carefully, like a thirsty man drinking sweet spring water, following its instructions in practice. Then life will be like water turning into wine, from tasteless to sweet, from "doomed to death" to "salvation and eternity." The last four stone jars are near the altar. Fang explained, "During every Eucharist, the priest will hold the bread and wine, which will be turned into the body and blood of Christ. The background of the altar has water patterns. That is because Jesus is the spring that nourishes our spirituality."

"May the Eucharist we receive be our power to subdue evil, prepare us for the resurrection of Christ, and fulfill our wish to live with and die with Christ." When everyone sings these lines at Communion, their celestial sound echoes in the air like the smoke of burning incense rising over the church.

有了信仰的这三年她形容自己"开始变得不那么狂妄了","没有信仰时自我意识膨胀得特别厉害,总觉得自己好像无所不能似的"。"原来就看过天主带梅瑟使红海分开带领以色列人逃离埃及的故事,觉得那是神话,当笑话听,但在慕道班再次听到时却觉得很合理,很真实"。现在她敬畏天主,凡事相信、感谢天主,遇到什么难事她会努力祈祷。圣经所言"把一切忧虑献给天主"(伯多禄前书5:7)、"你们祈求就给你们"(玛窦福音7:7),她觉得在她生活中确实如此。"真正的天主教徒不会自杀,因为圣经中描写了很多天主的奇迹,所以心中总有希望",她说。哪怕期间她经历了癌症和手术,也没有丢失信仰和埋怨天主。她深信天主的意念高过人的意念,在她身上发生的一切定有其心意。这其中她既有痛苦,也有感恩。

共融

经过重生的洗礼池,人成为基督徒,就必往前走向祭台,参与羔羊的婚宴(弥撒)。祭台侧后方有一盏长明灯,提示人们耶稣就在圣体柜中。弥撒有两个最重要部分:圣道礼和圣祭礼,分别在读经台和祭台两个位置举行。第二口水缸就在读经台上,寓意教友聆听圣言,有如干渴的人喜饮甘洌的泉水,照此教导去践行,生活就像水变酒一样,从无味变甘甜,从有死变为得救、永生。而最后四口水缸在祭台,"每次举祭时,神父都会举起面饼和酒祝圣,饼和酒就成为耶稣的体和血。背景还有水纹,因为耶稣是滋养我们灵性生命的活水。"方老师解释道。

"愿我们领受的圣体,成为我们制服邪恶的力量,准备我们分享基督的复活,实现我们与基督同死同生的愿望。"当弥撒中全会众唱起领主曲,那声音像上腾的烟雾般缭绕在圣堂上空。

在教友心中,"主的圣体"既是善度今世丰盛人生的食粮,也是迈向天上永生的"天路行粮",直到在天上参与新郎(基督)的婚宴;"将来能在天主的国里吃饭的,才是有福的!"(路加福音14:15)而人领受耶稣的圣体,就是与基督"合一",犹如夫妻的合一;而神父和每位教友领受同一个基督的身体,也成为一个合一共融的整体。这在张神父与教友们的关系中也能看到。

冯红说,张神父在她心里是一位特别宽容的长者,他对教友从出生到成年坚振、结婚、生病、悔罪、送终的陪伴和关心让她感受到"天父般的慈爱"。临近端午节我采访张神父,问及弃俗修道这些年遇到的困境,张神父笑说他当神父20几年以来从不觉艰辛,但他知道堂里一些教友自发每周固定有几天会为他禁食祷告祈求,这让他很感动。当我们聊到最后,有一位老教友笑着带她的小孙子走进大门,那小孩一见神父就开心地跑了过来,亲昵地叫着"神父,神父,我给你带端午节的粽子啦",就抱住神父。那一瞬间,我忽然意识到,眼前这位没有婚姻、子嗣、私财的人,其实是有家的:他有更多的家人、更广泛深入的关系和更宝贵的财宝。

盼望与喜乐

2019年6月9日,是《西堂加纳》周刊发行七周年纪念日。"七年,365期,记录了美丽西堂……2500多天的历程:
夜晚钟楼十字架放射的光芒……圣母抱耶稣对世人的垂视;
还有圣诞节平安夜涌入圣堂的人群,复活节阿肋路亚的欢呼声,以及院中大屏幕

101. 弥撒圣祭中教友领受圣体 Receiving the Eucharist in Mass

In the minds of the church members, "the Eucharist of the Lord" is food not only for living and enriching this life but also for the "heavenly road" to eternity, which lasts until we attend the wedding feast of the bridegroom in Heaven. "Blessed is the one who will eat at the feast in the kingdom of God" (Luke 14:15). Whoever eats the bread communes with the body of Christ, like husband and wife. Priests and church members receive the same body of Christ and therefore become one in communion. This concept is reflected in the relationships between Priest Zhang and the church members.

According to Feng, Priest Zhang is a very tolerant elder. He cares about every church member, from birth, to confirmation, marriage, illness, confession, and terminal care. His love is like that received from the Heavenly Father. I interviewed Priest Zhang on a day close to the Dragon Boat Festival. When asked whether he experienced lots of difficulties during the twenty years of being a priest, Priest Zhang smiled and said that he never felt it was hard. But when he learned that some church members fast and pray for him periodically, he was very moved. Just then, a senior church member came in with his grandchild. Upon seeing Priest Zhang, the child could not stop his excitement, "Father, Father, I brought *zongzi* [a traditional Dragon Festival dish] for you." The boy went on to give Priest Zhang a hug. Suddenly, I came to realize that the man in front of me, without spouse, children, and wealth, actually has a family. He has many more family members, more and closer social connections, and an abundance of wealth.

Aspirations and Joy

June 9, 2019 was the seventh anniversary of the publication of the "West Church Cana" weekly magazine, which printed 365 issues over those years. Fang recalled the life of the church during that time:

实时播放的弥撒盛况，圣堂内管风琴悠扬的旋律；

还有……每周一次坚持数年的圣经讲授，以及适时开办的礼仪音乐课，管风琴课，合唱指挥课，为更好理解圣经举办的拉丁语课，希腊语课；

还有每月一次的彻夜圣体朝拜，堂区各团体的信仰分享，以及常规性地关爱残婴院儿童，持续捐助贫困地区失学的孩子们；

还有对边远地区贫穷学生的关心，对受灾地区民众的及时援助，以及每人每月两本圣经捐款，常年不断的每天一点爱；

还有对教外朋友的圣经无偿恭赠，对堂区教友的圣书免费发放，以及认真准备的堂区教友避静，精心组织的各地朝圣。"

方老师在周刊纪念版深情回忆西堂七年生活，这是他们信仰从言到行的缩影，正是张神父特别强调的。

"张神父在西堂7年多特别让我钦佩的是，他很多事都亲力亲为，尽心尽力为教友服务，包括搬东西，很多很脏的，他都乐呵呵地做，从来没有把自己放在高高在上的位置，就是像耶稣说的你想成为最大的你就是最小的（路加福音9:48）。而且他经常组织教友的联谊，在交流中我们就能知道一些教友的需要，可以给他们探望、送圣体。"冯红说道。

而另一位教友张芳（化名）在新年伊始跟随张神父和方济各基金小组前往河北山湾子地区探望贫困孩子，送学习、生活用品和食品，问及孩子们最大的愿望是什么，没想到他们的回答是"吃一次方便面"。还有一个很有礼貌的孩子忘记出来送客人，张芳在车上知道原因竟是她从来没见过这么多好吃的，要在屋里守着，以致于忘记出来送客时，不禁潸然泪下。

从一进门、经过彩窗、读经台、祭台，步步深入到尽头，举头仰望到最璀璨夺目的一处，即三联圣像，画中是这场婚礼的终末：新天新地的红色帐幕中耶稣为新娘即圣教会戴上璀璨的冠冕，天使吹奏、歌唱，两边的历代众圣徒围绕、赞美。

方老师解释道："耶稣和圣教会的关系就像新郎和新娘那样的密切，结为一体。耶稣说：你们来吧，这是新郎召唤新娘，我们都是新娘。经过我们在世当跑的路跑尽了，美好的仗打完了，最终耶稣会给我们教会加冕，这样，天国的宴会，这个婚宴，最后就完成了。"

在这年圣周六弥撒的最后，张神父邀请所有人共同诵读圣方济各和平祷词。我想这或许就是来赴羔羊婚宴的西堂教会，历经苦难、得享饱足以后，带着对将来得着新天新地新郎冠冕的盼望，在世间所要完成的最后的部分。

- the journey of the beautiful West Church over 2500 days;
- the glow of the clock tower cross at night, and the Virgin Mary looking at the world with Jesus in her arms;
- people flooding into the church on Christmas Eve, the cheers of "Hallelujah" at Easter, the broadcast of the Mass on the courtyard screen, and the music from the pipe organ;
- weekly lectures on the Bible and routine classes about etiquette, music, the pipe organ, the choir, Latin, and Greek;
- the monthly Eucharistic Adoration throughout the night;
- group discussions about faith, routine visitation of nurseries for disabled children, and repeated donations to children in less developed areas;
- care for students in poor and remote areas, donations to disaster-stricken areas, the bi-weekly "Two-Bible Donation" by church members, and the "A Little Love Every Day Campaign";
- free Bibles for non-Catholics, free holy books for church members, and the meticulously planned retreats and pilgrimages for church members.

Fang concluded, "These are just some snapshots of our practice of the faith. Practice is what Priest Zhang has always been advocating."

"What I admire most about Priest Zhang is his humility. He always takes a hands-on approach and tries his best to help the church members. He even helps with moving, even when things are dirty. He has no complaints. He never places himself in an inaccessibly lofty position. Rather he follows what Jesus said, 'It is the one who is least among you all who is the greatest' [Luke 9:48]. He organizes many social events for church members. Through these activities, we learn about the needs of some members, so we visit them or bring them Eucharist," said Feng.

Another member of the church, Zhang Fang (pseudonym), accompanied Priest Zhang and the "Francis Fund" team to visit the poor children in the Shanwanzi area of Hebei Province at the beginning of the new year. They brought pens and paper, food, and other necessities. When asked about their biggest wishes, the children said they wanted to eat instant noodles. When the time came to leave, a very polite child did not follow them out of the room to say goodbye. Zhang later learned that the child had never seen so much good food. She was glued to the food and forgot to leave the room. Zhang welled up with tears when he heard this.

Returning to the church, I scanned through the door, noting the stained-glass windows, altar, and lectern, finally fixing my eyes on the most stunning sight at the far end of the nave—the three-fold holy painting, which pictures the end of the wedding. Sitting in a red tabernacle, Jesus is putting a crown on his bride (the holy church). Angels are singing and playing music. The saints surround the scene, offering praise from all around.

Fang explained: "The relationship between Jesus and the Holy Church resembles that of the bridegroom and the bride. Jesus said, 'Come to me' [Matthew 11:28]. This is the bridegroom's calling of the bride. We are all brides. When we complete our running in this world, when we finish fighting for what we must, Jesus will crown us. Then the celestial feast, the banquet, will be complete."

At the end of the Saturday Mass, Priest Zhang invited everyone to chant the Franciscan peace prayers. Having endured hardships, the West Church is coming for the wedding feast of the lamb, to enjoy the banquet, wishing to be crowned by the bridegroom in the new world. But before that, it has one more task to perform. That is love, I think.

雍和宫

宗喀·益西丹佛

历史

雍和宫坐落在北京内城的东北角,是二环路(北京的城市核心环城快速公路)沿线最显著的古典地标,也是清朝乾隆年间由王府改建的藏传佛教皇家寺院。其前身是四皇子胤禛(即后来的雍正皇帝)的王府及其登基后的行宫。在中国,著名人物的故居通常会被赋予"居住"以外的新功能,雍和宫在雍正皇帝逝世后被乾隆皇帝改建为藏传佛教寺院,由世俗王府变成神圣庙宇,是全中国仅有的两个以"宫"命名的藏传佛教场所之一。

雍和宫由宫改寺后,雍正皇帝的后继者乾隆皇帝对它的管理非常重视,成立专门机构,委派亲王担任最高行政首长"领雍和宫事务大臣",这是当时宗教场所少有的特殊待遇。乾隆皇帝还经常莅临雍和宫巡视调察、听法受戒,雍和宫的喇嘛也定期在寺院或前往紫禁城等皇家园囿为皇帝及皇室成员诵经祝寿、祈福、开光。清代,雍和宫作为皇家寺院,除了承载"弘扬佛法、利乐众生"的宗教使命外,还被赋予了安抚民众、治理蒙藏,稳定一统、巩固统治的政治功能与桥梁纽带作用。

清政府对于藏传佛教最大的贡献之一就是设立了"金瓶掣签"制度,这一制度与雍和宫有着密不可分的联系。"金瓶掣签"是藏传佛教遴选活佛转世灵童的一种方法。活佛转世是藏传佛教寺院为解决其首领的继承而采取的一种制度设计,是藏传佛教特有的传承方式。但在西藏和蒙古地方的传承过程,逐渐出现了营私舞弊现象,甚至影响到了边疆地区的政局稳定。乾隆皇帝为了革除其中的弊端,实现既尊重和护持藏传佛教,又要依法依规加强管理的政治理念,制定了金瓶掣签制度。在拉萨大昭寺与北京雍和宫各放置一个"金瓶",用于遴选认定蒙藏地区的大活佛。他还亲撰《喇嘛说》,刻石立碑于雍和宫,意在宣诏天下:活佛转世,金瓶掣签,永为定制。这是藏传佛教活佛转世管理体制的创新之举,既体现了中央权威与国家主权,又保证了活佛认定的公开、公正、合法,这一制度选择及其实施过程也标志着藏传佛教活佛转世制度在国家层面走向制度化与规范化,并且沿用至今。

空间布局

因为是由皇家王府改建的寺院,雍和宫的空间布局与一般中国藏区佛教寺院明显不同,我们在它的入口处就有这种感受。首先映入眼帘的是一个影壁墙和东、西、北三个方向的三座牌坊围合成的庭院,这代表了一种高级别的清代建筑起始模式。之后通过一条长长的辇道,始到达雍和宫的正门:昭泰门。清代,朝廷在这条辇道的两侧及其周围设置有七个佛仓:驻京呼图克图(蒙古语对高级活佛的称谓)的府邸,有七位来自蒙藏地区的大活佛在此居住。他们都是享誉一方、地位尊贵的宗教领袖,但能在此居住,也是莫大殊荣。

进入昭泰门后是雍和门殿,这是原先雍亲王府的大门。雍和门殿的后方是雍和宫殿,这两个建筑与左右配殿围成了一个庭院结构,正中间是一座四角碑亭,其内的御

Yonghegong Temple

Zongka Yixidanfo, with Madelyn Bjork, editor

History

Located in the northeast corner of Beijing's inner city, Yonghegong Lama Temple is the most remarkable classical landmark along the Second Ring Road—a princely mansion converted into a Tibetan Buddhist temple during the Qianlong reign (r. 1735–1796) of the Qing Dynasty. Prior to conversion, it first served as the mansion of Prince Yinzhen, Emperor Kangxi's fourth son who later became Emperor Yongzheng (r. 1722–1735), then functioned as the royal palace for a short period after he succeeded to the throne. In China, the former residence of distinguished people is later given a new function. After Emperor Yongzheng passed away, Emperor Qianlong converted Yonghegong into a lamasery. It is one of only two lamaseries containing the name *gong* ("palace") in China.

Emperor Qianlong attached great importance to the administration of the Lama Temple. He set up a special agency and designated a prince to assume the role of Yonghegong General Affairs Minister, the chief administrator of the temple, a prestige rarely seen at other religious sites. Emperor Qianlong visited Yonghegong, inspected the temple, listened to the preaching, and took precepts himself. The lamas at the temple later held routine rituals for the emperors and their royal families, such as scripture

102. 雍和宫的外部景观 Exterior view of Yonghegong (Lama) Temple

103. 戒台楼里的乾隆皇帝像 Statue of Emperor Qianlong in Jetai Building

碑就是著名的《喇嘛说》碑。它记载了藏传佛教活佛转世金瓶掣签制度的由来，为乾隆皇帝亲自撰写，并用汉、满、蒙、藏四种文字篆刻而成。

雍和宫殿相当于汉传佛教寺院的"大雄宝殿"。但与大雄宝殿中常见的佛像配置：释迦牟尼佛、阿弥陀佛和药师佛不同，此殿供奉的是"竖三世佛"，即主持现在世的释迦牟尼佛、主持过去世的燃灯佛、主持未来世的弥勒佛。雍和宫殿后的永佑殿，则主供无量寿佛，这是清代皇家祝寿祈福常用的供奉题材。无量寿佛东侧的狮吼佛，也是汉传佛教寺院所没有的。

永佑殿之后是法轮殿，这里原先是王府时期"嫡福晋（王爷的妻子）"的寝殿，现在是雍和宫僧众每日诵经和举行重大佛事活动的主要场所。里面主供宗喀巴大师坐像。其后的殿宇是万福阁，它是雍和宫内最高的建筑。当年七世达赖喇嘛向乾隆皇帝进献了一根罕见的巨型白檀木，乾隆皇帝命宫廷造办处将其雕造为一尊弥勒佛像，并在雍和宫造高阁供奉，这就是今天万福阁中的巨型弥勒佛立像。该佛像已载入吉尼斯世界纪录，是世界独木雕造最高大的佛像。

雍和宫最后建成的殿堂是法轮殿东西两侧的班禅楼和戒台楼。其修建缘于1780年六世班禅进京为乾隆皇帝祝寿。其中，戒台楼是乾隆皇帝为六世班禅传法授戒而专门修建的。这两座殿堂的修建，体现了乾隆皇帝对藏传佛教的信仰和对六世班禅的敬重之情。

chanting, birthday celebrations, prayers, and consecration, whether at Yonghegong Temple itself or at royal palaces and gardens like the Forbidden City. As a royal temple, Yonghegong not only undertook the mission of "promoting Buddhism and benefiting the people" but also assumed other political functions to appease the people, manage Mongolia and Tibet, maintain the unification of the country, and solidify the regime.

One of the greatest contributions the Qing Dynasty (1644–1912) made to Tibetan Buddhism was the establishment of "drawing lots from the golden urn," a system closely tied to Yonghegong Temple. "Drawing lots from the golden urn" is a way to determine the reincarnation of Living Buddhas, a succession system unique to Tibetan Buddhism. Corruption, however, gradually impaired its implementation in both Tibet and Mongolia, at times causing instability at the borders. To reform the succession system without losing respect and protection for Tibetan Buddhism, as well as to strengthen the political concept of managing by law, Emperor Qianlong set up the system of "drawing lots from the golden urn." To select the Living Buddhas in Tibet and Mongolia, one golden urn was placed at Jokhang Temple in Lhasa, another at Yonghegong Temple. Emperor Qianlong also drafted 喇嘛说 ("On Lama") and had it inscribed on a stela at Yonghegong Temple to announce to the world that the incarnation of Living Buddhas was to be determined by the system of "drawing lots from the golden urn." This was an innovative move. It assured the authority of the central government, the sovereignty of the country, and the openness, fairness, and legitimacy of the Living Buddha selection process. This marked the beginning of the institutionalization and standardization of Living Buddha incarnation at the national level. The system is still effective.

Space

Because the temple was converted from a mansion, its layout is very different from other Tibetan Buddhist monasteries. This difference can be noticed at the entrance. After passing through the main gate, one immediately arrives at a courtyard composed of a screen wall and three ornamental-arch gateways, which are located on the east, west, and north sides of the courtyard. This is elite Qing architectural style. A long imperial passageway then leads to Zhaotai Gate, the main gate of Yonghegong. In the Qing Dynasty, seven Buddhist residences were built along this passageway and its surrounding area. These were the residences for the Khutughtu, the Mongolian Living Buddhas, who were stationed in Beijing. Ever since, this has been the residence of the seven Khutughtu, reputable and prestigious religious leaders in their regions. For them, the opportunity to stay at Yonghegong Temple was a great honor.

After Zhaotai Gate comes Yonghemen Hall, which was originally the main gate of Prince Yinzhen's mansion. Behind Yonghemen Hall is Yonghegong Hall. These two halls, together with their side halls, constitute another courtyard. In the middle, there is a four-corner stela pavilion. The inscription on this stela, the work of Emperor Qianlong, is "On Lama", which records the origin of the system of "drawing lots from the golden urn" in four languages: Chinese, Manchurian, Mongolian, and Tibetan.

Yonghegong Hall is equivalent to the Daxiong Treasure Hall in a Chinese Buddhist monastery. However, instead of housing the statues of Śākyamuni Buddha, Amitābha Buddha, and the Pharmacist Buddha (Bhaiṣajyaguru), this hall is dedicated to the Trilokya Buddhas—Śākyamuni, who presides over the present realm, Dīpankara, who presides over the past, and Maitreya Buddha, who presides over the future. Behind Yonghegong Hall is Yongyou Hall, which is dedicated to the Buddha Amitāyus, who is frequently worshipped by Qing royal families for birthday celebrations.

104. 雍和门殿与拜佛的信众 Worship of statues of Buddhas in Yonghegong Hall

仪式活动

历史上，雍和宫的仪式活动众多，但最为北京居民喜闻乐见的是"金刚驱魔神舞"与"腊八舍粥"。更为可贵的是，这两项活动内容相沿成习，一直保留到了今天，并成为北京市民生活中重要的宗教与民俗文化活动。

清代，每年的腊八节，雍和宫都会举行大型的舍粥活动。农历腊月初八这天，北京城的佛教信徒与普通市民，甚至外地的信众都会从四面八方赶往雍和宫，参与这一盛会。如果说清代雍和宫的舍粥活动还有些许接济穷苦百姓的意味，那么今天的雍和宫腊八节，则是借助这一历史传统节日活动，更多的体现北京民俗活动中祈福求祥的文化特色，且有为春节增加浓厚年味儿的成分。北京曾有一首童谣"小孩儿小孩儿你别馋，过了腊八就是年"就反映了孩童们对过年（春节）的无限期盼。

为了搞好这一年一度的节庆活动，雍和宫的僧人与工作人员们要提前进行准备，采购配齐熬制腊八粥的大米、小米、红豆、绿豆、大枣、桂圆等近30种原料，初七晚上开始熬粥。初八一大早，众多信众与游客就已在雍和宫门口排起了长长的队伍，寺内的僧人与工作人员们则将一桶桶熬煮好的腊八粥抬到昭泰门院，备好餐具。开门以后，大家纷纷奔赴舍粥处，僧人们将热气腾腾的腊八粥盛入碗中，递给等候多时的群众。隆冬的北京，人们喝着香甜、热乎乎的腊八粥，满足、喜悦与幸福之情溢于言表。

从清代开始，也是在每年的正月，雍和宫都会举行跳金刚驱魔舞仪式，俗称"打鬼"，并且一直延续到今天。金刚驱魔神舞历史悠久，相传是印度的莲花生大师以西藏传统的舞蹈为基础，吸取藏族传统宗教苯教仪轨和印度瑜伽面具舞的部分形式，

The Siṃhanāda (Roaring Lion Buddha) on the east side of the Buddha Amitāyus is also not found in Chinese Buddhist temples; this is another difference between the Tibetan Lama temple and a Chinese Buddhist monastery.

After Yongyou Temple comes Dharmacakra Hall, which was originally the resting place of Difujin, the wife of the prince. It is currently the main site for chanting and other major Buddhist activities. The hall houses a statue of Je Tsongkhapa, founder of the Gelugpa school of Tibetan Buddhism. Behind the hall is Wanfu Pavilion, the tallest structure inside Yonghegong, which houses an enormous statue of Maitreya Buddha. The seventh Dalai Lama presented a rare piece of giant white sandalwood to Emperor Qianlong, who ordered a Maitreya Buddha statue to be carved out of it and a tall pavilion to be built to house it. This is the giant Maitreya Buddha statue we see at Wanfu Pavilion today. The statue is listed in the *Guinness Book of World Records* as the world's largest wooden Buddha statue.

The most recent halls to be built are the Panchen Lama and Jietai buildings, which are on the east and west side of Dharmacakra Hall. When the sixth Panchen Lama arrived in Beijing in 1780 for the birthday celebration of Emperor Qianlong, the Jietai building was built for him to teach sutras and perform ordination ceremonies. Emperor Qianlong's reverence for the sixth Panchen Lama is fully displayed in these two buildings.

Rituals

Although there have been many ceremonial activities at the Lama Temple over the years, the most popular among Beijing residents are "Laba Porridge Giving" and "Vajra Exorcism Dancing." These traditions continue today, offering important religious and cultural activities for the people of Beijing.

During the Qing Dynasty, large-scale porridge-giving activities were held at Yonghegong on the Laba Festival. When the eighth day of the twelfth month of the lunar calendar arrived, people from Beijing and the surrounding areas flooded to Yonghegong Temple to participate in the ceremony. At the time, porridge-giving was a form of alms-giving. Today, however the Laba Festival serves more as a preparatory celebration for the new year, an occasion to pray for blessings, which is characteristic of folk traditions in Beijing. There is even a children's rhyme for the festival: "Children, children, don't crave for food. Spring Festival is right around the corner after Laba Festival."

To prepare for the festival, the lamas and staff begin well ahead of time, readying all thirty ingredients for the porridge, which include rice, millet, red beans, mung beans, jujube, and longan. The boiling of the porridge begins on the seventh night. On the early morning of the eighth day, believers and visitors form long lines at the gate of Yonghegong. Buckets of Laba porridge are brought to the yard at Zhaotai Gate. When everything is ready, the gate is opened, and people rush in. The lamas bring the warm bowls of porridge to the hands of each visitor. On a chilly winter day, nothing brings more happiness than sweet, warm, and fragrant Laba porridge.

In the first lunar month of the year, Yonghegong Temple holds the Vajra Exorcism Dancing ceremony, commonly known as "fighting the ghosts." Vajra dancing has a long history, having begun during the Qing Dynasty. It is said that the Indian Padmasambhava (8th c.) created this Tibetan Vajrayāna dance on the basis of a traditional Tibetan dance, also integrating Tibetan Bon rituals and Indian Yoga mask-dancing. Vajra dancing is used mainly to dispel devils and bring peace, prosperity, and good luck. From a Buddhist point of view, dancers are saints who protect Dharma, chase away evil spirits, and ensure the flourishing of Buddhism and peace of the common people. The "evil spirits" refer mostly to the weaknesses and evil

雍和宫

105. 法轮殿里的宗喀巴大师像 Statue of Tsongkhapa in Falun Hall

创造了这一藏传佛教密宗舞蹈。该舞的主旨是驱除妖魔邪祟，祈祷吉祥平安、万事如意。从佛教的意义上来讲，跳舞时，舞者的身份是圣者与护法，消灭的是恶魔邪障，以此达到保护佛教事业兴旺和百姓安居乐业的目的。就此舞本义来讲，所要去除的"邪魔"，主要指人类本身的弱点和恶念，也就是佛教中所讲的"我执"。这一节日已经成为北京城春节期间重要的宗教民俗文化活动之一。每年都会吸引大批来自全国乃至世界各地的信众前来观看。2007年，雍和宫"藏传佛教金刚驱魔神舞"已列入北京市东城区非物质文化遗产名录。

新时代的雍和宫

神圣与世俗这两个标签似乎是每一个宗教场所都要面临与调和的身份认同，宗教的内容是神圣与超然的，但毕竟它无法独立于世俗社会，有时候作为旅游景点，僧人们不得不与普通的游客进行社交活动，雍和宫也不例外。现如今，雍和宫的神圣与世俗更多的反映在寺院僧人身上。身处北京这样的国际化大都市，而每天又生活在一个传统味道浓厚的藏传佛教寺院之中，这种神圣与世俗的交叉感的确很值得体味。

由于雍和宫身兼佛教寺院、博物馆和旅游景点三重身份，僧人们的日常生活与传统寺院相比有了很大变化。他们每天早晨5至7点间上殿诵经。初一、十五及佛教节庆日白天也要上殿诵经，为国泰民安、世界和平祈福。这些法会与诵经活动举办的时候，都会有北京及外地的信众前来参加。每天上午9点雍和宫正式对外开放，僧人们或看护殿堂，为游客信众服务，或从事其他工作。晚上，他们要到寺院自办的佛学院

thoughts of humans—ātma-grāha (obsession with self-ego). This festival is an important religious and folk-culture activity during the Chinese New Year celebration in Beijing. In 2007, Vajra dancing was listed as a cultural heritage of the Dongcheng District of Beijing.

Yonghegong in the New Era

Every religious site has two sides: sacred and secular. Every place of worship exists in secular society, while the content of religion is itself sacred and transcendental. Monks sometimes have to socialize with the secular, especially at tourist sites for ordinary people. This is true also for Yonghegong Temple, whose double identity affects the lives of the lamas, who continuously switch between identities associated with a traditional Tibetan Buddhist monastery and a tourist destination in a modern city.

Since Yonghegong is a temple, museum, and a tourist site, the lamas' daily life differs greatly from that in a traditional temple. From 5:00 to 7:00 a.m., they chant scriptures. On the first and fifteenth day of the lunar month, as well as on Buddhist festivals, they hold rites to chant and pray for the peace of the country and the world. Followers from Beijing and visitors from outside the city attend the rites. At 9:00 a.m., Yonghegong then opens to the public. Lamas look after the halls and offer services for visitors and Buddhist believers. After the temple closes, the lamas study Buddhism in the evening at their own Buddhist institute, where different Buddhism classes are offered based on the education level of the lamas. The classes serve to help the lamas improve their proficiency in Buddhism, so they are more professional when teaching sutras, answering questions, and correcting the misunderstandings of followers.

Two administrative agencies currently take care of temple management. One is the Yonghegong Management Office, which is composed of secular staff who are in charge of administration, logistics, and the security of the temple. The other is the Yonghegong Temple Affairs Committee, a democratic self-managed team organized by lamas, which is responsible for the religious affairs of the temple. The two teams have a clear division of labor, coordinating their work appropriately. The lamas actively explore modern temple management, with patriotism as the principal guide, setting up democratic management systems and developing the talents of fundamental assurance.

People

Yonghegong Lama Temple is the largest Tibetan Buddhist Monastery in China. A number of senior lamas practice and lecture here. We were given the privilege to interview three masters, Tubdan, Hu Xuefeng, and Danbei Jianzan.

Master Tubdan is a ninety-five-year-old man who is a Mongolian from Erdos, Inner Mongolia. Master Tubdan became a monk at age seven. At seventeen, he arrived at Ta'er Temple in Qinghai. There, he spent the next seventeen years systematically studying Buddhist theory, especially the "Five Classics and Four Continuations" (of Vajrayāna Buddhism), eventually achieving the level of Geshe, the equivalent of a doctoral degree. In 1981, he was invited to teach sutras at Yonghegong Temple, later attaining promotions to vice abbot and abbot. He also served as the vice director of the Chinese Buddhist Association and the vice chair of the Advisory Committee of the Beijing Buddhist Association. He is currently the vice chairman of the Advisory Committee of the Chinese Buddhist Association, a standing committee member of the Beijing Political Consultative Conference, the honorary president of the Beijing Buddhist Association, and the honorary

106. 万福阁内供奉的一尊高18米的弥勒佛像 Eighteen-meter statue of Maitreya Buddha in Wanfuge Pavilion

进行晚课学习。佛学院按僧人的佛学文化水平分班授课,帮助僧众依师闻法、精进学修,不断提高为信众讲经说法、解疑释惑的能力和水平。

雍和宫现有两个管理机构共同负责寺院各项事务。一个是由世俗工作人员组成的"雍和宫管理处",主要负责行政、后勤和安保等管理工作。另一个是由僧人组成的僧团自我民主管理组织"雍和宫庙务管理委员会",负责寺院宗教事务管理。二者同心协力、分工合作,以爱国爱教作为工作方针,通过采用有效的民主管理和制度建设,在人才培养和队伍建设做出了很大的努力,建立起一套较为有效的现代寺院管理模式。

人物

雍和宫现在仍然是中国内地规模最大的藏传佛教寺院,有不少高僧在此学修弘法。我们有幸采访到了图布丹、胡雪峰和丹贝坚赞三位法师。

图布丹法师来自内蒙古鄂尔多斯,蒙古族,今年95岁。他7岁出家为僧,17岁到青海塔尔寺,学经习律长达17年,系统修学了藏传佛教五部四续等显密经典,达到"格西"(博士)学位学识水平。1981年,他应邀到雍和宫做经师,后升任副住持、住持,还曾兼任中国佛教协会副会长、北京市佛教协会副会长等职务。现任中国佛教协会咨议委员会副主席、北京市政协常委、北京市佛教协会名誉会长、雍和宫

107. 持香拜佛的人 Woman worshipping with incense

abbot of Yonghegong Lama Temple. Master Tubdan is a very kind and knowledgeable man. As a scholar of Buddhism who is proficient in Mongolian, Tibetan, and Sanskrit, he has made great contributions to the resumption of Buddhist activities at Yonghegong and the development of Tibetan Buddhism in China.

Hu Xuefeng is the current abbot of the Yonghegong Lama Temple. A Mongolian from Fuxin City in Liaoning Province, Master Hu is fifty-three years old. He was one of the first monks at Yonghegong when the temple resumed religious activities in 1981. He was very clever as a child, a devout, hardworking, and patriotic Buddhist. He graduated from Advanced Tibetan Buddhism College of China, where he built a solid foundation in Buddhist studies and accumulated a rich experience in temple management. As an abbot, he advocates discipline and honesty. He promotes the concept of "Three Goods"—to do good things, speak good words, and keep good thoughts. He removed all the internal commercial activities from the temple, creating a "pure, peaceful, and reverent" environment for it. He strengthens his team by focusing on developing scholastic and practitioner-oriented Buddhist talents, while also equipping them with management skills. He holds an annual conference on sutra interpretation to enhance the temple's capacity to promote Buddhism, serve society, and benefit the general public. He is actively engaged in various charitable causes, such as providing student aid, organizing free medical diagnosis events, helping the poor, and participating in poverty-relief projects. He spreads compassion and love everywhere he goes, building connections with diverse groups. Under his influence, the management and social influence of the temple was brought to a higher level. In recent years, Yonghegong has won numerous awards including "Model Team of the First National Campaign of Creating Harmonious Religious Sites," "Demo Organization of Promoting the Unity and Progress of Ethnic Groups of the Capital City," and "Model Organization of the Capital City." In August 2014, Hu Xuefeng was elected as the chairman of the Beijing Buddhist Association. In April 2015, he was elected as the vice chairman of the Chinese Buddhist Association.

Master Danbi has also lived an interesting life. He is a Tibetan from Qinghai Province, born in 1952. Master Danbi became a monk as a child and is well versed in Tibetan, Chinese, and the philosophy of Tibetan Buddhism. In the 1960s, he returned to secular life. At the end of the 1980s, his former monastery resumed religious activities. After some consideration, he decided to return to the temple. About this decision, he later said,

> My ancestors were all Buddhists. The seed of Buddhism was planted in my heart at the time I was born. Although it was a family decision [for me] to become a monk at six, I

名誉住持。他为人善良、学识渊博，精通蒙、藏和梵文，是中国佛教界著名学者型高僧，为雍和宫佛事活动的恢复和各项事业的发展做出了重要贡献。

胡雪峰是雍和宫现任住持，全国政协委员，北京市政协委员。他来自辽宁省阜新市，蒙古族，今年53岁，是1981年雍和宫重新恢复宗教活动后第一批来此出家的僧人。他天资聪慧、信仰虔诚、修学刻苦、爱国爱教，是中国藏语系高级佛学院毕业的高材生，佛学功底深厚，寺院管理经验丰富。他担任雍和宫住持以来，着重引导僧众遵规守戒、正信正行，树立"做好事、说好话、存好念"的"三好"理念；通过撤销商业摊点、免费赠香等举措，努力打造"净、静、敬"的"三境"寺院；通过重点培养"学问型、修持型、管理型"僧才，不断强化僧团队伍建设。这既是他的管理理念，也是他对团队的要求；每年举办一届讲经交流会，提高寺院弘扬佛法、服务社会、惠及大众的水平和能力；积极投身助学义诊、扶贫济困、对口帮扶等公益慈善事业，广结善缘，把佛教的慈悲与爱心播撒到了四面八方，寺院管理水平和社会影响力进一步提升。近年来，雍和宫先后荣获"首届全国创建和谐寺观教堂活动先进集体"、"首都民族团结进步先进单位"、"首都文明标兵单位"等荣誉。2014年8月，胡雪峰被推选为北京市佛教协会会长，2015年4月，又当选中国佛教协会副会长。

丹贝法师有着非常有趣的经历。他出生于1952年，藏族，自幼出家为僧，通晓藏、汉语文和藏传佛教。20世纪60年代，因特殊的社会原因，丹贝法师曾一度还俗在家。80年代末，他原来出家的寺院恢复了正常运转，经过一段时间的思考，他再次出家当僧人。他说："我们家祖祖辈辈都信佛，信佛的种子从小就播撒在我的心里，这是与生俱来的，因此我6岁就出家了。这虽然是家里的决定，但我当时心里也非常愿意。后来尽管由于各种原因还俗在家，但我对藏传佛教的信仰情结始终没有改变过。所以又一次出家为僧，也算是我的佛缘吧。"1987年，丹贝法师从青海塔尔寺来到北京，成为雍和宫的一名僧人，至今已度过了32年的时光。现在，他的主要工作是整理、校对雍和宫所藏佛教经版和古籍文献、印制经书。经过多年不懈努力，2016年，他编辑和创制的雍和宫藏文字库和输入法问世，受到社会广泛好评。

雍和宫这座昔日的皇家寺院，今天已经成为国内外信众与游人有缘必朝的佛教圣地，成为中国对外开放、展现中国宗教信仰自由政策的一扇重要窗口。自1981年重新开放以来，雍和宫已接待来自世界各地的游客信众5000多万人次，其中包括数百位国家元首、地区领导人以及国际宗教组织和宗教界领袖。近年来，每年有近300万国内外信众和游客入寺礼佛参观。在充分发挥佛教场所固有功能和作用的同时，雍和宫积极服务于国家文化和外交事业，为国际社会了解中国宗教政策和宗教状况，促进中外友好交往、文化交流发挥了特殊作用。

在未来的岁月中，雍和宫这座历经270多年岁月的寺庙建筑，仍然会在北京这座多元文化兼容并蓄的城市中，继续发挥独特功能，展现人文新魅力。

108. 释迦牟尼的壁画 **Fresco of Śākyamuni** *(photo by He Yinglong)*

was happy for that decision. During my years of being a secular man, I never changed my faith in Tibetan Buddhism. It was because of my connection with Buddhism that I chose to become a monk again.

In 1987, Master Danbi arrived in Beijing from Ta'er Temple in Qinghai and became a lama at Yonghegong. He has been resident here for thirty-two years now, and his main responsibilities are editing and proof-reading the Buddhist scriptures and ancient classics as well as printing scriptures. In 2016, he designed and launched the Yonghegong Tibetan language database and input method, which has become highly acclaimed.

A former royal temple has become a holy pilgrimage site for Buddhists at home and abroad. It is a window to showcase to the world China's open policy and practice of religious freedom. Since the resumption of activities in 1981, Yonghegong has received over fifty million tourists and followers from all over the world, including hundreds of heads of state, regional leaders, and heads of international religious organizations. In recent years, the temple has received about three million visitors per year. While ensuring its Buddhist functions and activities, Yonghegong is actively engaged in the country's cultural and diplomatic causes. It plays an important role in introducing China's religious policies to the world and promoting friendship and cultural communications between China and other countries. The unique functions of Yonghegong, a Lama Temple with a 270-year history, will no doubt continue, and its cultural charms will remain.

Index

Anneiertiao Faming Temple 安内二条法明寺, as one of the "Four Major Official Mosques" in Beijing, 71
Asbury, Bishop Francis (1745–1816), 47
Asbury Church. *See* Chongwenmen Church

Bai Shouyi 白寿彝, and the planning of Fuad Library at Dongsi Mosque, 77
Baiyunguan Temple 白云观, location of, 9
Baiyunguan Temple 白云观—architecture (*kongjian* 空间):
 architectural symmetry of (Ch. *duanzheng* 端正) and simplicity of, 9, 15–17
 Caishen 财神 ("Money Deities") Hall, 9
 Laolü Hall 老律堂 (aka "Temple of Seven Immortals"), 15
 Lingguan Hall 灵官殿, 9
 Yuanchen Temple 元辰殿 featuring Doumu Yuanjun 斗姆元君, Mother Goddess of the Big Dipper, *13*f6, 17
 Yuanjun Hall featuring the Goddess of Sunlight from the East (Bixia Yuajun), 17
—Daoist rituals:
 birthday ceremony of Wenchang Emperor at, 17–19
 celebration of the birthdays of deities and founders of Daoism at, 15
 and Quanzhen Daoism 全真 at, 15
Beiding Niangniang Temple 北顶娘娘庙:
 Bixia Yuanjun worshipped at, 25–29, *28*f13
 Imperial Edict 敕建 on its Mountain Gate 山门, 21
 "Long Lasting Incense" 长眠香 sold at, 25, *27*f12
 and the name "*ding*" 顶 (top), 21
 Temple of Heavenly Kings 天王殿, 25
Beijing 北京:
 "Beijing Drifters," 109, 111, 149, 165
 as the Great Capital (Dadu 大都) of the Yuan, 57, 183
Beijing Buddhist Association 北京市佛教协会:
 Hu Xuefeng 胡雪峰 as chairman of, 209
 and Tubdan 丹贝坚赞, 207
Bible 圣经:
 banquet table symbolizing the presence of God in the Hebrew Bible, 189, *189*f97
 displayed with a cross 十字架 at Haidian Church, 109, 113
 donations of, 199
 and foreign literature studies, 55
 lectures and reading classes at Xizhimen Church, 197
 stained-glass windows with scenes from the Bible, 181–185, *183*f95, 191, 193, 199
 verses on "Resurrection Egg" gifts at Easter, 115
—quotations from:
 Matthew 1:21, 113
 Matthew 7:7, 195
 Matthew 10:33, 187
 Matthew 11:28, 199
 Luke 9:48, 199
 Luke 14:25, 197
 Luke 23:34, 193
 Luke 24:7, 115
 John 6:35, 191
 1 Peter 5:7, 195
Bixia Yuanjun 碧霞元君 (Goddess of Sunlight):
 evolution of worship of her, 21
 and fertility, 27
 Robe Changing Day (Ch. *huanpao ri* 换袍日) of, 27–29
 temples to Bixia Yuanjun built during the Qing, 21
 as Tianxian Niangniang ("Goddess of Heavenly Immortals"), 25
 worship at Baiyunguan Temple, *12*f5, 17
 worship at Beiding Niangniang Temple, 25–29, *28*f13
Boxer Rebellion (1899–1901):
 and Chongwenmen Church, 47
 and Guangji Temple, 93
 and Housangyu Church, 119
 and Xishiku Church, 179, 191
Buddhism 佛教:
 introduction to Beijing around 300 CE, 6
 Lü Zong 律宗 tradition at Guangji Temple, 93
 principles of the Noble Eightfold Path compared with tea brewing and tasting, 145
 Pure Land Buddhism (Ch. 净土宗), 155
 and Quanzhen Daoism 全真, 15
 See also Guangji Temple 广济寺; Yonghegong Temple 雍和宫
—Tibetan Buddhism 藏传佛教:
 Living Buddhas (Tib. *tulku*) determined by "drawing lots from the golden urn" 金瓶掣签制度, 203
 Miaoyin temple 妙应寺 built in the early Yuan Dynasty, 3
 prayer wheel 转经筒 at Tanzhe Temple, 137
 See also Ta'er Temple in Qinghai 青海塔尔寺 (Tib. Kumbum Jampa Ling)
Buddhist deities:
 Amitābha 阿弥陀佛 at Tianning Temple, *158*f82
 Amitāyus 无量寿佛 at Yonghegong Hall, 205
 bodhisattva Skanda (Ch. 韦陀菩萨) at Tianning Temple, 155
 enlightenment of Śākyamuni 释迦牟尼, 151
 guardian deities (Ch. 金刚力士, Skt. *Dharmapāla*) at Tianning Hall, *154*f80, 155
 Maitreya Buddha 弥勒佛 in, 97, *97*f48, 155, 205, *208*f106
 Past Buddha 过去佛像 (Skt. Kaśyapa) at Guangji Temple, 98, 99
 Siṃhanāda (Ch. 狮吼佛, Roaring Lion Buddha) at Yonghegong Hall, *158*f82
 See also Pharmacist Buddha 药师佛 (Skt. Bhaiṣajyaguru)
Buddhist nuns (Ch. 比丘尼, Skt. *bhikkunī*):
 alternative to familial life offered by the *bhikkhunī* system, 153
 Bamboo Forest Temple 竹林寺 as the first female monastery in China, 153
 Bao Chang's *Biographies of Bhikkhunī* 比丘尼传, 153
 Master Jingjian 净检法帅 (291–361), 153
 Master Xinhui's 心慧法帅 transition from a secular individual to a religious person, 159–163
 See also Tianning Temple 天宁寺
Buddhist practices:
 "Amitābha 阿弥陀佛" recitation at Guangji Temple, 105
 captive-animal releasing rite at Tianning Temple, 157
 clockwise circumambulation of the pagoda at Tianning Temple, 155
 devoutness and kindness practiced at Guangji temple, 99–103

Cai Yuanpei 蔡元培, and the planning of Fuad Library at Dongsi Mosque, 77
candles 灯:
 candle lighting at Mass, 125
 candlelight symbolism of Easter, 115
 lotus candles (Ch. 莲灯), *147*f77
Changping Mosque 昌平清真寺:
 and the first Muslim settlers in Beijing, 33
 as a Major Historical and Cultural Site Protected, 33
 moon-watching tower, 望月楼, 37–39
 Ramadan (Ch. 莱麦丹) celebrated at, 39
 three gateways of, 35–37, *40*f18
Chen Guangyuan 陈广元 (aka Hillalundin, b. 1932):
 on Dongsi Mosque during the Cultural Revolution, 71
 as imam of Changping Mosque, 35
 inscription on the lintel of the middle gate at Changping by, *37*f16
Chen You 陈友 (d. 1460), funding of Dongsi Mosque, 71
Chengda Teachers College 成达师范学院:
 Fuad Library 福德图书馆 at, 77
 location at Dongsi Mosque, 71
Chinese Daoist Association 道教协会, and Huode Zhenjun Temple, 131

Chinese Islamic Association:
Chen Guangyuan 陈广元 as president of, 35, 37, 71
Yang Faming 杨发明 as director of, 73
Chinese tradition:
and attitudes of those who lived through the Cultural Revolution, 87
burning of paper money, 13, 85
Chinese culture reflected in the names of mosques, 70
"Five Ridges and Six Beasts" 五脊六兽 from Chinese architectural tradition featured in Dongsi Mosque, 75, 75f36
and governance by the "Tianzi" 天子 (the emperor, a.k.a. the "son of Heaven"), 11, 65
important festivals celebrated at Haidian Church, 113
integration of Confucianism, Buddhism, and Daoism in Quanzhen Daoism 全真, 15
and legendary Bi Xi 贔屃, 181
and Lu Xun 鲁迅 on the roots of China in Daoism, 19
moon-watching towers 望月楼 compared with minarets in the Arab world, 73
and "Praise the Mountain Village" 山村咏怀 by Shao Kangjie 邵康节 (1011–1077), 91
tangyuan 汤圆 distributed at the Yuanxiao Festival 元宵节, 137
and Tanzhe Temple as a cultural center, 151
and the traditional Chinese architectural planning of the Forbidden City, 141
"Vajra Exorcism Dancing" (Ch. 金刚驱魔神舞) listed as a cultural heritage of the Dongcheng District of Beijing, 205–207
Xishiku Church's combination of Chinese and Western architecture, 179–181
See also Confucian classics; Confucianism; festivals; folk religions 民间宗教; immortals; *Journey to the West* 西游记; Spring Festival 春节
Chongwenmen Church 崇文门教堂, 47f21, 48f22, 50f23
accessibility of, 47–49
choral program at, 49–51, 51f24, 55
international orientation of, 47
Xu Yüfa 徐玉发 (member of), 51, 51, 52
—history (*lishi* 历史):
and the Beijing Christian Council, 47–49
and Bishop Francis Asbury, 47
and the Boxer Rebellion, 47
as the first Protestant church in Northern China, 47
Christianity 基督教:
Christians in Beijing noted by Marco Polo, 6
See also Chongwenmen Church 崇文门教堂; Evangelical Christianity; Haidian Church 海淀教堂; Housangyu Church 后桑峪教堂; Protestantism
—Roman Catholicism 罗马天主教 or 天主教,

arrival in Beijing, 3
and Matteo Ricci, 3, 183
See also Xishiku Church 西什库教堂; Xizhimen Church 西直门天主堂
Christmas (Ch. 圣诞节):
at Haidian Church, 113–115
at Xizhimen Catholic Church, 199
Confucian Classics 儒家经典:
and elite education at the Imperial College, 61
and *guoxue* 国学, 59, 67
and the revival of Confucianism, 67
rituals recorded in the Rites of Zhou and the Book of Rites, 17
Stella garden of thirteen Confucian Classics, 64f32, 65
See also Yijing
Confucianism:
and Quanzhen Daoism 全真, 15
spiritualization by Zhu Xi, 朱熹, 59
Confucian Temple 孔庙:
memorial tablet 牌位 for Confucian Sage Bu 卜子, 61f29
and worship of Confucius, 孔子, 57–59 57f27
—Dacheng Hall 大成殿, 58f28
plaques praising Confucius by nine emperors in, 63
Cui Hao 崔颢 (704–754), "Yellow Crane Tower" by, 9
Cultural Revolution (1966–1976):
clock-tower at Xizhimen Catholic Church destroyed during, 193
Daoist temples associated with feudalism and superstition, 87
Dongsi Mosque ordered to remain open during, 71
and Housangyu Church, 119–121, 123
the Temple of Heavenly Kings at Beiding Niangniang Temple during, 25
Tianning Temple Buddhist statues smashed during, 157
worship of Confucius considered superstition during, 59

Dalai Lamas:
7th Dalai Lama 七世达赖喇嘛, 205
and the system of "drawing lots from the golden urn" 金瓶掣签制度, 203
Daoism:
Dao of Heaven 道天 explained by Priest Chen at Dongyue Temple, 91
presentation in movies and soap operas, 133
Quanzhen Daoism 全真, 15
"Ten-Direction Residence System" 十方丛林, 17
and the views of many Chinese people, 87
yin 阴 and *yang* 阳, 11, 19, 135
See also Baiyunguan Temple 白云观; Huode Zhenjun Temple 火德真君庙
Daoist deities:
and attitudes towards life and the secular world, 11–13
Doumu Yuanjun 斗姆元君, Mother Goddess of the Big Dipper, 13f6, 17

Huode Zhenjun 火德真君 ("Fire God"), 138f30
Lightning Mother and Thunder Father, 15
"Money Deities" 财神, 9, 133
"Three Officer Great Deities" (*sanguan*), 131
Wang Lingguan 王灵官, 130f66
Xuanwu 玄武, 15, 135
Yühung 玉皇 ("Jade Emperor"), 11
Zhao Gongming (God of Wealth), 133
See also Bixia Yuan jun 碧霞元君 (Goddess of Sunlight); immortals (Ch. *shenxian* 火德真君); Tai Sui deities 太岁神; "Three Officer Great Deities" (*sanguan*)
Daoist ritual practice:
daily activities of Daoist priests at Biayunguan Temple, 15
Daoist Priest Ma on the life of Daoist priests, 87–89
and sound, 9, 17–19
Daoist temples:
Xianghuo temple 香火寺 on "Three Official Temple Hutong," 35
See also Huode Zhenjun Temple 火德真君庙
Dongsi Mosque 东四清真寺:
Imam He 何阿訇, 77–79, 78
location of, 69
See also Chengda Teachers College 成达师范学院; Imam He 何阿訇
—history (*lishi* 历史):
during the Cultural Revolution, 71
as one of the "Four Major Official Mosques" in Beijing, 71
"Qing Zhen Temple" (清真寺) on a plaque from 1450, 71
since the establishment of the PRC, 71
Yue hua 月华 Chinese Muslim newspaper formerly located at, 71
—Prayer Hall, 69f33, 73–75
amplification of sound by the domes in sound, 75
Arabic calligraphy featuring *Kufa* (Ch. 库法体) and *Naskh* (Ch. 纳斯赫体 on beams of), 75
"Five Ridges and Six Beasts" 五脊六兽 from Chinese architectural tradition featured in, 75f36
Imam He 何阿訇 giving a sermon in, 78f38
women's prayer hall at, 77
—space (*kongjian* 空间):
Ablution (*wudu*) room at, 70f34
"Dongsi Pailou—Four Ornamental Arches on the East" 东四牌楼 as its full name, 69
moon-watching tower 望月楼, 41f35, 73, 79,
stone monument named 清真法明百字圣号 ("The Life of Muhammad in 100 Characters") at, 75
Dongyue Temple 东岳庙:
cats at, 85, 91f45
founding by Zhang Liusun 张留孙, 85
prayer wheels at, 90f44
Tai Sui Deities worshipped at, 85

214   INDEX

Zhandai Gate ("Watching Mount Tai Gate") at, *81*f39

Easter (Ch. 复活节):
  candlelight symbolism of, 115
  Good Friday Cross at Chongwenmen Church, *53*f26
  at Haidian Christian Church, 113, 115
  at Xizhimen Catholic Church, 195, 199
Emperor Jiaqing 嘉庆帝 (r. 1796–1820), and damage to Xizhimen Catholic Church, 191
Emperor Kangxi 康熙帝 (r. 1661–1722):
  inscription on the Main Gate of Guangji Temple, 93, *94*f46
  and the plaques praising Confucius at Beijing's Confucius Temple, 63
  Tanzhe Temple endowed with the title "royal temple" by, 143
Emperor Shunzhi 顺治帝 (r. 1644–1661):
  and Guangji Temple, 56
  and worship of Confucius, 59
Emperor Qianlong 乾隆皇帝 (r. 1735–1796):
  and "Fruit of Realization and Sound of Emptiness" in Daxiong Hall of Guangji Temple, 99
  and Imperial College 国子监, 63–65
  reverence for the 6th Panchen Lama, 205
  statue in Jetai Building 戒台楼 of Yonghegong Temple, *202*f103
  temples to Bixia Yuanjun built during the reign of, 21
  and the Tibetan Buddhist system of "drawing lots from the golden urn" 金瓶掣签制度, 203
  and the white sandalwood Maitreya Buddha in Wanfu Pavilion at Yonghegong, 205
Emperor Xuande 宣德 (aka Emperor Xuanzong, r. 1425-135), and Beiding Niangning Temple, 15
Emperor Xuantong 宣统 (r. 1908–1912), and the plaques praising Confucius at Dacheng Hall in Beijing's Confucius Temple, 63
Emperor Yongle 永乐 (r. 1402–1424):
  capital Dadu 大都 established in Beijing, 33
  and Yilun Hall at the Imperial College, 65
Emperor Yongzheng 雍正 (r. 1722–1735)—as Prince Yinzhen 胤禛, residence in the Yonghegong Temple, 201
Emperor Zhu Qiyu 朱祁钰 (r. 1449–1457), inscription on Dongsi Mosque, 71
Emperor Zhu Yuanzhang 朱元璋 (r. 1368–1398):
  and Imperial College, 35
  and the text of the stone monument at 清真法明百字圣号, 75
Empress Dowager Cixi 慈禧太后 (1835–1908), and Xishiku Church, 179
Evangelical Christianity:
  Chongwenmen Church visited by William Franklin ("Billy") Graham, Jr., 47
  See also Haidian Church

Feng Youlan 冯友兰, and the planning of Fuad Library at Dongsi Mosque, 77
festivals:
  Chongyang 重阳 (Double Ninth Festival), 113, 137
  Duanwu 端午 (Dragon Boat Festival), 113, 197
  Zhongqiu 中秋 (Mid-Autumn Festival), 113, 137
  Qingming 清明 (Tomb-Sweeping Day), 113, 137
  Yuanxiao 元宵节 (Lantern Festival), 113, 137
  See also Christmas (Ch. 圣诞节); Easter (Ch. 复活节); Laba Festival 腊八节; Spring Festival 春节
Five Pillars 五功. *See* Islam 伊斯兰教—Five Pillars
folk religions 民间宗教:
  and answers to prayers, 131
  and Bixia Yuanjun 碧霞元君 (Goddess of Sunlight), 21
  and combining Confucianism and Daoism, 13
  and divination practices, 135
  multifaceted social function of, 135
  See also immortals; Tanzhe Temple 潭柘寺
Forbidden City 故宫:
  Dongsi Mosque in relation to, 69
  Guangji Temple in relation to, 93
  Houde Zhenjun Temple in relation to, 137
  Taihe Hall (Ch. 太和殿) construction standards, 63
  and traditional Chinese architectural planning, 141
  Xiyuan Palace 西苑 in relation to, 179
Four Heavenly Kings 四大天王:
  and China's traditional religions, 135
  in the *Journey to the West*, 25
  statue of a Heavenly King at Guangji Temple, *97*f48
  Tianwang Hall at Tanzhe Temple, *141*
Fuad I 福阿德 (1868—1936), funding provided for Fuad Library at Dongsi Mosque, 77

Gu Jiegang 顾颉刚, and the planning of Fuad Library at Dongsi Mosque, 77
Guangji Temple 广济寺:
  and contemporary Buddhism, 99–103, *103*f52
  Emperor Kangxi's inscription on the Main Gate of, 93, *94*f46
  location of, 93
  Lü Zong 律宗 tradition at, 93
  social function of offering tranquility and health for seniors, 99
  statues of Maitreya and a Heavenly King at, 97, *97*f48
  —Daxiong Hall 大雄宝殿, *102*f51
  "Amitābha 阿弥陀佛" recitation at, 105
  daily worship at, 103, 105
  eighteen *arhats* (Ch. 罗汉), *95*f47, 99
  "Fruit of Realization and Sound of Emptiness" mural in, 99, *100*f50
  statue of the Past Buddha 过去佛 (Skt. Kaśyapa) at, 98, 99
Guanyin Bodhisattva, 观音菩萨 (Skt. Avalokiteśvara), six-character mantra "Om Mani Padme Hum" 唵嘛呢叭咪吽, 143

Haidian Church 海淀教堂, *107*f53
  bible 圣经 displayed with a cross 十字架, 113
  Easter (Ch. 复活节) at, 113, 115
  Taize-style (Ch. 泰泽) prayer service held during Holy Week (Ch. 复活节的圣周) at, 115
  youth choir at, *108*f54, 115
hajj (Ch. 朝功) pilgrimage to Mecca (Ch. 麦加朝觐):
  and the Japanese attempt of cover up crimes during the Sino-Japanese War, 77
  as one of the Five Pillars, 171
Heavenly Kings. *See* Four Heavenly Kings 四大天王
Housangyu Church 后桑峪教堂:
  Chinese traditions celebrated at, 125
  church band, *122*f62
  during the Cultural revolution, 119–121, 123
  location of, 117, *117*f58
  Mass at, 121–127, *121*f61
  Sacred Heart of Jesus Hall, 121, *125*f64
  —and Virgin Mary:
  Mount Virgin Mary, *118*f59, 119, *120*f60, 123, 127
  Virgin Mary statue in the courtyard, *120*f60, 121
Hui people (Ch. Huimin 回民):
  and the halal catering industry (Ch. Qingzhen canyingye 清真餐饮业), 41, 42, 165, 175
  surnames of, 167
  zhemati 哲马提 (residential community centered around a mosque), 167
  Zhongcang community 中仓社区 in Beijing, 165
Huode Zhenjun Temple 火德真君庙 ("Fire God" Temple):
  and the Chinese Daoist Association 道教协会, 131
  Daoist Priest Wei "Intern Immortal" 实习神仙, 129, 133
  front courtyard of, *128*f65
  location of, 129, 137
  Moon Elderly Immortal Hall of, 135, *137*f69
  secularization with the founding of the PRC, 129
  statue of Huode Zhenjun at, *138*f30
  Wealth God Hall 财神殿, 133, *134*f68
  and the Zhengyi Sect of Daoism (Way of Orthodox Unity), 131
  —rites and activities at:
  answers to prayers, 131, 135
  Chinese New Year at, 129
  "competing for the first stick of incense" (*qiang tou xiang* 抢头香), 129
  festivals celebrated throughout the year, 137
  worshiping with incense at, 137, *139*f71
Hu Xuefeng 胡雪峰, 207

promotion of the "Three Goods" (三好) as abbot (住持) of Yonghegong, 209

Imam He 何阿訇, 76f37
    on functions at Dongsi Mosque, 79
    giving a sermon (*khutbah* 呼图白) in the prayer hall and Dongsi Mosque, 78f38
immortals (Ch. *shenxian* 神仙们):
    Bixia Yuanjun as Tianxian Niangniang ("Goddess of Heavenly Immortals"), 25
    and Daoist self-cultivation, 89
    Moon Elderly Immortal, 135, 137
    Yühung 玉皇 ("Jade Emperor"), 11
    Zhenwu 真武, 15
    See also Wenchang Emperor 文昌帝
Imperial College 国子监:
    establishment as an "Imperial School" (Guozixue 国子学), 59
    Paifang 牌坊 with 圜桥教泽 ("School Surrounded by a Circular Pool Connected outside by Bridges"), 62f30, 65
    Piyong Hall 辟雍殿, 63f31, 65
    Yilun Hall 彝伦堂 of, 65
incense and incense burning (Ch. *shaoxiang* 烧香):
    burning incense at Tianning Temple, 157, 161f83, 163
    celestial sounds of singing at Eucharist compared with, 195
    "competing for the first stick of incense" (*qiang tou xiang* 抢头香) at Huode Zhenjun Temple, 129
    incense lighter at Dongyue Temple, 89f43
    "Long Lasting Incense" 长眠香 at Beiding Niangning Temple, 25, 27f12
    offering by a Daoist priest at Baiyun Temple, 11
    on Robe Changing day, 29
    on Sundays and holy days at Housangyu Roman Catholic Church, 125
    worshipping with incense at Guangji Temple, 99
    worshipping with incense at Yonghegong Temple, 209f107
Islam 伊斯兰教:
    creation of life not depicted in art of, 75
    Eid al-Adha (Ch. 古尔邦节), 39, 73, 77
    Eid al-Fitr (Ch. 开斋节), 39, 73, 77
    introduction to Beijing, 6
    Jumu'ah worship on Fridays (Ch. 聚礼), 37, 39, 77, 171, 173
    mosques (*libaisi* 礼拜寺 or *Qingzhensi* 清真寺 [Arabic *masjid*]). See Dongsi Mosque; Niujie Mosque
    Muslim hat and prayer beads, 168f87
    as "Qing Zhen Gu Jiao" 清真古教, 69–70
    See also Chinese Islamic Association; minarets; *salat* (prayer)
—Five Pillars (Ch. 五功):
    and *duwayi* 杜哇宜 inscriptions, 167
    sawm (Ch. 课功) fasting during Ramadan, 171
    shahada (Ch. 念功) Muslim profession of faith, 171
    zakat (Ch. 斋功) alms to benefit the poor, 171

See also *hajj* (Ch. 朝功) pilgrimage to Mecca; *salat* (prayer)

Jetai Building 戒台楼. See Yonghegong Temple 雍和宫
Jinshifangjie Pushou Temple 锦什坊街普寿寺:
    as one of the "Four Major Official Mosques" in Beijing, 71
    and the term *pushou* ("May all have a long life"), 71
Journey to the West 西游记 by Wu Cheng'en 吴承恩:
    and the four heavenly kings, 25
    and Thunder Father and Lightning Mother, 15

Kublai Khan 忽必烈汗 (1215–1294), Dadu 大都 (Great Capital) established by, 57

Laba Festival 腊八节:
    evolution of, 149
    at Tanzhe Temple, 149–151
    at Yonghegong Temple, 205
Lu Xun 鲁迅 on the roots of China in Daoism, 19

Marco Polo, 3
    marriage and weddings:
    and blessings by the Goddess of Sunlight (Bixia Yuanjun 白寿彝), 17
    Cana wedding feast miracle depicted on carvings at Xizhimen Catholic Church, 189
    Cana wedding feast miracle stone jar replicas at Xizhimen Catholic Church, 193
    and conversion rites at Dongsi Mosque, 79
    and "Long Lasting Incense" (Daoist blessing cards) at Beiding Niangning Temple, 27
    and Moon Elderly Immortal, 135, 137
    symbolism of the wedding tabernacle behind the banquet table at Xizhimen Church, 189, 189f97
minarets (Ch. 宣礼塔 or 敏纳热):
    and the courtyard of Tongzhou Mosque, 169
    and the "moon-watching tower" at Dongsi Mosque, 71, 73
    smaller size of Chinese minarets compared with those in the Arab world, 73
Ming Dynasty 明朝 (1368–1644):
    and Bixia Yuanjun, 21
    construction of Dongsi Mosque during, 71
    emperors. See Emperor Yongle 永乐; Emperor Zhu Qiyu 朱祁钰; Emperor Zhu Yuanzhang 朱元璋
    Master Puhui's 普慧法师 rebuilding of Guangji Temple, 93
    names for mosques during, 71
Mongolia and Mongolians:
    Khutughtu (Ch. 呼图克图) Mongolian Living Buddhas at Yonghegong Temple, 203
    Kublai Khan 忽必烈汗 (1215–1294), 57
    meeting of Genghis Khan 成吉思汗

and Qiu Chuji 丘处机 at Snow Mountain, (1220s), 15
Montecorvino, Giovanni da, Bishop (孟高维主教), arrival in Beijing in 1294, 3, 117, 183

Nanluoguxiang 南锣鼓巷 (International Trade Center), Huode Zhenjun Temple in relation to, 137
Niujie Mosque 牛街礼拜寺:
    establishment in Beijing (996), 3
    as one of the "Four Major Official Mosques" in Beijing, 71
North Church. See Xishiku Church 西什库教堂

Pharmacist Buddha 药师佛 (Skt. Bhaiṣajyaguru):
    hall at Tianning Temple dedicated to, 157f81, 162f84
    worship at the Daxiong Treasue Hall in Chinese Buddhist monasteries, 203
prayer wheels 转经筒:
    at Dongyue Temple, 90f44
    at Tanzhe Temple, 142f73, 143–145
Protestantism:
    arrival in Beijing, 3
    churches. See Chongwenmen Church

Qing Dynasty 清代 (1644–1912), emperors. See Emperor Jiaqing 嘉庆帝; Emperor Kangxi 康熙皇帝; Emperor Qianlong 乾隆皇帝; Emperor Shunzhi 顺治帝 (r. 1644–1661); Emperor Xuantong 宣统; Empress Dowager Cixi 慈禧太后
Qur'an (Ch. 古兰经):
    chanting by the imam while entering the prayer hall, 39
    on fasting during Ramadan, 39
    reading of, 41f19
    reciting verses during *salat*, 74, 77, 171
    revelation by Allah during the month of Ramadan, 39
    translation of *Selected Translation of the Qur'an Classification* by Yang Pinsan 杨品三, 35
    verse 17:1, 173
    verses inscribed on bronze plates in the hutong near Tongzhou Mosque, 167

Ramadan (Ch. 莱麦丹):
    iftar (Ch. 开斋饭) served at the end of, 39
    revelation of the Quran by Allah celebrated during, 39
    sawm (Ch. 课功) fasting during, 171
Roman Catholicism 罗马天主教 or 天主教. See Christianity 基督教—Roman Catholicism

salat (prayer):
    fajr (Ch. 晨) dawn prayer, 171
    dhuhr (Ch. 晌功) midday prayer (aka *Salat al-Zuhr*), 43f20, 77, 171
    asr (Ch. 晡) afternoon prayer, 171
    magrib (Ch. 昏) sunset prayer, 45, 171, 173
    isha, nighttime prayer (Ch. 宵), 171
    and *duwayi* 杜哇宜, 167

Jumu'ah worship on Fridays (Ch. 聚礼), 37, 39, 77, 171, 173
 as one of the Five Pillars, 39, 171
 reciting of verses from the Qur'an during, 74, 77, 171
 and the women's mosque at Tongzhou Mosque, 169, 171, *171*f88
 and the women's prayer hall at Dongsi Mosque, 77
Silk Road 丝绸之路, and the introduction of foreign religions to Beijing, 3
Song Dynasty 宋朝 (960—1279):
 Confucianism during, 59
 Daoism during, 13, 15
sound:
 amplification by the domes in Dongsi Mosque, 75
 and "bell sound, good luck," 9, *10*f3
 call to prayer from minarets, 73
 and the choral program at Chongwenmen Church, 49–51, *51*f24
 of Christmas carols at Haidian Church, 113–115
 and the expression of spirituality, 17
 and "Fruit of Realization and Sound of Emptiness" in Daxiong Hall of Guangji Temple, 99, *100*f50
 and the Housangyu church band, 121–123, *122*f62
 music at Xizhimen Church, 191, 199
 of quiet eating at a ritual of cultivation at Guangji Temple, 105
 of red praying-cards in the wind, 16
 in rituals and music at Confucius Temple, 57, 59, 63–65
 of singing during Eucharist at Xizhimen Church, 195
 of wind chimes at Tianning Temple, 155, 163
 of the wooden fish in Daxiong Hall, 103, 105
Spring Festival 春节:
 and a children's rhyme for Laba Festival, 205
 celebration at Haidian Church, 113
 celebration at Housangyu Church, 125
 and Chinese New Year at Huode Zhenjun Temple, 129

Ta'er Temple in Qinghai 青海塔尔寺 (Tib. Kumbum Jampa Ling):
 and Master Danbe, 110
 and Master Tubdan 丹贝坚赞, 207
Tai Sui Deities 太岁神:
 and New Year's festivities at Huode Zhenjun Temple, 129
 worship at Dongyue Temple, 85
 Zhandai Gate ("Watching Mount Tai Gate") at Dongyue Temple, *81*f39
Tang Dynasty 唐代 (618–907):
 Baiyun Temple constructed during, 9
 Bixia Yuanjun as Tai Mountain Jade Maiden during, 21
 and Chan-Tea culture, 145
 evocative imagery from poetry of, 9
Tanzhe Temple 潭柘寺:
 and Chan-Tea culture, 143–145, *144*f75

 endowed as a "royal temple" by Kangxi, 143
 founding in 307 CE, 6
 Laba Festival 腊八节, 149–151
 prayer wheel at, *142*f73, 143–145
—space (*kongjian* 空间), 141
 Guanyin 观音菩萨 (Avalokiteśvara), *149*f78
 Imperial Trees at, 143
 stone fish at Dragon King Hall, *143*f74, 145
 symmetrical layout of, 141
Teodorico Pedrini (1671–1746), 191
"Three Officer Great Deities" (*sanguan*):
 at Baiyunguan Temple, 9–10
 at Sanguan Hall in Huode Zhenjun Temple, 131
 and the spiritual nature of the Chinese people, 13
Tianning Temple 天宁寺:
 accessibility to the public, 86, 162
 burning incense at, 157, *161*f83, 163
 captive-animal releasing rite, 157
 clockwise circumambulation of the pagoda at, 155
—history (*lishi* 历史):
 construction and reconstruction of, 155
 destruction during the Cultural Revolution, 157
 occupation by different factories, 155
—space (*kongjian* 空间):
 Amitābha 阿弥陀佛 at, *158*f82
 location in Beijing, 155, 159, 163
 Mountain Gate Hall, 山门殿, 155
 pagoda stupa 佛塔 at, *153*f79, *154*f80, 155
 Pharmacist Buddha Hall 药师殿, *157*f81, *162*f84
 sound of wind chimes at, 155, 163
Tibetan Buddhism 藏传佛教. *See under* Buddhism 佛教
Tongzhou Mosque 通州清真大寺:
 ablution (*wudu*) room at, 169, *175*f91
 stone tablet commemorating the reconstruction of, *166*f86
 surrounding hutong 胡同, 167
 women's mosque at, 169, 171, *171*f88
Tubdan 丹贝坚赞, 207

Wenchang Emperor 文昌帝:
 birthday ceremony at Baiyunguang, 17–19
 influence in Daoism and folk religions of, 19
 statues of his riding the horses at Dongyue Temple, 83, *85*f41
West Church. *See* Xizhimen Church 西直门天主堂
Western Jin Dynasty 西晋 (266–317):
 Bamboo Forest Temple 竹林寺 established during, 153
 "Imperial School" (*Guozixue* 国子学) established, 59
 Tanzhe Temple 潭柘寺 built in the first year of, 141

Xishiku Church 西什库教堂:
 combination of Chinese and Western architecture at, 179–181

 stained-glass windows at, 181–185, *183*f95,
 visibility from Xiyuan Palace of the Forbidden City, 179
Xizhimen Church 西直门天主堂:
 baptisms at, *190*f98, 195
 destruction during the Cultural Revolution, 193
 music at, 191, 199
 publication of "the West Church Cana" weekly magazine, 197
 stained-glass windows at, 191, 193, 199
 symbolism of the wedding tabernacle behind the banquet table at, 189, *189*f97

Yang, C. K., on the multifaceted social function of Chinese traditional religions, 135
Yang Pinsan 杨品三 (aka Nuraq, 1921–1983), 35
Yijing 易经 (*Classic of Changes* or 周易):
 as one of the thirteen Confucian Classics, 65
 "Tai" 泰 hexagram of, 29
Yonghegong Temple 雍和宫:
 exterior view of, *201*f102
 Fresco of Śakyamuni at, *211*f108
 Khutughtu (Ch. 呼图克图) Mongolian Living Buddhas in residence at, 203
 Laba Festival 腊八节 at, 205
 "Vajra Exorcism Dancing" (Ch. 金刚驱魔神舞), 205–207
—history 历史:
 and the 6th Panchen Lama 六世班禅, 205
 inscription on stele recording the origin of the system of "drawing lots from the golden urn" 金瓶掣签制度, 203
 and Prince Yinzhen 胤禛, 201
 three masters interviewed at. *See* Hu Xuefeng 胡雪峰; Tubdan 丹贝坚赞
—space (*kongjian* 空间):
 Falun Hall 法伦殿 (aka Dharmacakra Hall), statue of Je Tsongkhapa (Ch. 宗喀巴), 205
 Jetai Building 戒台楼, statue of Emperor Qianlong 乾隆, *202*f103
 Wanfu Pavilion 万福阁, white sandalwood Maitreya Buddha 弥勒佛 in, 205, *208*f106
Yuan Dynasty 元朝 (1279–1368):
 Bixia Yuanjun accepted as a Daoist deity during, 21
 and Christianity. *See* Montecorvino, Giovanni da
 establishment of Imperial College and the Confucian temple, 57
 founding of Dongyue Temple, 85
 and Islam. *See* Changping Mosque Miaoying temple 妙应寺 built during, 3
 Roman Catholicism arrives in Beijing, 3
 stela by Zhao Mengfu at Dongyue Temple, 83

Zhou Dynasty (1046–256 BCE), and Imperial College, 65

www.ingramcontent.com/pod-product-compliance
Ingram Content Group UK Ltd.
Pitfield, Milton Keynes, MK11 3LW, UK
UKHW050006230326
469204UK00005B/48